Martin Fárek

India in the Eyes of Europeans
Conceptualization of Religion in Theology and Oriental Studies

KAROLINUM PRESS
PRAGUE, 2021

KAROLINUM PRESS
Karolinum Press is a publishing department of the Charles University
www.karolinum.cz

First English edition

Designed by Jan Šerých
Set and printed in the Czech Republic by Karolinum Press

Cataloging-in-Publication Data is available from the National Library
of the Czech Republic

This book is published with the financial support from the University
of Pardubice and the Technical University of Liberec.

ISBN 978-80-246-4755-5
ISBN 978-80-246-4891-0 (pdf)

Table of Contents

Acknowledgments

To meet a mind that fundamentally changes our perception of the world is one of the most amazing experiences in one's life. At the same time, when the person who developed his critical thinking so considerably is a straightforward and truly charitable character, you are attracted to the path this person has opened. I consider myself to be very lucky to meet such a teacher in S. N. Balagangadhara fourteen years ago. It has truly been a delight to step off the prescribed paths of research and discover new ways, in fact, new horizons.

All my encounters with Professor Balu, as he suggested people call him, were refreshing in the best sense of the word. They brought me to new experiences of cultural otherness and their very sincere reflections; they made me think along the routes I could not imagine existed before; they shattered some of my dearly held and deeply ingrained beliefs and attitudes; they also gave me hope for a new kind of research into understanding between cultures. And above all, they showed me the richness a friendship can offer, the special kind of friendship that Balu extended to many people. Balu, this is to say—thank you so much!

These fourteen years have been an exhilarating journey through many experiences and places: from New Delhi, Bengaluru, Mumbai, Chennai, Mangaluru, Ujire, and other cities and towns in India, to Ghent, London, Krakow, Tartu, Erfurt, Bratislava, and other European places. I have enjoyed each day with the research group which has formed because of the inspiration taken from the work of professor Balu. On this journey, it was my honor to become a partner in debates, research, writing, conferences, and India Platform projects undertaken by the Ghent team of Comparative Science of Cultures, as well as groups of researchers from India. Jakob, Sarah, Marianne, Nele, Anne, Sarika, Esther, Jolien, Dunkin, Sufiya, Prakash, Rajaram, Sadananda, Sandeep, Chaitra, Tess, Venkat, and many others, I am very grateful for your friendship, hospitality, and care. I am looking forward to new work and experiences we will undertake in the years to come.

My former colleagues in the Department for the Study of Religions at the Faculty of Art and Philosophy, University of Pardubice, endured my excitement for the discoveries of the Comparative Science of Cultures Programme, and also for all the initiatives aimed at co-operations with universities in India and Europe. Not only that: Ivan Štampach, Štěpán Lisý, Viola Pargačová, Zuzana Černá, Vít Machálek, and Henryk Hoffmann took interest in all of these attempts and offered their own thoughts, encouragement, and lots of practical support. What shall I say to you and to the group of doctoral students of the same department who took a more or less active part in all that? Thank you, friends. The support for India Platform which several leading personalities of the University of Pardubice have shown has been crucial on this way. It was also a pleasure to work with professionals from the International office as well as with several colleagues from other faculties of the same university.

Debates with many scholars have been an important part of this research. I would like to thank namely Naomi Goldenberg, Geoffrey Oddie, Richard King, Laurie Patton, Elizabeth Clark, Róbert Gáfrik, Dušan Deák, Pavel Hošek, and Jana Valtrová.

I express my appreciation to my new friends and colleagues at the Technical University of Liberec for their support and understanding during the period of my final work on this book. You are a great team and I am happy to be able to work with you. And finally, I would like to express my gratitude to Eva, the woman of my life, to our children, parents, and the whole family. Without your support, this book would simply not have materialized.

Martin Fárek, Liberec, June 2021

A Note on the Transliteration of Indian Words and on the Translation from Czech

To make the text more accessible to a wider audience, Indian words in this book have been anglicised, following a common usage in this kind of academic literature. The closest English equivalent is given upon a word's first occurrence. Full transliterations with diacritical marks are listed in the index. Anglicised words that have been in common use for a very long time are an exception, and although their transliteration does not come as close to the Indian original as possible, they became more usual than their linguistically desired closer transliterations; e.g., it would be more accurate to write "Brahmans," but the colonial "Brahmins" has been commonly used for a very long time. Indian names have also been anglicised according to the common use and I think there is no need to give transliterations for them. Because of the research focus, there are numerous translations from the Czech original texts in this book. It was ongoing effort of the author to assure that the translations give precise meaning of the original Czech paragraphs or sentences.

Introduction

How Do Europeans Approach the Otherness of Indian Traditions?

Is this hymn possibly a memory of the pre-Vedic religion, when God the strict, the powerful, the just, ruled people who had not dispersed all over Asia yet? . . . If it is so, then the peak of Indian religion is to be found in prehistory, and everything that followed, the Vedas, Brahmanism, Buddhism, and Hinduism, was only a journey down the hill.
(Emanuel Rádl, *The West and the East*)

The fascination with India has been a remarkable and long-lasting phenomenon all over Europe, including the Czech Republic, my homeland. European scholarship dealing with India represents an immense library that encompasses the results of research in many disciplines: linguistics, history, religion, ethnography and anthropology, art history, philosophy, politics, economics, and others. Even a nation as small in number as we are, we can pride ourselves on a relatively great number of scholars who devoted their work to the Indian subcontinent and who still continue to do so. There is a considerable amount of books, articles, and other resources on the topic. Czech Indologists, for example Dušan Zbavitel, Kamil Zvelebil, Vladimír Miltner, Hana Preinhaelterová, and others, have won acclaim among Western as well as Indian scholars. It would appear that we have excellent knowledge of India's history, culture, religions, and its many languages. However, is that really the case?

What kind of knowledge does Indology and other related disciplines actually offer as branches of Oriental studies? Over the last forty years, the very nature of Oriental studies has become the subject of critique, which shook the foundations of some seemingly self-evident findings and truths. Several influential scholars have paused to reflect and asked themselves: How have Europeans actually understood the thought and behaviour of Indian people? And how have they approached the otherness of Indian culture?[1] Searching for answers, these scholars have pointed out problems in intercultural understanding that is hampered by the creation of deformed images of another culture.[2]

A very important question arises: How to proceed in intercultural research? This is the question that I am going to ask myself, arguing that we are still trapped by our cultural limitations despite the impressive efforts of several generations of European scholars. Whilst travelling in India, studying and taking part in discussions abroad and at home, I have become increasingly surprised by how the specifically European treatment of the Indian culture's radical differences precludes their perception. I intend to argue that understanding and perception of this culture is overwritten with our own story. We take it for granted that people in India developed basically the same understanding of themselves and the world as we did. A significant factor in the failure to comprehend the otherness of India is the European treatment of religion. Conceptualisation of Indian traditions as "religion" caused numerous problems which will be the main subject of my analysis. By discussing the selected topics, I hope to point to a solution leading to intercultural understanding as an alternative to what is commonly followed not only in the Czech context, but also in other countries.[3]

What experience and reflections bring me to analyse the conceptualisation of religion in the Orientalist discourse? It was on the pages of

1   See for example S. N. Mukherjee, *Sir William Jones: A Study in the Eighteenth Century British Attitudes to India* (Cambridge: Cambridge University Press, 1968); P. J. Marshall, *The British Discovery of Hinduism in the Eighteenth Century* (Cambridge: Cambridge University Press, 1970); Ronald Inden, *Imagining India* (Oxford: Blackwell, 1990).

2   See especially S. N. Balagangadhara, *"The Heathen in His Blindness...": Asia, the West and the Dynamic of Religion* (Leiden: Brill, 1994).

3   Some of the problems with the religious perspective of European research and its influence on the ideas of non-believers has been hinted in analyses of travelogues written by people from different European nations. See, for example, Róbert Gáfrik, "Representations of India in Slovak Travel Writing during the Communist Regime (1948–1989)," in *Postcolonial Europe? Essays on Post-Communist Literatures and Cultures*, ed. Dobrota Pucherová and Róbert Gáfrik (Leiden and Boston: Brill Rodopi 2015), 283–298.

the books written by Vladimír Miltner, Dušan Zbavitel, Miroslav Krása, and Milada Bartoňová that I first encountered Indian traditions. Ever since 1994, I have had a number of experiences on my trips to India that made me doubt the explanations that I have read since I began my studies of Western Orientalist work. Most European authors would maintain that in order to become a Hindu, one has to be born a Hindu. Yet, I have witnessed inhabitants of several regions of India respecting foreigners who practised one of the various local traditions. Moreover, some Indians would accept *diksha* from these Europeans or Americans, a ritual initiation into traditional Indian practices such as mantra recitation, visualisation, etc. Hinduism is said to be a religion unifying most of India's inhabitants, but I have observed a great number of often very different traditions. Concepts such as *religion*, *faith*, or *confession* have proved to be particularly confusing in India. It is true that these and similar words are used in everyday parlance in Indian English. However, if you engage in extended conversation with Indians, you will find that the so-called Hindus have no common faith. Furthermore, they have difficulties understanding what this concept actually means in Europe. Indologists have claimed that Buddhist and Jain traditions were a revolt against the Brahmins and their ritualism. I have talked to Jain Brahmins in Shravanabelagola, who maintain a large number of rituals that bear a considerable resemblance to those of "Hinduism," including names and characters of "Hindu" deities.[4]

During my first substantial research, I found that since the arrival of Christian missionaries in India European literature exhibits a notable continuity of topics, questions, and explanations. It became clear that many Western interpretations of Indian traditions originate in the works of Protestant missionaries from the turn of the 18th and 19th centuries. Whatever the differences were between the stances of the first British Orientalists such as William Jones or Henry T. Colebrooke, and those adopted by the so-called Anglicists, these two groups still shared some fundamental views of Indian society and religion. Surprisingly, despite increasing secularisation of humanities, they in one way or another

---

4   Similarly, there are also Buddhist Brahmins, see for example Christiaan Hooykaas, *Balinese Bauddha Brahmins* (Amsterdam: North Holland, 1973). If Western scholars explain the existence of Buddhist or Jain Brahmins by reference to syncretism, they ought to clarify what has changed so fundamentally in Buddhist and Jain lore that these supposed criticisms or even revolts against the Brahmins have given rise to traditions that have their own Brahmins. The question of whether the ascetic movements reacted against Brahmin orthodoxy will be dealt with in the first chapter.

retained many of the original Christian ideas which are in use even today. Those include differentiating the "moral" Krishna of the *Bhagavadgita* from the "immoral" Krishna of the *Puranas* and subsequent traditions, or the search for parallels between the New Testament theology and the Indian understanding of the *Bhagavadgita*.[5] However, I was mistaken in presuming that the secularisation of humanities had by itself emancipated scholars to achieve a deeper understanding of Indian traditions.[6] I attributed some problematic assertions solely to colonial ideology. It was only later that I would encounter theoretically more plausible and useful explanations. I have gradually come to realise that the results of Western scholarship tend to ignore the groundwork on which the whole structure rests. Our generation can hardly catch sight of the basis that supports the framework of dominant explanations of India.

Paradigms and Theories in the Study of Indian Culture

Before tackling the problem of European understanding of Indian traditions, I shall briefly describe my basic theoretical approach as well as explain a few terms, starting with *Indian traditions*. Subsequently, the current scholarly discussion will be presented as a meeting point of arguments developed in the Oriental and postcolonial studies and in the newly conceived comparative study of cultures. Finally, I will present an outline of particular problems in the order in which I will further elaborate on them in their respective chapters.

It is, above all, the post-war development of philosophy, or theory, of science that has provided significant insights into the process of generating, establishing, and refuting scientific theories.[7] The image of science

---

5   See, for example, David Haberman, "Divine Betrayal: Krishna-Gopal of Braj in the Eyes of Outsiders," *Journal of Vaisnava Studies* 3, no. 1 (1994): 83–111, and Vincent Pořízka, *Opera Minora: Studies in the Bhagavadgita and New Indo-Aryan languages*, ed. Jaroslav Strnad (Prague: Oriental Institute, Academy of Sciences of the Czech Republic, 2000).

6   See Martin Fárek, *Haré Kršna v západním světě: Setkání dvou myšlenkových tradic* [Hare Krishna in the western world: Meetings of two traditions of thought] (Pardubice: Univerzita Pardubice, 2004). The choice of the title was unfortunate as it seems to suggest that the book focuses on the Hare Krishna movement, whereas it actually deals with the historical typology of Western, especially Anglo-Saxon, scholars' approach to the Chaitanya tradition. Nevertheless, the typology provides a general picture of the Western approach to the "Hindu" traditions.

7   Thomas Samuel Kuhn, *The Structure of Scientific Revolutions* (Chicago: University of Chicago, 1970); Imre Lakatos, "Falsification and the Methodology of Scientific Research Programmes,"

as a process of accumulating factual knowledge which is only elaborated or improved on by new theories, has been called into question. It was in particular T. S. Kuhn and I. Lakatos who have developed an important criticism in this respect. The first of the famous philosophers of science points out that scientific knowledge is developed as a process of establishing paradigms and elaborating on them before finally abandoning them for new ones. He describes this process as a repetitive cycle of three stages: normal science–crisis–scientific revolution. Kuhn's claim that there is usually one paradigm within a given scientific discipline has been criticised by many. Lakotos was apparently the first to develop the idea that individual scientific disciplines actually comprise of several paradigms that co-exist and compete with each other. Instead of paradigms, Lakatos speaks of research programmes. Despite Lakatos' pronounced criticism of Kuhn's analyses, both thinkers arrive at an important conclusion that rejects the previous model of science as cumulative knowledge. Rather than just individual theories, science involves the competition of whole paradigms, or research programmes, that determine the starting points of their many theories.

Another topic is the relationship among theory, observation, and facts. European sciences have long relied on the assumption that there are empirically proven, and therefore neutral facts that, in theory, can be generalised by means of induction. At the root of this was another assumption, namely, that individual facts have a certain basic atomic nature that makes them unrelated to each other. They only become related to each other via theory.[8] This conviction has been called into serious doubt, starting from the Duhem-Quine thesis on the indeterminacy of theories by empirical data, to Popper's discard of the empirical basis of science, referring to the theoretical nature of data (the so-called bold hypothesis), to Kuhn's argument concerning the central role of paradigm in acquiring data and construing reality, to Feyerabend's radical thesis regarding the parasitic nature of observation. This critique gave rise to the currently largely accepted view that facts, or data, arrived at by observation are fundamentally determined by theories:

in *Criticism and the Growth of Knowledge*, ed. Imre Lakatos and Alan Musgrave (Cambridge: Cambridge University Press, 1970), 91–196; Peter Godfrey-Smith, *Theory and Reality: An Introduction to the Philosophy of Science* (Chicago: University of Chicago, 2003); Břetislav Fajkus, *Filosofie a metodologie vědy: Vývoj, současnost a perspektivy* [The philosophy and methodology of science: Development, current situation and the perspectives] (Prague: Academia, 2005).

8   Břetislav Fajkus, *Současná filosofie a metodologie vědy* [Contemporary philosophy and methodology of science] (Prague: Filosofia, 1997), 22.

The main role of theory is in determining (1) what can be measured or otherwise observed, especially in terms of data, (2) what data are relevant, (3) how are crude data processed, (4) how are they interpreted, and (5) how the interpreted data are used legitimately in constructing and confirming theories, etc.[9]

Another insight developed out of a debate concerning the ways of confirming or refuting theories: Popper argues against the assumption that theories can be validated by the frequency of observations. He points out that some hypotheses have been accepted as a consequence of a single observation. By logical inference, he concludes that the verification of theories by observation poses considerable problems and postulates his famous criterion of falsifiability. To put it simply, theories ought to be able to predict a particular phenomenon and if the phenomenon is not observed under stated circumstances, the theory is therefore falsified. However, Popper also argues that observing the predicted phenomenon does not amount to verification of the theory. Supposedly, it only means that the theory has not been falsified. Although the last pronouncement is open to many objections, Popper's contribution is considered important inasmuch as any truly scientific theory must be falsifiable, and consequently at risk of being refuted. This criterion was later emphasised by Laudan.[10] If a thesis does not fulfil this condition, then it is highly probable that it is pseudoscientific.[11]

I find all of these three findings—the existence of competing paradigms (and not just theories), the dependence of data and their evaluation on theories, and the falsifiability criterion—crucial to my further argument. Shortly, I will summarise three different theoretical approaches to the study of Indian traditions. I consider them to be competing paradigms, or research programmes. Every programme is characterised by a specific constellation of theories, rooted in its basic axioms. Each has its strong points as well as less sufficiently developed arguments and unresolved problems. This constellation will be called *a metastructure of ideas*, made up of several rival or just co-existing theories.

In order to avoid any misunderstanding, I will clarify a few terms that will be used in this book. The term *Western* is used as equivalent to

---

9   Fajkus, *Současná filosofie a metodologie vědy*, 132–133.
10 Larry Laudan, *Science and Relativism: Some Key Controversies in the Philosophy of Science* (Chicago: The University of Chicago, 1990).
11 Godfrey-Smith, *Theory and Reality*, 57–74.

Euro-American, because the development of disciplines relating to India in the US and in Canada has been derived from the European research, and it is still linked to the corresponding scholarship in Europe. The term *Indian traditions* refers to the traditions that had developed in South Asia before the invasion of various conquerors under the flag of Islam since the 10th century. It also includes these traditions that have been preserved in India during the Muslim ascendancy, developing in the various Sultanates, later under British colonial rule, and now in the independent Republic of India, alongside the increasing number of Muslims. This is not to say that these autochthonous traditions have not been influenced by Islam at all, for there is enough evidence that the opposite was true in many cases.[12] The mutual influence of the "Hindus" and Muslims on the Subcontinent in itself represents a vast field of research and it will not be discussed here.[13] On the other hand, many Indologists and anthropologists will attest that the so-called Hindu, Buddhist, and other communities have lived and continue to do so in accordance with their own rituals and festivals. They cultivate their own intellectual traditions and pass on their own stories of the past that are fundamentally different from those of Muslim communities. Research into the long-term continuity of autochthonous Indian traditions is therefore justified. I use the singular form of *Christian thought* and *Christian theology* intentionally, with an awareness of the varying dogmas, changes in interpretation, and other differences among the theologies of particular denominations. All these streams of thought share a number of basic themes that become more visible when compared to as different a culture as the one represented by Indian traditions, which sufficiently justifies the use of this umbrella term. If need be, a more precise differentiation between particular Christian ideas will be applied in specific points of argument.

The first paradigm are the Oriental studies, in which theories of various disciplines of humanities meet and interact. With regard to India, linguistics has for a long time been given unequivocal primacy due to the ground-break-

---

12 For example, in the poems of North Indian Sants or in the teaching of Nanak, the founder of Sikhism.

13 Those who are interested in this matter can consult, for example: Richard Eaton, *The Rise of Islam and the Bengal Frontier, 1204–1760* (Berkeley and Los Angeles: University of California, 1993); Dušan Deák, *Indický svätci medzi minulosťou a prítomnosťou: Hladanie hinduistov a muslimov v Južnej Ázii* [Indian sages between the past and present: On searching for Hindus and Muslims in South Asia] (Trnava: Univerzita Sv. Cyrila a Metoda, 2010).

ing discovery of the Indo-European language family. In Popper's terms, this success was the exemplum of the whole paradigm, initiating, as it is well known, the fundamental development of Western comparative linguistics. However, 19th century Orientalists such as Horace H. Wilson, Eugène Burnouf, Friedrich Max Müller, and many others, were also involved in the study of religion, instigating the birth of religious studies. Among intellectuals dealing with India, we can find historians such as Mountstuart Elphinstone and Vincent Arthur Smith, anthropologists such as H. H. Risley who examined Indian traditions in the perspective of nascent physical anthropology, and many others. Since these disciplines were not as specialised and separate as they are today, it is reasonable to examine Indian traditions in a wider range of fields. Other influential thinkers who drew on Orientalists' work must also be taken into account. India featured in the works of philosophers such as Voltaire, Friedrich von Schlegel, Hegel, Schopenhauer, and others. Topics related to India were touched upon by Marx and Engels. Indian religions were discussed by Max Weber. Indeed, it would be possible to extend this list of both significant and less prominent personalities almost ad infinitum. The purpose of this introduction is not to give an account of Western intellectuals who have dealt with India, nor to outline the topics that they worked on. Instead, the characteristics and certain problems of specific paradigms will be addressed.

An important feature of European Oriental studies is the still predominantly accepted cumulative model of science and the use of induction and deduction. A linguistic competence, ideally, knowledge of Sanskrit and at least of one modern Indian language, is considered to be the main qualification for research, and a warrant of great authority for the Orientalists. Literature and poetry have been frequent fields of research. Translations of both the older and modern Indian texts and articles regarding linguistic topics have formed a huge part, if not the majority, of their publications. If someone from a different field deals with matters pertaining to India, they tend to rely on Orientalist scholarship. As for the Czech Indologist production, it includes translations from both the older and modern Indian literature, historiographical works, and more recently, a number of engaging anthropological and religious studies. After the Velvet Revolution of 1989, our leading Indologists claimed that their goal was:

> to continue to eradicate the remains of some habitual opinions, such as applying European criteria to the reality of India, or using European con-

ceptual categories in relation to the 'Orient' which has always formed the basis of simplifying and often confusing Eurocentric clichés.[14]

It is therefore surprising how few of our scholars reflect upon some important debates that have occurred globally. It will be argued that the majority of our scholarly output actually remains entrenched in the European categories of thinking, both in general framework and in respect to specific questions. It will be showed that the basic structure of seemingly modern interpretations is, in fact, very old; although many theses were formulated in the 19th century and even later, their origins are significantly older. It will also be argued that if we really are to see beyond the horizon delimited by European categories and to achieve better understanding of another culture, we must obtain a better understanding of our limitations first. In other words, in order to cross the horizon of our cultural confines, it is necessary to first realise that there is one.

Those "habitual opinions" will be the core subject of my discussion, the aim of which is not to eradicate them, but rather to investigate the role they have been playing in the meeting of cultures. These opinions and problematic categories of thinking will be analysed with the arguments of a new theory in comparative study of cultures. My goal does not consist of deconstructing either Hinduism or Buddhism.[15] If individuals of various European nations and groups appear to give practically the same account of Indian traditions, irrespective of their particular beliefs or philosophical stances, one can conceive of a new type of research. While the research approach envisioned here can open up new insights into our own intellectual tradition, it can also inform the people of India as to why and how their own traditions have been explained by foreigners. Postcolonial critique has shown that Indian people have adopted and still are frequently adopting the Western view of their culture.

In *Indie a Indové*, our Indologists aver that they are going to present the outcomes of the most recent research, "emphasising what has been newly discovered and methodologically re-evaluated."[16] However, this has happened to a small extent only. Moreover, this promise has arguably not been fulfilled in the more recent works either. Currently, there are, at least in the Czech context, another two paradigms that

---

14 Miroslav Krása, Dagmar Marková, and Dušan Zbavitel, *Indie a Indové: Od dávnověku k dnešku* [India and the Indians: From the ancient times till today] (Prague: Vyšehrad, 1997).
15 This is how several colleagues understood my objections in personal discussions.
16 Krása, Marková and Zbavitel, *Indie a Indové*, 16.

are scarcely known or reflected upon in relation to the study of Indian traditions. Be that as it may, the last three decades have seen new trends forming into fairly well-defined research programmes dealing with not only Indian traditions, getting involved plenty of scholars in Europe, America, India, and elsewhere. What is also important is that by making a conscientious effort towards a broad theoretical evaluation of the accomplishments and shortcomings of both research programmes, these scholars build a meta-theoretical framework of research. Historically speaking, this is related primarily to the rich output of the postcolonial critique initiated, above all, by the works of Edward Said. Postcolonial critique explains the genesis of concepts such as Hinduism, and to some extent Buddhism, as constructs of colonial science, which are portrayed as results negotiated between the rulers and the ruled. The theological basis of European interpretations of Indian traditions is analysed in the research programme of comparative science of cultures pioneered by the Indo-Belgian scholar S. N. Balagangadhara. Let me present a concise overview of the arguments used in these approaches, focusing primarily on what is relevant to the European treatment of Indian traditions as religion.

Instigated by Said's *Orientalism*, postcolonial critique now enjoys considerable popularity. This paradigm has launched an open critique of Orientalist disciplines, questioning the objectivity of their theories and practise. Theoretically speaking, the postcolonial paradigm is heavily influenced by the philosophical stance generally called Postmodernism, which results in the rather unsatisfactory nature of Said's argumentation. Said's work is undoubtedly stimulating and I will defend the fruitfulness of some of his insights later. However, it is difficult to put up with the quite a chaotic way of his writing which makes it difficult to understand his ideas and to follow their continuity. His work, primarily, consists of intuitive statements connected with empirical examples serving as an evidence material. Said's analysis is largely determined by his academic subject—literary studies. The main concern of this paradigm consists in examining the political bias of Orientalism.

Although Said's critique is predominantly linked to the Western interpretations of Islam and the countries where this religion prevails, he also studied the formation of Western representations of Indian and other traditions. Inspired by the Foucaultian and Marxist thought, his critique of Orientalism pinpointed several fundamental problems in the Western study of Asian and partly of African cultures as well. They all construe the Orient as "different to Europe." It is difficult to justify the presumed unity of both larger and smaller cultures that can be found in the geographical area subsumed in the term Orient. The European construct of Oriental "otherness" was built on the erroneous supposition of a generally widespread character of the "Orientals," although there are fundamental differences between the cultures of a Palestinian Arab, a Carnatic Indian and a Japanese inhabitant of Kyushu, to name only three random examples. No less doubtful is the belief in some unchangeable essence of these cultures. Said draws attention to academic Orientalism, "a manner of thought based upon an ontological and epistemological distinction made between *the Orient* and (most of the time) *the Occident*."[17] Furthermore, he pointed out a liaison between the academics and the particular interests of the colonial powers and the latter 20th century great powers, describing Orientalism in short as "a Western way of dominating, restructuring, and having authority over the Orient."[18] He thus considered the relationship between the Oriental countries and the West an uneven one, a relationship between the ruled and the rulers. It is primarily in this light that the cumulative tradition of Orientalist science needs to be scrutinised.

The main problem of Orientalism is the creation of Western representations of the Orient, largely disjointed from the indigenous way of life and understanding, but firmly established in the academic discourse. In this respect, Orientalism has its own given structures, classical authors, and recognised methods. It has become "a system for citing works and authors."[19] The issue is that the rulers' interpretations were in the colonial period accepted by the emerging intellectual elites of the subjugated countries as a valid insight into their own culture. The political emancipation of the former colonies did not necessarily entail a change in the inherited explanations. As a result, decolonisation of humanities and social sciences is still a pressing issue in these countries.

As a professor of English literature, Said focused on analysing fiction and travelogues, which was presented especially in his *Culture and Imperialism* (1993). He threw doubt on the autonomy of fiction:

> . . . as I shall be trying to show throughout this book, the literature itself makes constant references to itself as somehow participating in Europe's

---

17 Edward W. Said, *Orientalism: Western Conceptions of the Orient* (New York: Vintage Books 1979), 2.
18 Said, *Orientalism*, 3.
19 Said, *Orientalism*, 23.

overseas expansion, and therefore creates what Williams calls "structures of feeling" that support, elaborate, and consolidate the practice of empire.[20]

Let us return to the analysis of European scholarship. Rather unfairly, the popularity of Said's work overshadowed earlier works that outlined the same problems, albeit within a particular topic or discipline.[21] I would like to bring attention to the insights made by S. N. Mukherjee ten years before the publication of *Orientalism*:

> A comprehensive study of the British ideas and administrative policies must take into account the history of the development of Indian studies. It is often forgotten that all Oriental studies in the 18th century had a political slant, and all political pamphleteers writing on East Indian affairs based their theories of Indian politics on Oriental researches, or so they thought. In textbooks the history of Indian studies has been presented as a story of a series of discoveries by the British officers, who spent part of their leisure in revealing the history and culture of the country. The scholarly activities of the British administrators and the European missionaries and travellers (as most of the early Orientalists were) are presented in isolation, almost without reference to the society in which the Orientalists were born and to the British administration which they served (or to which, as in the case of some French scholars, they were actively hostile). *For a better understanding to the British response to Indian civilization we should study it within the context of the British and European economic system, social structure, and intellectual movements, and with reference to the problems of the British administration in India. Early Orientalists were not an isolated group. They were involved in the political conflicts of the time and their "theories" about Indian history and culture were influenced by their respective political positions and intellectual convictions* [emphasis added].[22]

The connection between Orientalist scholarship and Western politics and culture became the focus of a number of works that drew on Said's *Orientalism*, as well as texts written by Said himself.[23] The frequently

---

20 Edward W. Said, *Culure and Imperialism* (New York: Vintage Books, 1994), 14.
21 The first analysis of Orientalism as the ideological basis of colonialism was probably carried out by Abdel Anwar Malek, "Orientalism in Crisis," *Diogenes* 44 (1963): 103–140.
22 Mukherjee, *Sir William Jones*, 2.
23 See the new foreword in the 25th anniversary edition of *Orientalism* in Edward W. Said, *Orientalism: Western Conceptions of the Orient* (New York: Vintage Books, 2003), xv–xxx.

cited and criticised authors include Homi Bhabha, Gayatri Chakravorty Spivak, Talal Asad or Gauri Viswanathan. The Subaltern Studies Group founded by Ranajit Guha won acclaim in the study of Indian past, while postcolonial critique of Western ideas regarding the role of India's religion and Indian studies was taken up by authors such as Ronald Inden,[24] Richard King,[25] and Sharada Sugirtharajah.[26] Postcolonial studies have also had a significant influence on American anthropologists. McKim Marriot, for example, is well known for his critique of Western interpretations and for his efforts to explain the Indian reality in local terms:

> It is an anomalous fact that the social sciences used in India today have developed from thought about Western rather than Indian cultural realities. . . . Attending to what is perceived by Indians in Indian categories should at least promote a more perceptive Indian ethnography.[27]

Originally, Marriott was the inspiration for a project of ethnohistory highly influenced by Foucault's and Said's thoughts, which allowed anthropologists of the Chicago school to oppose Dumont's interpretation of the caste system.[28] Drawing on those insights, Nicholas Dirks advocated the thesis that *jatis*, sub-castes in their present form, developed from a specifically colonial organisation of the Indian society, rather than being directly inherited from ancient India.[29]

Said and other postcolonial scholars have been criticised for inadequate simplification, deficiency in historical knowledge, and also because they factually adopt the theories and methods of European humanities which are the subject of their critique. The major criticism came from scholars such as Ernest Gellner and Bernard Lewis. Amongst Indologists, the first to react was probably David Kopf. He refuted Said's critique as

---

24   Inden, *Imagining India*.
25   Richard King, *Orientalism and Religion: Postcolonial Theory, India and "the Mystic East"* (London: Routledge, 1999).
26   Sharada Sugirtharajah, *Imagining Hinduism: A Postcolonial Perspective* (London: Routledge, 2003).
27   McKim Marriot, "Constructing an Indian Ethnosociology," *Contributions to Indian Sociology* 23, no. 1 (1989): 1.
28   For an overview of this debate see Saloni Mathur, "History and Anhropology in South Asia: Rethinking the Archive," *Annual Review of Anthropology* 29 (2000): 89–106.
29   Nicholas B. Dirks, "Castes of Mind," *Representations. Special Issue: Imperial Fantasies and Postcolonial Histories* 37 (1992): 56–78.

anti-historical and "irreconcilable with responsible historical research." According to Kopf, British Orientalists worked on modernising Indian traditions "from within" so that Indian people could establish their identity in a changing world. He saw a fundamental difference between the first British Orientalists and the so-called Anglicists who did not find any worth in Indian traditions and endeavoured to implement the English model of education in the areas controlled by the British.[30] A little later, Eugene Irschick argued against the postcolonial authors' criticism, saying that research into Indian traditions is not merely a Western imposition because, in one way or another, it has involved Indian scholars and the local population in general. According to Irschick, Orientalist discourse, along with its findings, is a continuous process of dialogue between the Europeans and the Indians.[31]

Apart from Irschick's dialogue argument, other objections have been raised against the postcolonial critique of the Western study of Indian traditions. They can be summarized in the following statements: Postcolonial critique does not consider the European study of the Orient prior to the times of Europeans' colonial hold over some more significant part of the Indian Subcontinent—that is when Bengal gradually came to be ruled by the East India Company after 1757. Postcolonial critique does not explain how Oriental studies happened to develop and enjoy considerable attention in countries such as Germany that had no colonies in the regions in question.[32] Postcolonial scholars are wrong in imputing Orientalism to British and other European thinkers who, in fact, disagreed with Orientalists and strongly criticised their opinions. Like D. Kopf before, T. Trautmann maintained as well that:

> In India the British Orientalists were by no means a unitary group, but Orientalists constituted the core of a distinct policy group who, as I have said, had been dominant since the times of Hastings and who had devised the Orientalizing policy. This group constituted a faction promoting education in the vernacular languages; these "Orientalists" were in opposition to the "Anglicists," Evangelicals, and others who promoted English

30 David Kopf, "Hermeneutics versus History," *Journal of Asian Studies* 39, no. 3 (1980): 501–503.
31 Eugene Irschick, *Dialogue and History: Constructing South Asia 1795–1895* (Berkeley and Los Angeles: University of California, 1994).
32 Among the first scholars who raised these objections were Lata Mani and Ruth Frankenberg, "The Challenge of Orientalism," *Economy and Society* 14, no. 2 (1985): 175.

as a medium of instruction. The Anglicists were also involved in the production of knowledge of a kind Said calls Orientalism.[33]

Trautmann argued against the supposed unity of thought of Orientalism. From the same position, he criticised Inden's claim that James Mill's and Georg F. Hegel's works constituted hegemonic Indological texts. According to Trautmann, it is impossible to call neither Mill nor Hegel Orientalists because they did not know any Oriental language, nor did they travel to the Orient. Most importantly, the two used their knowledge of Orientalist scholarship to argue against the opinions of early British Orientalists and against the enthusiasm for India that was spreading amongst European intellectuals of their times. According to Trautmann, Said was aware of these discrepancies, but wanted to draw attention to the basis that was common to the contending parties. Trautmann proposed to rather pay attention to the relation between Orientalist and "anti-Orientalist" scholarship and to "examine and problematize" it. Moreover, he found fault with Said's approach in that it passes judgment on Orientalist knowledge while refusing to judge its content.[34]

To what extent are all the above mentioned objections justified? It is true that Said sometimes made historically erroneous generalisations or was deficient in factual knowledge. For example, he claims that Duperron's translations of the *Avesta* and of several *Upanishads*—based on Persian translations—were the first case of "the Orient being revealed to Europe in the materiality of its texts, languages, and civilizations."[35] As a matter of fact, prior to that Europeans had already been acquainted with Chinese texts translated by Jesuits. These texts were assiduously studied by European intellectuals at the turn of the 17th and 18th centuries, some even tried to learn Chinese, for example Leibniz.

On the other hand, I do not consider the rest of the objections to Said's work interesting, nor appropriate as the critics impute to him what he did not say and overlook what he, in fact, did say. To accuse the postcolonial critique of turning the local people into passive participants in the growth of Orientalist scholarship is to trivialize Said's argumentation. He aimed at researching how European, and later also American

---

33 Thomas R. Trautmann, *Aryans and British India* (Berkeley and Los Angeles: University of California, 1997), 23.

34 Trautmann, *Aryans and British India*, 25.

35 Said, *Orientalism*, 77.

representations of the "Orient" depended on established opinions, practices, exigencies, and trends in the Western culture. He pointed out the limitations that these opinions bring about in any dialogue. One of those was the widespread notion of the 19th century, that the "Orientals" were childish, backward, and barbarian, and therefore the Europeans had nothing to learn from them. With these assumptions as starting points, it was truly a strange dialogue![36] Said did not deny the idea of Orientalist scholarship deriving from some sort of dialogue, a communication, in which the controlled peoples also had a good deal to say, thus enriching Orientalist scholars with knowledge. He asked what was the role of the whole series of European assumptions in this dialogue with which Orientalists entered the conversation: "Every writer on the Orient (and this is true even of Homer) assumes some Oriental precedent, some previous knowledge of the Orient, to which he refers and on which he relies."[37] We should not be confused by Said's talking of writers. Every European Orientalist who embarks on a research trip during which he is to converse with the "Orientals" has always had his own understanding, acquired by previous education.[38] In brief, it is important to realise and reflect on the European presumptions that significantly predetermine the direction and outcome of any such dialogue.

Said disclosed a basic problem: In the colonial era, the newly forming intellectual elites of the subjugated regions adopted the Western interpretations of their "Oriental" cultures which have in turn become the basis of their own educational systems. Said expressed this in the following words: "The modern Orient, in short, participates in its own Orientalising."[39] In non-European societies, the ascendency of Western education has marginalised the local intellectual traditions. Although some Hindu and Jain traditional schools survive in today's India, there is very little contact between their scholars (Pandits) and university intellectuals. More often than not, academics do not go through the traditional education and they only know their traditions through the prism of the currently accepted Western representations. In this case, exemptions

36 Said, *Orientalism*, 22, 24, 37–38.
37 Said, *Orientalism*, 20.
38 This also holds true for laymen who travel to the "Oriental" countries. For example, the Czech painter Jaroslav Skřivánek studied Hindi with V. Pořízka and read works of the Czech scholarship on Indian religions. See Jan Marek's afterword in Jaroslav Skřivánek, *Za krásami Indie* [For the beauties of India] (Prague: Albatros 1988), 172–173.
39 Said, *Orientalism*, 325.

really prove the rule. Traditional scholars are not usually interested in Western interpretations, but it is only fair to ask why they should.[40]

It is not true that postcolonial critique does not reflect upon the precolonial period of European study of "Oriental" countries. Said drew attention to cultural stereotypes handed down in Europe from Antiquity, including, for example, the lamenting Persian women of Aeschylus' drama, some motifs in Euripides' *The Bacchae*, or the medieval condemnatory image of Islam. The question is to what extent and with what results has the postcolonial critique analysed this period—a problem I will look into later.

If Trautmann wanted Said's thesis to "help elucidate the extraordinary enthusiasm of Germans for Orientalist studies,"[41] it is a rhetorical figure rather than an argument. What exactly should postcolonial critique help elucidate in this case? Should it be examining *the causes* of German enthusiasm: Why was it the Germans who took so much interest in Oriental studies in the first place? Or should it be looking into *the ways* German Oriental studies developed, what was their starting point, or analyse *the contributions* they made? Furthermore, Trautmann failed to mention that Said considered studying German as well as Swiss, Italian, Russian, and other nations' Orientalist scholarship to be important for further research.[42] Neither did he mention that although Said considered his own meagre treatment of German scholarship to be a shortcoming, he argued that German Oriental studies owed a great deal to British and French scholarly productions, sharing with them the same type of intellectual authority over the Orient.[43]

The criticism accusing Said's *Orientalism* of being overly generalising and disregarding various often contradictory positions found in European discussions (Kopf, Trautmann), actually, is itself overly generalising, and therefore confusing. The whole problem consists of two distinct matters of a different order. Said argued in favour of the thesis that Western Orientalist production exhibits certain common features, thus creating a fairly unified framework for the interpretation and treatment of

40   This gulf between traditional scholars and Indian academics was pointed out, for example, by Walther Eidlitz, *Krsna Caitanya: Sein Leben und Seine Lehre* (Stockholm: Almqvist & Wiksell, 1968), 19.
41   Trautmann, *Aryans and British India*, 22.
42   Said, *Orientalism*, 24.
43   Said, *Orientalism*, 16–19.

the "Orientals." He suggested that Western culture's explanation of the "Oriental" otherness bears characteristics of a long-term continuity that need to be analysed. In this respect, one can talk of a basic distinction between cultures and the way they relate to each other. Examining particular discussions and differences of opinion within one cultural framework is another task altogether. Moreover, one can ask to what extent could such separate arguments be analysed without understanding their common basis. Kopf and Trautmann adduced the example of the Anglicist-Orientalist dispute over the content of education in British India. Inasmuch as they both took the Anglicists and the Orientalists as two opposing factions, they disregarded the fundamental characteristics both of these factions had in common. Both of these groups thought that the contemporary state of Indian society and education was dreary, attributing that to the degenerated condition of Indian religion and believing in the positive role of the British rule in India. Both parties thus shared the conviction that reform was necessary, although they differed on the particulars of how it should be carried out.

Although Said's insights are more intuitive than theoretically well developed, it is plausible to take them as a point of departure and test them within a theory-based framework. I consider the focus of postcolonial critique on the relationship between power and knowledge unfortunate, because it overshadowed another Said's idea. I find it crucial since it poses the question of how the European conceptualisation of religion influenced the explanation of Indian traditions:

> My thesis is that the essential aspects of modern Orientalist theory and praxis . . . can be understood, not as a sudden access of objective knowledge about the Orient, but as a set of structures inherited from the past, secularised, redisposed, and re-formed by such disciplines as philology, which in turn were naturalized, modernized, and laicized substitutes for (or versions of) Christian supernaturalism. In the form of new texts and ideas, the East was accommodated to these structures.[44]

Said's text does not explain what exactly he means by "Christian supernaturalism," but he was evidently drawing attention to the heritage of Christian theological thinking and its role in the formation of secular humanities. He pointed out that a long-term continuity of theological

---

44 Said, *Orientalism*, 122.

thought structures is much more likely than an abrupt revolution that suddenly provided the Europeans with access to objective knowledge about the Orient. There is a prevalent modern myth claiming that since the 18th century Enlightenment, humanities and social sciences have not been dependent on Christian theology. This is relevant to the birth and development of Indology and other disciplines inasmuch as William Jones (1746–1794) and other early British Orientalists are referred to as impartial scientists.[45]

Therefore, the subsequent development of Indian studies is viewed as a growth of independent scientific research. I will show that Said was right in pointing out a "set of structures" of Christian thinking, which can be observed in the European approach to Indian traditions for hundreds of years and which fundamentally determines research in its secularised form until today. I want to stress that there is a basic difference between Christian thought as the initial pre-theoretical framework used by Europeans to interpret their experience with other cultures and the imperialist ideology of European powers that used Christian ideas to their own ends. Throughout the 19th century, British people were largely convinced of their role as the supreme nation of the world whom Providence endowed with special tasks, including ruling India.[46] However, the question of how the Christian teaching of various denominations became the colonialists' ideology is different from the central topic of this treatise which explores how the Christian theological understanding of themselves and the world constituted the basis for the modern explanations of Indian traditions.

---

45 For example, W. Halbfass claimed that William Jones and other founders of the Asiatic Society of Bengal established "a tradition of exploring Indian thought in its original sources and contexts of understanding." The German Indologist contrasted here the research conducted by Jones, Wilkins and Colebrooke to the work of J. Z. Holwell and Alexander Dow. I will show in chapter one that this description is untenable. Wilhelm Halbfass, *India and Europe: Essay in Understanding* (New York: SUNY Press, 1988), 62.

46 See for example Michael Edwardes, *British India 1772–1947: A Survey of the Nature and Effects of Alien Rule* (London: Sidgwick & Jackson, 1967), 32–37; Ronald Hyam, *Britain's Imperial Century 1815–1914: A Study of Empire and Expansion* (London: B. T. Batsford, 1976), 47–69. The Foreign Secretary to the Government of India Seton Kerr made a telling statement when he said that all the British people in India were convinced that they belonged to "a race whom God has destined to govern and subdue." This speech, made in 1883, is cited by Jawaharlal Nehru, *The Discovery of India* (Delhi: Oxford University Press, 1994), 326.

The Problematic Concept of Religion

The constructivist explanation of Indian religions is a specific theory in postcolonial studies which stresses a dialogic interpretation and tries to show the specific way in which European Orientalists and traditional Indian scholars cooperated to construe Hinduism. Scholars like Richard King, Romila Thapar,[47] and Brian Pennington[48] emphasised the major role the local inhabitants have played in the conceptualisation of Indian religions:

> This is not (to restate my position) to argue that Hinduism is a Western colonial invention but rather to point out that the modern notion of "Hinduism" was framed initially by European observers of Indian cultural traditions and emerged OUT OF THE COLONIAL ENCOUNTER between Indians and Europeans (particularly the British). Recognition of the disparity of power relations precipitated by British colonial rule is not the same as suggesting that the British simply imposed their ideas about religion onto a largely passive native population.[49]

King claimed that two major representations of Indian traditions can be identified in Western scholarship: *the mystical Orient*, soaked with spirituality and ancient wisdom, which some think the West is lacking, and *the militant fanaticism*, the image of religious fundamentalists who are currently condemned for acts of communal violence in India. According to King, both representations derive from the Western thinking and are inadequately essentialising the indigenous traditions.[50] The concept of Hinduism as a religion was introduced into India via the Judeo-Christian category of religion with the Protestant emphasis on the role of sacred texts. In the constructivist explanation, a certain segment of Indian elites, especially Brahmins, grabbed the opportunity and cooperated with the colonial rulers to canonise the core of their traditions.[51]

---

47 Romila Thapar, "Syndicated Hinduism," in *Hinduism Reconsidered*, ed. Günther-Dietz Sontheimer and Hermann Kulke, 4th revised ed. (New Delhi: Manohar, 1997), 54–81.

48 Brian Pennington, *Was Hinduism Invented? Britons, Indians, and the Colonial Construction of Religion* (Oxford: Oxford University, 2005).

49 Richard King, "Colonialism, Hinduism and the Discourse of Religion," unpublished position paper, Roundtable Session, *Rethinking Religion in India I*, New Delhi, January 21–24, 2008, p. 5.

50 Richard King, "Orientalism and the Modern Myth of 'Hinduism'," *Numen* 46, no. 2 (1999): 146–185.

51 Apart from King, this argument is also in Robert E. Frykenberg, "The Emergence of Modern Hinduism as a Concept and as an Institution: A Reappraisal with special reference to South

The rise of new local elites who were educated at schools of the European type and generally adopted the Western image of their own culture has thus become an important research field. Postcolonial critics speak of colonisation of the ruled people's minds as they embraced Western education along with a new image of themselves created by the colonisers. In A. Nandi's words:

> This colonialism colonizes minds in addition to bodies and it releases forces within the colonized societies to alter their cultural priorities once and for all. In the process, it helps generalize the concept of the modern West from a geographical and temporal entity to a psychological category. The West is now everywhere, within the West and outside; in structures and in minds.[52]

To go back to the topic of Indian religions, postcolonial critique considers the approach of British missionaries and scholars led by their Protestant experience inadequate in their search for pivotal texts in Indian traditions. For instance, Sugirtharajah pointed out the erroneous way of such a hermeneutic approach that identified some texts as pan-Indian. In the British Protestant perspective, those texts were thought to represent the opinions of the priestly class, the Brahmins.[53] However, instead of examining the British attitude, postcolonial critics dwell on how the Brahmin elites allegedly used this opportunity and created modern Hinduism in cooperation with the British rulers.

Balagangadhara and Gelders have recently responded to this claim by analysing the postcolonial critique itself. If it accepts the existence of a priestly class, it perpetuates the Orientalist construction of Indian traditions as religion. The Brahmin elite is said to have existed, although Hinduism had not yet come into being. "Furthermore, the constructionists continue to give primacy to textual sources and fail to take into account that the 'sacred texts of Brahmanism' were unknown to the majority of the Brahmins when the British began to create a colonial state."[54] Balagangadhara and Gelders explained that the constructivists

India," in *Hinduism Reconsidered*, ed. Günther Dietz Sontheimer and Herman Kulke (New Delhi: Manohar, 1989), 82–107.

52 Ashis Nandy, *The Intimate Enemy: Loss and Recovery of Self Under Colonialism* (New Delhi: Oxford University Press, 1983), 11.

53 Sugirtharajah, *Imagining Hinduism*, 25.

54 Raf Gelders and S. N. Balagangadhara, "Rethinking Orientalism: Colonialism and the Study of Indian Traiditons," *History of Religion* 51, no. 2 (2011): 104.

effectively adopt the Orientalist strategy of identifying one doctrinal core of manifold traditions. The problem of Hinduism's inner diversity was treated in this way, for example, by Monier Monier-Williams in the second half of the 19th century.[55] In order to better understand the basis for this new critique as well as the solution it offers in the discussion of Indian traditions, a more detailed overview is necessary.

The newly conceived Comparative Science of Cultures, a research programme conducted by S. N. Balagangadhara and his team, focuses on problems related to the concept of "religion" and its use in the study of non-European cultures. The Indo-Belgian scholar is engaged in a thorough analysis that delves deep into European intellectual past. He introduced his analysis in the book *"The Heathen in his Blindness…" Asia, the West, and the Dynamic of Religion*.[56] In his works, Balagangadhara endeavours to develop arguments consistent with the new findings in philosophy of science as well as with the principles of modern logic, influenced above all by Tarski. In contrast to postcolonial critique, he considers the European thinking on religion a crucial topic, irrespective of how it was treated by colonial ideology at a particular stage. Balagangadhara's argumentation reveals the importance of the fourth paradigm that I have not yet mentioned—Christian theological thinking. The influence of this frequently neglected paradigm has become the main theme of his analysis:

> I argue two interdependent theses: first, the constitution and identity of the Western culture are tied to the dynamic of Christianity as a religion; second, because of this, it is possible to provide a different description of non-Western cultures and 'religions' than those prevalent in the West.[57]

The Indo-Belgian scholar showed that the theological paradigm has had a fundamental influence on Oriental studies and other disciplines dealing with the study of India and other non-European traditions. In this respect, the concept of religion (*religio*) has played a major part, having been the Europeans' way of self-conceptualisation and self-definition in relation to other traditions and cultures. Balagangadhara argued that the dynamics of early Christian apologetics created a paradigmatic

---

55 Gelders and Balagangadhara, *Rethinking Orientalism*, 105.
56 S. N. Balagangadhara, *"The Heathen in His Blindness…": Asia, the West and the Dynamic of Religion* (Delhi: Manohar, 2005).
57 Balagangadhara, *"The Heathen in His Blindness…"*, 5.

framework that transformed the radical otherness of ancient traditions into a negative image of Christianity itself (*vera religio—falsae religiones*).

This interpretation of the Early Church Fathers was revived by Protestantism, and although there was a growing and better informed awareness of non-European cultures, they were unanimously understood as heathen, or false, religions. At times, recourse was made to speculations about natural religion; they were given a new momentum especially by the Deist movement. The belief in the universality of religion was preserved by the Enlightenment's transformation of natural religion into a field of religious experience shared by all humankind. Thence we can trace the various modern theories founded implicitly or explicitly on the conviction that religion is universal. These moments in the intellectual history of Europe formed the ideas conceiving of Indian traditions as religions. *By imposing this universal claim on explicating both Christianity and all the other traditions and cultures of the world, the theological paradigm bars us from appreciating and comprehending their otherness.*

Within this framework, it is only possible to study variations of the same theme. The particularity of Europeans' treatment of Indian traditions' differences is precisely this transformation of radical otherness to an imperfect image of their own culture. Before presenting Balagangadhara's argumentation concerning the particular stages of the Christian conceptualisation of religion, I will briefly outline the contribution of this approach to the current issues of religious studies and other humanities.

Balagangadhara cast doubt on the commonplace assumption of the universality of religion. In doing so, he pointed out a fundamental problem in the modern research of religion: On the one hand, we presuppose universality of religion, on the other hand, we are not even able to produce a satisfactory theory of religion. Nevertheless, we not only study religion of the various cultures whereof we possess written records, but there is an increasing number of publications dealing with religion in prehistoric times. Religion has been widely discussed by historians, anthropologists, Orientalists, sociologists, psychologists, geographers, and scholars of other various disciplines. Religious studies came into being as a specialised discipline devoted to the study of religion. Remarkably, as religious studies and related disciplines developed in the 20th century and as they exhibited an increasing tendency to set themselves apart from theological thought, they found it more and more difficult to define their subject of study:

Any attempt at an anatomy of religious life immediately faces the vexed question of a definition of religion. The field of religious studies is bestrewn with corpses of rejected definitions, found to be either too vague to be of any foundational value, or too specific to include types of religion that are found at the other end of the spectrum; or perhaps too cumbersome to be anything other than a summary description of typical features found in traditions which by general consent are part of comparative field of religious studies.[58]

As of now, many scholars have given up on defining the category that they use in their research. Others at best admit that there are all kinds of difficulties in efforts to define religion. In the Czech academic context, definitions of an ostensibly theological character are prevalent: relationship with the sacred, relation to transcendence, and suchlike. Others still try to "extend" the concept so as to include various traditions, almost as if it were a balloon that can be blown up as much as we need. One of these attempts at extension is the so-called polythetic definition of religion.[59]

Balagangadhara has proposed a more promising procedure: If we find fundamental problems with the definitions of religion, let us analyse the theoretical background and evidence that formed our understanding of religion. What is it that makes something into a religion? His analysis brought the following results:

1. The very concept of religion stems from centuries of Christian thought. It is absolutely necessary to analyse it in relation to other important concepts of the theological paradigm, such as the specific ideas of deity, the creation of the world, worship, etc. In other words, it must be considered in the optics of continuous axioms that form this metastructure of ideas.

2. The concept of religion thus became part and parcel of the theoretical apparatus used by European conquerors, missionaries, travellers, and others as they produced reports regarding the distant cultures.

---

58 Eric J. Lott, *Vision, Tradition, Interpretation: Theology, Religion and the Study of Religion* (Berlin: Mouton de Gruyter, 1988) 15, quoted in Balagangadhara, *"The Heathen in His Blindness…"*, 154.

59 The polythetic approach is inspired by Wittgenstein's thesis of *family resemblance*. It has also been applied to the problem of defining Hinduism. However, the polythetic definition leaves the issue unresolved. See Martin Fárek, "Hinduismus: reálné náboženství nebo konstrukt koloniální vědy?" [Hinduism: A real religion or a construct of the colonial science?] *Religio. Revue pro religionistiku* 14, no. 2 (2006): 227–242.

Individual experiences were explained through this optic and systematised in a structure of ideas that Europeans found comprehensible. The supposition of the universality of religion has therefore never been tested in a systematic empirical manner.

3. The cumulative description of European experience with other cultures seemingly confirms the presence of religion in other parts of the world. However, it rather evidences lasting influence of the theological paradigm within which Europeans systematised and interpreted their experiences with the otherness of Indian and other cultures.[60]

It would be beyond the scope of the present study to elaborate on Balagangadhara's effort to establish a new theory of religion. The first three theses will be sufficient in pursuing the main object of this treatise, which consists in discussing the European treatment of the otherness of Indian traditions. Let me summarise the arguments that the Indo-Belgian scholar used in order to defend the three above-stated points. It will then become clear how Balagangadhara reached the conclusion that the European interpretations of Indian traditions bar us from comprehending their fundamental otherness. In order to make the following overview readable and clearly arranged, only a necessary amount of reference will be made to Balagangadhara's work.

The change of phenomenon described as religio in Antiquity under the influence of Christian apologetics. The surviving sources show that the usage of the word *religio* in Ancient Rome referred primarily to maintaining traditional practices, and not necessarily to the belief in the existence of gods. It is well known that Roman intellectuals frequently embraced scepticism; the mocking of certain cults is well documented (Plutarch, Lucian, and others). It is noteworthy that some sceptical intellectuals (e.g. Cicero) who doubted or denied the existence of gods were also augurs and performed traditional rituals. How is it possible to elucidate this contradiction which is by modern thought, starting from Montesquieu and Gibbon, to this day considered to be the Roman intelligentsia's compromise in relation to their traditions? Referring to ancient authors as well as modern studies, Balagangadhara proposed a different solution: Rituals were not based on any metaphysical ideas, such as the belief in gods. The validity and necessity of rituals were defined by tradition itself,

---

60 For detailed discussion of this topic, see Jakob De Roover: "Incurably religious? *Consensus Gentium* and the Cultural Universality of Religion," *Numen: International Review of the History of Religion* 61, no. 1 (2014): 5–32.

by practices handed down from generation to generation. One could embrace opinions of various philosophical schools, believe in gods, be doubtful, or even agnostic, but that had nothing to do with religio which was simply a continuation of ancient traditions specific to a particular group. In Cicero's words, it was *"wise and reasonable for us to preserve the institutions of our forefathers by retaining their rites and ceremonies."*[61]

Jews were able to defend their practices of religio in the same manner. Although Roman intellectuals raised many objections to them and some straightforwardly poured scorn on Jewish customs, they eventually recognised this group to be an authentic religion because they abided by their old traditions (e.g. Celsus and Tacitus). In this way, Jews succeeded in averting allegations of atheism—a suspicion that they did not have their ancient tradition or did not abide by them. Early Christianity faced a bigger problem in this respect. In the first decades of its existence, Christian believers set their hopes on the immediacy of the Christ's Second Coming. Apparently, they did not engage in disputations with the critics of their creed. As the expected apocalypse was not occurring, a number of apologies appeared affirming that Christianity was a religion. Like the Jews, the Church Fathers invoked the antiquity of Biblical tradition and pointed out that Moses had come long before Homer or even his predecessors. However, the First Christians could not appeal to any antiquity of their practices because they had deliberately abandoned the Jewish rituals. How did they defend their new practices then?

By "transforming the very question: Instead of proving that they were following the true and original traditions of their ancestors, they claimed that their doctrines were ancient, and therefore true."[62] Earlier Christian polemics with Jewish scholars had paved the way to this claim; most importantly, the apology of Jesus as the foretold Messiah should have been a fulfilment of not just the Jewish expectation, but that of all humankind. New philosophy of history was born, *praeparatio evangelica*, which included not only Jewish prophets, but also important Greek and Roman philosophers. The apologists' response brought two fundamental ideas: It postulated a new relation between beliefs and practices, and turned the history of one specific group, the Jews, into the framework of global history. Christian teachings were presented not only as old, but also as the original and the only true religion that legitimises the practices

---

61 Cicero, *De Divinatione* (II.77), quoted in Balagangadhara, *"The Heathen in His Blindness…"*, 44.
62 Balagangadhara, *"The Heathen in His Blindness…"*, 48.

of the Church. *Rather than tradition as such, the basis for religious practice was doctrine, according to the Church Fathers.* They endowed the word religio with this new meaning and set it in opposition to the current Roman traditions.[63] A number of traditions, ranging from rituals relating to Juno, Ceres, or Jupiter, to the imported cults of Isis, Mithra, and others, became the object of Christian criticism. In the optics of the nascent Christian theology, tales involving these various goddesses and gods were tales about false gods. Following the Judaic concept of idolatry, representations of ancient deities were interpreted as the work of deluded people. All practices related to them were therefore false, in contrast to the teaching and practice of the Church. One quote from an overview of the history of theological thought will suffice here:

> Of course, the Fathers do not talk about non-Christian religions, but rather about idolatry, about cults of false gods, or later about pagans. They demonstrate that the religions of the Graeco-Roman world are untrue and contain deep-rooted perversities. Amongst those, the chief place is given to idolatry, a myth understood as an unreal and delusive lore and immorality of 'sacred' representations. The relationship between Christianity and other religions is thus construed in a way similar to that between the truth and error . . . The Father's judgement is therefore overwhelmingly negative: idol-worshipping religions are devil's work, a fruit of sin, a hodgepodge of error, superstition, and eccentricity. Idols are considered deified creatures, evil spirits, or figments of man resulting from his sin: "All pagan deities are demons," declares Augustine.[64]

The Church Fathers did not speak of non-Christian religions, but of false religions, in opposition to their concept of true religion. The conceptual framework of the developing Christian theology did not allow for a different interpretation of originally distinct traditions. Either there is a true religion, or various forms of false religions synonymous with paganism. In the philosophy of Christian history, Roman traditions became the

---

63 This change is well represented by the difference in the etymologies given by Cicero and Lactantius respectively. While Cicero derived religio from re-legere, *to gather together, to collect again, to consider carefully* (as opposed to neglegere *to neglect, to disregard*), that is to say to ensure the preservation of ancestral traditions by careful selection, Lactantius traced the meaning from re-ligare, *to bind*, interpreting it explicitly as "a bond with God" in doctrinal terms.

64 Vladimír Boublík, *Teologie mimokřesťanských náboženství* [Theology of the non-Christian religions] (Prague: Karmelitánské nakladatelství, 2000), 23.

prototype of paganism. Importantly, this polar distinction between the true and false religions, which was constructed as a totality of all possible explanations, provided the basis for the later medieval and early modern taxonomy of religions.

Protestant movements considerably resuscitated the theme of paganism both in terms of internal disputes within Christianity and on the outside in relation to other traditions. Frequently connected to eschatological expectations, late medieval anti-clerical movements had already prepared the ground for the 16th century Reformation. Wide-ranging as the agenda of these movements was, the point here is that it strengthened the focus on idolatry and heresy within the Western Church. This was part of passionate discussions about the general decline in piety, a search for the true and original meaning of the Scripture, and a quest for a true relationship between man and God. All these topics were connected with the question of which doctrines were true and which were false. On these grounds, Protestants criticised the Roman Church for the proliferation of pagan practices. Already adapted by the Church Fathers, Euhemeros' old thesis on the origin of gods was invoked to fight against the Papacy and its clergy. However, how does one worship the true God in the true manner? By returning to the Scripture, Zwingli and Calvin argued. In doing so, humankind will be able to respond to the repeated calls from God and will not degenerate into an animal state. Theologians of the Reformation thereby developed the old idea of natural religion, that is to say, the inner capacity bestowed on man at the time of Creation to search for God and to find Him.

The return to the Scripture and to early Christianity gave new importance to the theme of paganism, which was further facilitated by the Renaissance contribution to the discovery, translation, and dissemination of ancient texts that used to be practically unknown in the Middle Ages. Nevertheless, as Balagangadhara pointed out, this renaissance of the topic of paganism continued the process of erasing the difference of the otherness of the other within the theological framework. While the Church Fathers dealt with the existing and truly different old traditions of Rome, which their apologetics transformed into a false image of their true religion, the 16th century theologians used the same apologetics to criticise the Roman Church. The different "other" was thus thoroughly domesticated: It became a degenerated pagan form of Christianity.[65]

---

65 Balagangadhara, *"The Heathen in His Blindness…"*, 82.

In the process of transforming their own history into "paganism," the European Reformation thinkers were sending out a signal that they were now, truly, unable to understand paganism. They had rediscovered the texts of the Ancients, but were unable to understand the messages.[66]

It is worth noting that it was precisely at that time when Europeans were encountering various cultures not only in Asia, but also in the New World. Cognitively, Catholics and Protestants alike were occupied with the same questions: Shall we find amongst these peoples the remains of the original monotheism that can be traced to the sons of Noah? Or has this monotheism degenerated, as can be expected from human nature burdened with sin? Moreover, they were looking for Christians on the Indian Subcontinent of whom there had been reports in ancient travelogues. Of course, they were already aware of the Jews and Muslims. The theological interpretative framework did not allow for other alternatives. It was a generally acknowledged truth that every human culture had some of these forms of religion. It is true that the rare voices of conquerors or missionaries who had discovered human groups who evidently had no religion stirred quite a lot of discussion. However, it was finally closed by the consensus of Religious Studies scholars about universality of religion at the end of the 19th century.

A closer encounter with Indian traditions began with missionary efforts. Converting the "pagans" of 16th century India to the true faith was not successful. Missionaries therefore had no alternative but to try and reach a more thorough understanding of local traditions. They started to pay more attention to the study of local languages, looking for the basis of the various rituals and practices in India. Relying on the long accepted general assumption that practices were based on doctrines, the missionaries tried to identify the sacred texts of India. In order to understand the "pagans," they looked for their theology.[67] Following the example of the Church Fathers, the missionaries entered into discussions with the Brahmins in an attempt to persuade them of the fallacy of their supposed doctrines and of the superiority of Christian teachings. Gradually, some "sacred texts" were identified and the Brahmins came to be considered priests responsible for preserving the doctrines. This is how

---

66   Balagangadhara, *"The Heathen in His Blindness..."*, 83.
67   Balagangadhara, *"The Heathen in His Blindness..."*, 88–89.

the basic structure of the modern interpretations of Indian traditions, later called Hinduism, came into being.

The Enlightenment saw a transformation of the old theological theme: Natural religion was transformed into the domain of religious experience common to all humankind. Although philosophers criticised various theological dogmas, they accepted the belief of previous centuries that religion was a universal human phenomenon. It is true that Bayle and Voltaire had a debate as to whether a nation could exist without religion. This discussion actually followed a controversy on the same topic that missionaries' reports from China had sparked off in the Catholic Church. Nevertheless, the belief in the universality of religion in the sense of a specific human experience common to all cultures remained generally unchallenged. Enlightenment thinkers also adopted the theme of paganism revived by the Protestant criticism. As a matter of fact, if Protestant theologians equalled the false religion of the ancient Romans to other contemporary forms of "paganism," Enlightenment philosophers took this as an established fact. The first Orientalists used ancient "paganism" to describe Indian traditions, as will be seen later in the case of the renowned William Jones.

The belief in the existence of a religious sphere of experience was also the starting point for considerations regarding the development of human thought. They resulted in the Enlightenment concept of the scale of civilisation development. Bernard Fontenelle, David Hume, and other thinkers developed the idea of primitive society, a savage state of human existence, out of which people can gradually aspire to higher forms of civilisation. To these philosophers and to Voltaire as well, the development of the concept of deity was also a condition of human evolution—from primitive fear to the personification of natural forces and to abstract thinking, which enables one to perceive the creation order and to meditate on its creator. This latter stage represented a "rational" way of thinking, in contrast to the thinking of "primitives." Ancient paganism and its supposed present forms were placed just one level above complete savagery. This "invention of the primitive" enabled the Enlightenment philosophers to measure the progress of Europe. Historiography, which was then undergoing the first stage of its secularisation, took these ideas as the basis for the great theories of the 19th century.

The 19th century saw the elaboration of both the old degeneration hypothesis of religion and of the Enlightenment and later Darwinian theories of evolution. Gradually, new classifications of religion were developed, dividing them, for example, into global and national, natural and ethical, or tribal and cultural. If Europeans talked of "the religion of the Gentoos"—the inhabitants of India whose religion was neither Islam nor Christianity—until the last third of the 18th century, then Charles Grant, an official of the British East India Company, by the end of that century already wrote about "Hinduism."[68] A little later, Buddhism and Jainism entered the discourse. However, all these concepts were directly built within the thought structures of Christian theological paradigm. Anthropology and other nascent disciplines followed the same scheme, adopting the interpretations given by missionaries and Orientalists. The religious explanation of Indian traditions has continued to this day.

As for the otherness of the other, Balagangadhara stresses that there is a difference between particular European experiences with the practices of people in India and the European explanation and systematisation of those experiences. Empirically, Europeans have doubtlessly experienced, for example, the wedding rituals; they have seen people standing with folded palms in front of a statue of Ganesha; they have looked at the ritual baths of poeple in the Ganges, etc. The point of our discussion, however, is the European explanation of these experiences. Since the 16th century, the number of Europeans who have experienced such practices in India has been on the rise. How have they understood these activities of the people of the subcontinent? What explanations have they developed about such a different culture?

In his newer book, Balagangadhara introduces a very illustrative simile featuring the idea of *hipkapi*. Let us imagine that our planet has been visited by an alien being who takes a lively interest in the following phenomena: the grass is green, milk turns sour after a while, birds fly, and some flowers are fragrant. The alien is convinced that these phenomena are closely interconnected and perceives them as hipkapi. The presence of hipkapi also explains how are these phenomena interlinked as well as why they exist in this way at all. Gradually, more aliens land on Earth and also perceive hipkapi in these phenomena and in others. It is their interpretation that lends structure to their experiences and makes them a coherent whole. Hipkapi becomes an empirical entity to them.[69] There are many reasons to believe that the European search for religion in Indian traditions is such a formation of an experience-based entity entirely alien to autochthonous Indian experience and thinking.

---

68 Geoffrey A. Oddie, "Colonialism and Religion in India," unpublished position paper, Roundtable Session, *Rethinking Religion in India 1,* New Delhi, January 21–24, 2008, 1.
69 Balagangadhara, *Reconceptualizing India Studies* (New Delhi: Oxford University, 2012), 52–53.

S. N. Balagangadhara is not the only one who has analysed the problematic heritage of theological thought in the human and social sciences' understanding of the non-European cultures. Particularly relevant is the work of Frits Staal, who also pointed out the Western origin of the concept of religion and its inadequacy in the study of Indian traditions. Staal brought new insights into understanding the role of ritual in India. After studying a unique enactment of a large Vedic ritual in South India,[70] he concluded that performance and practice stood in the centre of Vedic tradition. We cannot talk here of any meaning that is attributed to the ritual by Western Indologists and anthropologists.[71] Before Balagangadhara, Staal argued that ritual was independent of any specific doctrines in Asian traditions.[72] If there are any interpretations of practices (doctrines) at all, they appear to be only secondary. In some cases, they were produced in response to Western questions and criteria. This argument appears to be what inspired the direction of Balagangadhara's arguments. Unlike the Indo-Belgian scholar, however, Staal did not deal with the question of how doctrines happened to be so important to Christian thinking. He therefore did not even attempt postulating an explanation of specific connection between doctrine and practice in Christianity.

The Dutch scholar wrote about Western monotheisms—Judaism, Christianity, and Islam—as the basis for a narrow concept of religion. This view offers three common characteristics of religion: belief in God, a sacred book, and a historical founder.[73] Staal showed that in this sense it is impossible to consider Asian traditions to be a religion:

> The inapplicability of Western notions of religion to the traditions of Asia has not only led to piecemeal errors of labelling, identification and classification, to conceptual confusion and to some name calling. It is also responsible for something more extraordinary: the creation of so-called religions. This act was primarily engaged in by outsiders and foreigners, but is sometimes subsequently accepted by members of a tradition. The reasons lie in the nature of Western religion, which is pervaded by the notion of exclusive truth and claims a monopoly on truth.[74]

70 Frits Staal, C. V. Somayajipad, and Itti Ravi Nambudiri, *Agni: The Vedic Ritual of Fire Altar*, 2 vols. (Berkeley: Asian Humanities Press, 1983).

71 Frits Staal, "The Meaninglessness of Ritual," *Numen. International Journal of the History of Religions* 26 (1979): 2–22.

72 Frits Staal, *Ritual and Mantras: Rules without Meaning* (Delhi: Motilal Banarsidass, 1996), 389.

73 Staal, *Ritual and Mantras*, 398.

74 Staal, *Ritual and Mantras*, 393.

In this argumentation, Staal in somewhat uncertain manner anticipated the importance of the analysis of how and why doctrine became such a crucial feature to the Western religions. He suggested how to better understand Asian traditions by pointing out the importance of their performative aspects.

> Thus there arises a host of religions: Vedic, Brahmanical, Hindu, Buddhist, Bon-po, Tantric, Taoist, Confucian, Shinto, etc. In Asia, such groupings are not only uninteresting and uninformative, but tinged with the unreal. What counts instead are ancestors and teachers—hence lineages, traditions, affiliations, cults, eligibility, and initiation—concepts with ritual rather than truth-functional overtones.[75]

However, Staal's further argumentation is rather vague. He chose to extend Durkheim's characteristics of religion. To belief and ritual, he added *mystical experience* without elaborating on that idea further. Since it is difficult to look for belief in a system of doctrines in Asians traditions, Staal omitted it as a defining feature, adding meditation as an important element of Asian traditions. In a rather vague discussion, the Dutch scholar concluded that "The trio of ritual, mediation, and mystical experience represents much more fundamental categories than religion as such."[76] In any case, the belief in the universality of religion was taken by Staal to be a prejudice of the Euro-American civilisation. He later summarised his thoughts on the Asian cultures, claiming: "There is no religion there."[77]

The Research Questions and Steps

Whilst the present treatise aims at testing several ideas stemming from Balagangadhara's Comparative Science of Cultures, the Orientalist and postcolonial paradigms will also be necessarily considered. The research questions and the theses to be discussed are as follows:

---

75 Staal, *Ritual and Mantras*, 393.
76 Staal, *Ritual and Mantras*, 401.
77 Frits Staal: "There Is No Religion There," in *The Craft of Religious Studies*, ed. John R. Stone (London and New York: MacMillan Press and St. Martin's Press, 1998), 52–75.

1. If the theological paradigm, albeit in an implicit and secularised manner, were to form the basis for the European Orientalist explanations of Indian traditions, in this respect Czech Orientalist scholarship will not be fundamentally different from that of Western Europe. What are the Czech explanations of the original Indian traditions? Does Czech Indology and other related disciplines share the same or similar positions regarding Indian religions with Western Oriental studies? Does it also face the problems caused by the largely overlooked influence of the theological paradigm?
2. By the time of the praised British Orientalists such as William Jones, Henry T. Colebrooke, and later Horace H. Wilson, the basic framework for understanding Indian traditions as pagan religion—and thus an inversion of Christianity—had long been established. As that period was a watershed for the genesis of modern Indology as a discipline, with considerable impact on the birth of modern religious studies several decades later, I am asking: Did the British Orientalists adopt the theological questions of the preceding generations? If they did, how did they deal with them and what influence did their treatment of them have on the modern explanation of Indian traditions as religions?
3. Balagangadhara's discussion of the Christian apologetic basis for the European historiography and its significance poses the following question: To what extent does the secularised European historiography depend on the basic assumptions of theological thought? If the structure of ideas in the European treatment of the past remained bound up with the theological metastructure, how is that reflected in the modern reconstruction of Indian history?
4. A major question in the history of ancient India is the arrival of the Aryans in India. The last few decades have seen very lively debates on this matter. It appears that the topic of the Aryans reveals some momentous problems in the European conceptualisation of human groups. What part did the theological considerations of religion, language, and the origin of humankind play in the formation of the theory about the Aryan invasion of India?
5. A crucial issue in the intercultural understanding is the cooperation of Indian scholars and Europeans in creating the image of Indian traditions. As we have observed, Orientalists as well as postcolonial scholars spoke of a dialogue which resulted in the creation of modern Hinduism. However, scarcely anyone has posed the question of whether and how did the Indian scholars understand the Western

concept of religion. In this respect, the work of the Bengali reformer Ram Mohan Roy, a key figure in the modernisation of India, will be analysed. In what way did Ram Mohan Roy understand Western religious thought?

These questions and thesis listed above are the topics of the individual chapters in the respective order. Only the first two—analyses of the Czech representation of Indian traditions and of the work of the first British Orientalists—are discussed in the first chapter. This way, it will be possible to reconsider the continuity of thought between the Czech Indological production and the questions and answers as they were pursued by the first British Orientalists. Furthermore, the first chapter will also include a note on the relationship between linguistic use and theoretical thinking in the explanation of experiences with a different culture. All these problems require a few additional notes:

1. First, Czech scholarship dealing with Indian religions will be analysed. In personal communication, I have encountered the argument that the critique of Orientalism cannot apply to Czech scholars because our small country has never been directly engaged in colonial expansion and in ruling the "Orientals." As true as that may be, if Czech Indologists and other researchers offer some basic interpretations dependent on the same theological preconceptions of scholars of former colonial powers, it will support Balagangadhara's theory: Interpretations of Indian traditions are inherited primarily from Christian thought shared by scholars irrespective of their particular geopolitical situation. The analysis of Czech scholarship will focus on the structure of ideas underlying the story of Indian traditions where descriptions of Hinduism and Buddhism are points of discussion. We shall see how Czech scholars dealt with these issues.
2. To this day, Indologists make implicit and sometimes even explicit claims that missionaries, travellers, and the first Orientalists were able to break away from their cultural limits and collected "facts" that can still be relied on. But is that so? For instance, David Kopf dubbed the Baptist missionary William Carey (1761–1834) "the first anthropologist of Bengal." Similar homage was paid to other missionaries as well. To this day, William Jones (1746–1794) is called the father of modern Indology and is celebrated for his discovery of the Indo-European language family. The Czech Indologist Vilém Gampert wrote in the same vein about the European scholarship

of the 18th century and its growing knowledge of Indian religion.[78] Apparently, this derives from the unspoken conviction that by the time of the Enlightenment philosophers, Western sciences had been purged of the theological principles and aims. I will argue that the first British Orientalists actually pursued the theological questions of their predecessors.

3. The Western construction of Indian history raises another important question: How exactly did the Indians approach their own past? Is it true that no kind of historiography was developed in India until the advent of Muslim conquerors and scholars? For example, Dušan Zbavitel was convinced that actual history did not exist in India for a long time due to the specific religious teaching of the law of Karman and the vision of immense temporal cycles of the world.[79] On the other hand, starting with Horace H. Wilson, some scholars have argued in favour of an ancient Indian historical consciousness. Or shall we consider a much different mode of awareness of the past, different from that of European thought?

4. Czech Indological texts have practically ignored the criticism of the dominant theory about Aryan invasion of, or migration into, India. Recent Czech scholarship describes the theory of invasion as based on archaeological findings and confirmed by linguistic evidence.[80] However, the last three to four decades of international research on the subject brought surprising insights and facts. I will show how the archaeological findings were interpreted through the prism of the already accepted invasion theory. Today, respected archaeologists and South Asian physical anthropologists are sceptical of associating any findings with Aryans. Is it the case that the invasion theory was formulated on the basis of linguistic research, or can we discover other theoretical foundations for the belief in the early arrival of Indo-European people in South Asia?

5. In the chapter on Ram Mohan Roy, I will consider the contribution Balagangadhara's new comparative method could make towards resolving the debates surrounding this important reformer. Czech Indological scholarship has until now neglected the international

---

78 Dušan Zbavitel et al., *Bozi, bráhmani, lidé: Čtyři tisíciletí hinduismu* [Gods, brahmins, people: Four millenia of Hinduism] (Prague: Nakladatelství ČSAV, 1964), 11.

79 Dušan Zbavitel, *Starověká Indie [Anceint India]* (Prague: Panorama 1985), 89.

80 For example, see the relevant passages by Jan Filipský in Jaroslav Strnad et al., *Dějiny Indie* [History of India] (Prague: Nakladatelství Lidové noviny, 2003), 38–44.

discussion over the understanding of Roy's opinions. While Dušan Zbavitel commended Roy's rationality and extensive erudition, he failed to consider the possibility that the Bengali reformer sought "the original sources of Hinduism, in order to find what had formed the very basis of the Hindu *Weltanschauung*,"[81] quite in the manner of the contemporary British Orientalists. It will be shown that Zbavitel was wrong in claiming that Roy's goal was to purge Hinduism of idolatry.[82] However, in the works of various foreign authors, opinions on Roy's understanding of religion differ. One way out of this maze of conflicting ideas could be in resolving the question of how Ram Mohan Roy understood the Western concept of religion. At the same time, I want to show how this analysis could provide a new way of understanding the differences in thought between European and Indian traditions.

The main subject of this treatise is mostly scientific publications, however, at times, it will be necessary to analyse older texts which are classified rather as historical sources today. There are, of course, many related topics that will not be discussed in this book. These include, for example, the descriptions of the Indian peoples as passive, lazy, dreamy, emotional, sensual, or even irrational. These stereotypes will be left for future research. Let us now look at how Europeans have been trying to understand traditions of India in religious terms.

---

81 Dušan Zbavitel, *Bengali Literature* (Wiesbaden: Otto Harrassowitz, 1976), 213. The Czech edition with a bibliographical essay on more recent literature to the topic, but without critical assesment of the Orientalist's perspective: Dušan Zbavitel, *Bengálská literatura: Od tantrických písní k Rabíndranáthu Thákurovi* [Bengali literature: From Tantric songs to Rabindranath Tagore] (Prague: ExOriente, 2008).
82 Zbavitel, *Bengálská literatura*, 214.

Europeans' Search for Religion in India

European Indology promotes the term Hinduism only in order to conceal
its ignorance where it has failed to advance further.
Ivo Fišer

What is the story of religion in India which is presented in Czech text-books and on which most specialised monographs rely? It goes as follows: Once upon a time, there used to be one Indian religion, the ancient Vedic religion. Its propagators were Aryans, the noble Indo-Europeans who arrived in India from their Indo-European homeland approximately in the centuries following the year 1500 BC. They had sacred scriptures, *the Vedas*, which they believed had been revealed to their ancient sages. However, the nature of their religion is a subject of discussion, some scholars speak of monism, some of polytheism, and some even of henotheism. They subdued the indigenous Dravidians and Mundas who had probably created the advanced civilisation of the Indus Valley. Seemingly, they pushed some of the indigenous people to the south of India. By approximately 500 BC, the Aryans occupied the north of India: from present-day Pakistan to Bangladesh, from the Himalayas down to the Vindhya Range. Inevitably, intermarriages between the conquerors and the subdued people occurred, which the Aryans attempted to check by codifying the caste system with the Brahmins at the top of the social pyramid. However, the Brahmin priestly elite had to accept many elements of the subdued Dravidians' cults and integrate them into the Vedic religion. Nevertheless, the Brahmins thus succeed-ed in maintaining a privileged social status, and by availing themselves of the advantages afforded by their knowledge of rituals, they seized power. This was the next phase in the development of Indian religion called Brahmanism. The empty ritualism of increasingly sumptuous offerings gradually ceased to satisfy people in general. Criticism was raised especially by ascetics called *Shramanas*. It was from their ranks where there emerged protesting religious movements, the Jains and, above all, the Buddhists, who spoke against Brahmanism and its caste system. Significant rulers of the Maurya dynasty converted to the protesting religions— Chandragupta Maurya converted to Jainism (allegedly, he is said to have become a monk in his old age) while his grandson Ashoka embraced Buddhism. Buddhism, in particular, became wide-spread due to royal patronage and superseded Brahmanism. However, as time wore on, Brahmanism gradually transformed into Hinduism, absorbing a number of Buddhist and Jainist elements, and thereby marginalising the two traditions. The cults of great gods and goddesses, especially those of Vishnu and Shiva, gained prominence and their adherents still form the two major movements, or sects, of Hinduism. Tantra emerged before the advent of Islam, while Buddhism had almost disappeared from India by the 13th century.[83] The story has not substantially changed in view of the more recently propagated opinion that all these changes represent the development of Hinduism.

A number of serious problems arise when one examines this explanation of Indian traditions either in the Czech scholarship or elsewhere as well. Half a century has passed since the leading Czech Indologist Dušan Zbavitel noted that nobody had, as of yet, managed to come up with a satisfactory definition of Hinduism and that huge disagreements were prevalent in determining what Hinduism encompassed. He mentioned *endless discussions* that had dealt with the topics in scholarly literature.[84] Academic debates have not ceased since then; actually, it is quite the contrary.

---

83   For example, see the section "Náboženství" [Religion] in the introduction of Jan Filipský et al., *Dějiny Bangladéše, Bhútánu, Malediv, Nepálu, Pákistánu a Šrí Lanky* [History of Bangladesh, Bhutan, Maledives, Nepal, Pakistan and Sri Lanka] (Prague: Nakladatelství Lidové noviny, 2003), 11–13; Blanka Knotková-Čapková, *Základy asijských náboženství* [The basics of Asian religions] (Prague: Karolinum, 2005), 1:107–135; the development of Hinduism is described in the same way by Karel Werner, *Náboženství jižní a východní Asie* [Religions of South and East Asia] (Brno: Masarykova Univerzita, 1996), 9–22; or Stanislava Vavroušková, "Tradice a moderní společnost: hinduismus" [Tradition and modern society: Hinduism"], in *Náboženství v asijských společnostech* [Religion in the Asian societies], ed. Dagmar Marková (Prague: AV ČR, 1996), 93–98.

84   Zbavitel, *Bozi, bráhmani, lidé*, 5.

It appears that, with respect to defining Hinduism, the situation is much worse today than it was in the 1960s. Even a cursory glance reveals a whole spectrum of differing opinions on the matter, ranging from Hinduism as a unified religion defined either in essentialist or polythetic terms, to Hinduism as a cultural area covering an array of particular religions, to a downright rejection of the term and its usefulness. Discussions of this topic fill up the pages of scholarly books and journals.[85]

Similarly persistent is the problem of defining Buddhism, by many authors counted amongst the world religions, by some considered to be a philosophical system of some kind, and by others spoken rather vaguely of a religious-philosophical system. Buddhism has often been interpreted as an originally atheist philosophy, which "in the process of transforming into the Mahayana teaching gradually came in all fundamental questions so close to Hinduism that it came to be considered an offshoot of Hinduism."[86] This is, in itself, a noteworthy claim that requires analysis. What exactly constitutes the problem in defining Hinduism and Buddhism? What kind of problems does it reveal? How did they arise? Finding answers to these questions will enable us to propose possible ways of solving them.

First, Czech definitions of Hinduism and Buddhism will be discussed in order to subsequently consider to what extent they share the principles and conclusions of primarily Anglo-Saxon Orientalists. How cogent are the arguments presented by Czech Indologists in favour of their explanation of Indian traditions? I will argue that their understanding is in no fundamental way different from that created by British Orientalists. After considering the role of theological language in the debate, the works of the first British Orientalists will be analysed. I will show that in that crucial period of development of Western humanities, the first Indologists took over the theological questions of their predecessors. Together with the French, German and other European Orientalists, they created a modern image of Indian religions within the structures of theologically shaped ideas, which is the prevalent interpretation of Indian culture even today.

---

85 Apart from the works mentioned in the introduction, a useful overview can be found in J. E. Llewellyn, *Defining Hinduism: A Reader* (London: Routledge, 2005). For a brief overview and selective analysis of the spectrum of interpretations, see also Fárek: "Hinduismus: reálné náboženství nebo konstrukt koloniální vědy?," 227–242.

86 See Jan Filipský in the section dealing with religion and philosophy in *Dějiny pravěku a starověku* [Prehistory and ancient times], ed. Jan Pečírka (Prague: SPN, 1989), 2:930.

The Czech Understanding of Indian Traditions

Definition Problems in "Endless" Discussions about Hinduism

Keeping Buddhism aside for a while, let us start by analysing the Czech characterisation of Hinduism. If the Czech definitions prove to be adequate for delimiting the subject of the study, we may abide by them. It is interesting to note that while providing a definition of Hinduism, Czech researchers often describe all that is *not* Hinduism as well, which might cause some confusion to the readers of the Czech Orientalist production. We shall return to this point later. Now, let us start with the definition of Dušan Zbavitel from a book published in 2009:

> Hinduism, the socio-religious organisation of the vast majority of more than billion inhabitants of the Republic of India and Nepal as well as of some religious minorities in Bangladesh, Pakistan, and in a great variety of other regions, is highly variable in respect to its religious side.[87]

It is hardly surprising that Krása, Marková, and Zbavitel expressed the same opinion in 1997:

> Even more telling, however, is the increased emphasis on the social organisation of the adherents. They are all . . . connected by belonging to one of the many castes that superseded the old system of the four varnas . . . It is therefore absolutely correct to think of Hinduism as the socio-religious organisation of most of the Indian population rather than as a religion.[88]

Similarly, Stanislava Vavroušková wrote in 1996:

> Hinduism is a worldview complex that includes religious and cultic ideas, philosophical teachings, and ethical and legal norms created in the course of the millennia-long social development on the Indian soil. Its legal norms and social institutions are inseparable from the doctrine itself,

---

87 *Mánavadharmašástra aneb Manuovo poučení o dharmě, [Manava-dharmashastra, or, the Manu's Treatise on Dharma]* (Prague: ExOriente, 2009), 14. (Translated by D. Zbavitel, from his Introduction.)
88 Krása, Marková, and Zbavitel, *Indie a Indové*, 37.

which is why Hinduism is often called a socio-religious system rather than just a religion.[89]

The authors actually repeat the definition presented by Zbavitel in 1964:

Far from being merely a religion, if it can be described in any simple terms at all, Hinduism is a *socio-religious organisation of the vast majority of India's inhabitants.*[90]

The same definition was already put forward in 1927 by Vincenc Lesný, a teacher of Dušan Zbavitel:

Hinduism is an Indian socio-religious system that evolved out of the older Brahmanism by absorbing elements of different origin. It is a body of rituals, religious practices and views, traditions, and stories which are directly or indirectly validated by the ancient books or precepts of the Brahmins.[91]

Likewise, Otakar Pertold wrote a year before that:

It is the religion which is now professed by the majority of Indian population. In its essence, it is a mixture of various and often heterogeneous sects unified by their faith in the Vedas as the basis of all divine and human law and also by the fact that they recognise the Brahmins as experts on religion and the supreme arbiters in all religious matters.[92]

It is a startling fact that the description of Hinduism has remained the same for over eighty years despite Czech Indologists' ostensible commitment to presenting the findings of current research. However, if the description happens to be useful for characterizing the phenomenon under scrutiny and if it is not contradictory to the gathered evidence, we can abide by it. Is it so? Is the explanation prevalent in Czech specialized

---

89   Vavroušková, "Tradice a moderní společnost: hinduismus," 93.
90   Zbavitel et al., *Bozi, bráhmani, lidé,* 11.
91   Vincenc Lesný, *Duch Indie* [Spirit of India] (Prague: Státní nakladatelství, 1927), 151–158. The author reiterated the definition almost verbatim in other publications, see Vincenc Lesný, *Indie a Indové: Pouť staletími* [India and Indians: A journey through centuries] (Prague: Orientální ústav, 1931), 18.
92   Otakar Pertold, *Perla Indického oceánu: Vzpomínky ze dvou cest na Ceylon (1910 a 1922)* [Pearl of the Indian Ocean: Memories from two journeys to Ceylon in 1910 and 1922] (Prague: J. Otto, 1926), 135.

literature clear and consistent with available facts and the recent state of research? First, the core claim of the definition will be examined: Hinduism is said to be a social organisation *defined by religion*. One would therefore expect the social system to be grounded in doctrine. The relevance of other claims, that is the central role of *the Vedas* and the Brahminical religious authority, will be considered later.

According to the works of four Czech Indologists (Zbavitel, Merhautová, Filipský, Knížková), Hinduism consists of "both doctrinal and social elements."[93] The doctrine of this Indian religion is said to be most tolerant, free from imposing any dogmas on the believers, and enabling extensive freedom of thought and opinion. Moreover, its adherents can enrich the heritage of the past with their original contributions, and it is even permissible for a Hindu to be atheist![94] The social element is thought to consist of the caste system and a series of rules determining the right conduct of an individual. Those are defined "by general ethical and moral principles as well as the individual's social status and his relationship with others."[95]

In contrast to doctrine, the social "element" is presented as highly rigid, especially because it is supposedly impossible for a Hindu to change his social status as defined by his birth in a particular group. Furthermore, besides dividing its adherents into castes and sub-castes, Hinduism instituted "a baffling plethora of commandments and prohibitions covering a great deal of social, domestic, and private life. In this respect, one can hardly speak of tolerance in orthodox Hindu communities."[96]

Let us first look at the alleged doctrine of Hinduism. We shall soon see how Czech scholars have contradicted themselves in this matter and reached untenable conclusions. Despite claiming that Hinduism has no unified doctrine, they still tried to describe it. For instance, Dušan Zbavitel said:

Hinduism is not a unified religion with firm dogmas. In its repertoire, we can find the most absurd ideas side by side with very rational attempts at interpreting the world that are in some respects considerably close to the

93 Dušan Zbavitel et al., *Bohové s lotosovýma očima: Hinduistické mýty v indické kultuře tří tisíciletí* [The gods with lotus eyes: Myths of the Hindus in the Indian culture of three millenia] (Prague: Vyšehrad, 1986), 8.
94 Compare Zbavitel et al., *Bohové s lotosovýma očima*, 9, with Zbavitel et al., *Bozi, bráhmani, lidé*, 6.
95 Zbavitel et al., *Bohové s lotosovýma očima*, 9.
96 Zbavitel et al., *Bozi, bráhmani, lidé*, 6.

most recent scientific hypotheses. It hardly imposes anything at all on its adherents in the area of thought. It does not resist the influence of other creeds or materialist views, nor does it condemn a member of its religious community for doubts, scepticism, or opinions differing from what is set down in the old scriptures. This is the reason why we find in Hinduism seemingly irreconcilable philosophical schools, belief in innumerable deities alongside to monotheism, absolute fatalism and determinism, as well as the belief that man creates his own fate and destiny . . .[97]

Although Czech scholars have often written about "Brahminical orthodoxy," or in other words "Hindu doctrine," Zbavitel was convinced that any firm dogmas do not form a substantial doctrine at all![98] On the contrary, as the quotations demonstrate, it is actually an indefinite complex of all possible as well as mutually exclusive positions. However, Czech Indologists have supposedly found several common characteristics of doctrines: the concept of a permanent component of human being (Zbavitel: "some kind of soul") and its transmigration, the law of Karman, the universal order of permanent creation, evolution and annihilation of the world, and the effort to free oneself from the cycle of rebirth.[99] Czech Indologists have also claimed that all the religious and philosophical positions of Indian traditions, including those of the early ascetic groups and later of Buddhism and Jainism, evolved from the teachings contained in *the Upanishads*. Therefore, they considered *the Upanishads* to be the central sacred texts of India:

In all the autochthonous Indian religions, i.e. Hinduism, Buddhism, and Jainism, these Vedas—or more precisely their younger part, *the Upanishads*—form the basis for the main articles of faith. For orthodox Hindu philosophy, they are the foundation of principles that have the validity of incontrovertible truths.[100]

---

97 Sómadéva, *Oceán příběhů: Kathásaritságaram* [Somadeva's Ocean of Stories] (Prague: Odeon, 1981), 1:17; from the Introduction of Dušan Zbavitel, the translator.

98 Compare e.g. Vavroušková: "Tradice a moderní společnost: hinduismus," 93.

99 Sómadéva, *Oceán příběhů*, 1:17–18. Similarly, on the "Hindu worldview" characterised by the belief in soul, the cycle of rebirth, the law of Karman, and the duty dictated by the *dharma*, see Zbavitel et al., *Bohové s lotosovýma očima*, 10. The teaching about the cycle of lives and the law of Karman was considered the "cornerstone of Hindu worldview" by Ivo Fišer, *Bohové s lotosovýma očima*, 32. See also the chapter "Základní články hinduistické věrouky" [The basic articles of Hindu doctrine] by Boris Merhaut, *Bohové s lotosovýma očima*, 43–44.

100 Dušan Zbavitel and Jaroslav Vacek, *Průvodce dějinami staroindické literatury* [The guide through history of the old Indian literature] (Třebíč: Arca JiMfa, 1996), 13.

For, indeed, there is no significant form of Indian thought that would not be ultimately rooted in *the Upanishads*, the ancient Indian philosophical texts whose scope and content are unparalleled worldwide. The heterodox Buddhism is no exception. As the British Indologist Rhys Davids succinctly remarks, after all, the Buddha was born and brought up a Hindu, he lived and died as one.[101]

Counter-arguments can be summed up in the following three points:

1. *A conjunction of such irreconcilable opinions can hardly result in any kind of orthodoxy.* Some of the traditions cited above actually refuted the proposed characteristics. Moreover, the supposed "main articles of Hindu faith" coexist with completely different views even today. The first discrepancy can be exemplified by opinions embraced by ascetic groups, supposedly grounded in *the Upanishads*. The ascetic Ajivikas argued against the law of Karman, the Charvakas refuted the law of Karman as well as the teaching about the cycle of lives, and the Ajnanikas doubted the usefulness of such discussions.[102] The oldest Buddhist teaching seems to be unequivocal in its rejection of the existence of a permanent component of man (the teaching of non-self, *anatta*).[103] Is it possible to maintain that a rejection of a particular "article of faith" implies its anchoring in it? Furthermore, freeing oneself from the cycle of lives, the supposed goal of all Hindus, is not a commonly held belief either. For example, in certain Bhakti traditions, Bhakti towards a beloved deity is by itself considered the highest goal of human life, something that the aspirant wishes to experience in the world, "birth after birth," whereas liberation from the cycle of lives is not the issue at all.[104]

---

101 Vladimír Miltner, *Indie má jméno Bhárat: Aneb úvod do historie, bytí a vědomí indické společnosti* [India's name is Bharat: Or, the introduction into the history, being, and consciousness of Indian society] (Prague: Panorama, 1978), 174.

102 See e.g. Vladimír Miltner, *Vznik a vývoj buddhismu* [The origin and development of Buddhism] (Prague: Vyšehrad, 2001), 39–43.

103 See Jiří Holba, "Buddhova nauka o ne-Já (*an-átman*)" [Buddha's Teaching about Non-Self], in *Pojetí duše v náboženskýc tradicích světa* [Concept of the soul in religious traditions of the world], ed. Radek Chlup (Prague: DharmaGaia, 2007), 295–329. Jiří Holba mentions here the evidence of Buddhist texts about Brahmins who did not believe in the existence of a permanent self (p. 311). It follows that in the early period of Buddhism there was no unanimous agreement on this "article of faith" even among the Brahmins.

104 Thus, for example, Chaitanya (c. 1486–1533), an important figure of Bengali Vaishnavism: "O Lord of the Univerise, I do not desire material wealth, followers, a beautiful wife or fruitive activities described in flowery language. All I want, life after life, is unmotivated bhakti unto

2. *In India, there have never been conditions that could form and sustain orthodoxy.* Balagangadhara pointed out a series of such conditions. A primary prerequisite for a worldview (doctrine) is the very existence of a standardized worldview to which all changes of interpretation relate. Another condition is the existence of an authority that would settle possible differences of opinion. This authority must be a human one because the mere existence of a normative text could hardly resolve such debates. The human authority must be somehow organised, which again implies the existence of an organisation ensuring the maintenance and proliferation of a doctrine.[105] Until the emergence of modern reform movements in the 19th century that evidently emulated the patterns of Christian missions, Indian traditions did not exhibit any of these conditions for the existence of orthodoxy. Not even the reform movements such as Brahmo Samaj, Arya Samaj, or the Hindoo Association have become the unifying organisation of the Hindu majority, which means that the basic conditions for preserving and transmitting any doctrine are non-existent in India to this day.

Czech Indologists themselves have observed that there are no churches, no heresies, nor councils in "Hinduism." How could it be possible then to create and maintain a unified worldview? Having pointed out the lack of any external central authority in "Hinduism," Karel Werner attempted to solve this problem:

> In Hinduism, central authority is only internal, individually experienced and understood in the sense of the term *Sanātana Dharma*, as derived from the traditional sacred scriptures, the Vedas, whose acceptance as a divine revelation or an inspired source of spiritual knowledge has therefore become a formal mark or a criterion of adherence to Hinduism.[106]

Werner thus proposed that the central authority of Hindus consists in the internalisation of doctrine and the individual experience of believers. However, it is evident that this cannot be substituted for a central authority in society inasmuch as it does not meet the above mentioned conditions for the existence and transmission of orthodoxy. I can only

---

you." (Verse 4) in *Sri Siksastaka: Eight Beautiful Instructions by Sri Caitanya Mahaprabhu*, ed. Sarvabhavana Dasa and Riktananda Dasa (Andheri: Harmonist Publications, 1991), 39.

105 Balagangadhara, "*The Heathen in His Blindness...*", 371–378.
106 Werner, *Náboženství jižní a východní Asie*, 8.

repeat that *the Vedas* have been and still are irrelevant to many Indian traditions and that there are no generally recognised "articles of faith." In reality, there is no unified doctrine that Indian people can internalise. Consequently, Werner's argument falls apart.

3. Both of the above discussed arguments are supported by the cumulative evidence of the Europeans' experience of India: *"Hindus" are generally unaware of their "sacred texts" and they are either unfamiliar with the putative doctrines or they consider them unimportant.* Many "Hindus" have held and still do hold completely different opinions and one can hardly speak of a unified worldview in their case. This objection is confirmed by Lubomír Ondračka's observation that the law of Karman has never been generally accepted and that many Indians do not desire to free themselves from the cycle of lives:

> In many important texts (e.g. the Mahabharata), we can see that human life is not influenced solely by the quality of preceding actions, but by a great variety of other factors as well: by the moods and interests of the deities, malicious demons, fate, etc. . . . And the same is true even today. In various catastrophes of life, Indians perceive the workings of displeased goddesses, evil demons or the spirits of prematurely departed ancestors, astrological circumstances, or they are simply vicissitudes of fortune. If considered at all, the law of Karman does certainly not take priority in interpreting the troubles of life ... Contemporary India offers a different picture: Most Indians do not yearn for a better rebirth but rather for a blessed abode in the heavens.[107]

Similar observations have been made, for example, by Otakar Pertold regarding the Katkari tribe who might have worshipped various Hindu deities, although ideas about evil malignant creatures were prominent features in their rituals. While Pertold did find some awareness of reincarnation among Katkari people, it was unrelated to the law of Karman and it certainly was not a fundamental belief:

> *They do not give much thought to how the world was created and what happens to man after his death; their views vary a great deal in this respect* depending on

---

107 Lubomír Ondračka, "Védské představy o posmrtném životě" [Vedic ideas about the life after death], in *Pojetí duše v náboženských tradicích světa*, ed. Radek Chlup, 252–253.

the influences they have been exposed to most. The common beliefs of the lowest Hindu classes are the most widespread among them. The Katkaris predominant idea of afterlife is a crude belief in reincarnation, which however does not entail causality or the idea of retribution. *It is utterly impossible to offer a precise rendering of their ideas in this respect.*[108]

One might object that the Katkari were a tribe who professed Hinduism only superficially. Nevertheless, how are we to explain that ignorance of *the Vedas* and *the Upanishads* (and thus the "articles of faith") has long been observed among the Brahmins who are said to be the creators and guardians of Hindu doctrines? Balagangadhara pointed out that as early as 1808, Chatfield summarised the British consensus regarding the Brahmins' ignorance of the content of their supposed sacred texts:

> In confirmation of this opinion of the general ignorance of the Brahmins, it is recorded, *that they cannot even read the books which contain their sacred records*, but are altogether immersed in such deep sloth and depravity, that immoral practices, which the most barbarous nations would have feared to adopt, are at this hour, openly allowed and sanctioned, in the most public places and polished cities of Hindoostan. . . . They are said to have as little acquaintance with the moral precepts of their Sastras, as the Samoeides, and Hottentots, with the elegant arts of sculpture and painting.[109]

Gelders and Balagangadhara pointed out that *the Vedas, the Upanishads*, and *the Bhagavadgita* became better known only in the colonial era, primarily because of the attention the European Orientalists paid to these texts, and later among some Indian reformers as well. For instance, when Ram Mohan Roy published his translation of some of *the Upanishads* in 1820, he was accused by a traditional Bengali scholar of having fabricated those passages. In the second half of the 19th century, the Sanskrit expert F. Hall noted that Bengali scholars could get along well without knowledge of *the Vedas*.[110] I found other statements bearing evidence that *the Vedas* were absolutely unknown to many "Hindus" in the 19th century,

---

108 Otakar Pertold, *Ze zapomenutých koutů Indie* [From the forgotten corners of India] (Prague: Aventinum, 1927), 39.

109 Robert Chatfield, *An Historical Review of the Commercial, Political and Moral State of Hindoostan*, 1808, quoted in Balagangadhara, *"The Heathen in His Blindness..."*, 374.

110 Gelders and Balagangadhara, "Rethinking Orientalism: Colonialism and the Study of Indian Traditions," 104.

and if the Brahmins knew them at all, they would use them ritually without taking any interest in their possible doctrinal content. Having spent many years in India and eventually holding the first Boden Professor of Sanskrit at Oxford, Horace H. Wilson expressed his disappointment with ignorance of the guardians of doctrine:

> In many parts of India, the Vedas are not studied at all; and when they are studied it is merely for the sake of repeating the words; the sense is regarded as a matter of no importance, and is not understood even by the Brahman who recites or chants the expressions. Now this is in itself a vital departure from the sacred institutes of the Hindus . . .[111]

Indians' general awareness of *the Vedas* was not any better and has hardly improved since. A. Bharati estimated that barely five per cent of "Hindus" are familiar with the titles of "the most important texts of Hinduism"![112] If over ninety per cent of "Hindus" do not even know about the existence of their sacred texts, how could they be familiar with the teachings enshrined in them? This is in stark contrast to Europe where even non-believers, with a few exceptions perhaps, know about the existence of the Bible. Moreover, among the "Hindu" schools that do make reference to *the Vedas*, there is no agreement as to what actually constitutes *the Vedas*. For instance, some Vaishnava traditions include the great epics and the *Puranas* among *the Vedas*.[113] This is why some Vaishnava schools consider the *Bhagavata Purana* the culmination of Vedic learning, while others are wholly unfamiliar with it. Therefore, *the Vedas* cannot be proved to be the only and most widely accepted authority since days of yore, as they are described in European literature; they are only the oldest preserved collection, consisting mainly of guidelines on ritual, and commentaries of varying nature.

The inevitable conclusion is that neither the doctrine of Hinduism nor its central scared scriptures exist. That is provided that the term "doctrine" retains its meaning and is not used vaguely as an empty concept, or paradoxes

---

111 Fitzedward Hall, *Works of the Late Horace Hayman Wilson* (London: Trübner, 1864), 2:49.
112 Agehananda Bharati, *Hindu Views and Ways and the Hindu-Muslim Interface* (New Delhi: Munshiram Manoharlal, 1981), 3.
113 The Vaishnavite compendium *Bhagavata Purana*, composed no later than the 10th century AD, gives a list of *Vedas* created by the god Brahma. As well as the four *Samhitas*, he is said to have created the epics and the *Puranas* which are called "the fifth Veda" (Bhag. 3.12.39). A. C. Bhaktivedanta Swami Prabhupada, *Srimad Bhagavatam, Third Canto, Part One* (Los Angeles: Bhaktivedanta Book Trust, 1993), 526.

such as doctrine/non-doctrine are not juggled. However, for the sake of further discussion, we should remember one thing: Czech researchers kept explaining how Indian traditions lack any unifying dogmas, while still attempting to discover and describe crucial doctrines of Hinduism. Because of that, they identified *the Vedas* and *the Upanishads* as the central "sacred" texts of "Hinduism" as well as other Indian traditions. However, what are these texts?

Only a promising direction of further analysis may be suggested here in brief. Frits Staal demonstrated that in India, rituals are transmitted either without interpretations or with constantly changing interpretations, their purpose consisting in the performance itself with a strong emphasis on correct recitation or chanting.[114] If we abandon the idea of doctrines that provide the foundation for practices, derived as that idea is from Christian thinking, there remain at least two research areas: the practices of Indian traditions and theoretical speculations in abundance interspersed with stories. The relationship between them is different from what it has so far been assumed to be.

For example, one research question will be how traditional Indian thought interpreted rituals and human actions in general. Frits Staal's work makes it clear that the performance of complex rituals coincided with the development of reasoning about rules and meta-rules which did not only deal with the execution of rituals as such, but also with the structure of language. Having been, thus far, overlooked by most Western scholars, the school of *Mimamsa* should be given much more attention. Staal claims that it is virtually impossible to properly understand *Vedanta*, *Vyakarana* as well as Buddhist thought without thoroughly comprehending *Mimamsa* inasmuch as all of these lines of thought reacted to that school.[115]

Let us return to our discussion about Hinduism. Describing it as socio-religious organisation is already doubtful at this stage. *If there is no unified religious doctrine, what makes the organisation of Indian society religious? What is it actually founded on? And furthermore, how does such an organisation function?* On the one hand, Indologists assume the existence of such an unimaginably contradictory and tolerant doctrine that it does not justify the use of the term, and on the other hand, the allegedly immutable practice covers all areas of human life. This leaves us with two possible

---

114 Staal, *Ritual and Mantras*, 400.
115 Staal, *Ritual and Mantras*, 419.

explanations. According to the authors cited above, the doctrinal element is not the basis of the social, familial, or personal practice, which of course does not answer the question of what forms that basis. There is no evidence of this approach among Czech Indologists, unlike the other explanation of which there is ample evidence: Doctrine is thought to be the reason for what is perceived as intolerance and rigidity. However, Indologists do not discuss *the Vedas* or *the Upanishads* in this case. The ideological basis of the social system is traced primarily to the *Manava-dharmashatra* and other texts and commentaries dealing with *dharma* that Indologists associate with the teaching of the law of Karman.[116] Czech scholars have attributed a central role to the story of Brahma which is considered to have given rise to the four well known *varnas* of the ancient Indian society: Brahmins, Kshatriyas, Vaishyas, and Shudras. The Brahmins are thought to have used this story ideologically to legitimise their exceptional social status:

> Once and for all, this established the basic framework of the whole social system—a framework which was unchangeable because it was laid down by a divine authority and was fully convenient to those who were its real founders, i.e. the Brahmins. It endowed them with a spiritual authority over all other members of the society, including the earthly rulers, and secured for them a monopoly in executing offerings that would be indispensable to everyone, and in teaching all others . . .[117]

This brings us to a claim crucial to not only Czech but to all Western Indological scholarship. *The main protagonists in the story of Indian religions are the Brahmins whom Europeans considered to be priests.* Whether scholars embraced the older interpretation of the three evolutionary stages of Indian religion (from Vedism to Brahmanism to Hinduism), or treated Hinduism as one religion that developed, presumably, since the birth of the Indus Valley Civilisation, is of little consequence here.[118] In both

---

116 See e.g. Strnad et al., *Dějiny Indie*, 171. Ivo Fišer found in the teaching on Karman "a unique instrument for the enslavement of a men within the caste system," in Zbavitel et al., *Bozi, bráhmani, lidé*, 36. Although one could object that this opinion was due to the contemporary Marxist ideology, the idea of a doctrinal "enslavement" of the Indian people by the Brahmins is recorded as early as the second half of the 18th century, in the work of J. Z. Howell who cannot be suspected of adopting the Marxist ideology. See more in the section concerned with the first British Orientalists further below in this chapter.

117 *Mánavadharmašástra aneb Manuovo poučení o dharmě*, 14 (Introduction by the translator D. Zbavitel).

118 See, for example, Gavin Flood, *An Introduction to Hinduism* (New Delhi: Cambridge University Press, 1998), 20–22.

views, the Brahmins are the spiritual leaders and supervisors of Indian society since the advent of Aryans in India.[119] As they subdued the Dravidians, they are said to have succeeded in integrating the indigenous cults in their own system:

> Thus began the process of mutual integration of the Aryans and the local population, which also included syncretism of the Indo-European people's religion and the native cults. Those cults were adopted and firmly incorporated into the foundations of nascent Hinduism. Today, it is impossible to ascertain the period when they merged with the religion of the Vedas (the Aryans' sacred texts).[120]

The Aryan priests thus allegedly succeeded in taking over and subsequently assimilating the indigenous religious ideas. However, the general view is that rather than becoming wise leaders and counsellors of their people, they are thought to have abused their position of ritual specialists to usurp more power:

> Having formerly instigated cultural and scientific progress, the Brahmins transformed in their majority into what might be called the spiritual guards of the caste society; they engaged in close surveillance so that nobody would deviate a single step from the path strictly outlined by commandments and prohibitions which they claimed to be "eternal" and "divine," and especially that nobody would impinge on their monopoly in mediating between people and gods and on deciding what is right and wrong.[121]

The first problem with this interpretation is the absence of any central organisation as has already been explained above. Hinduism is envisioned to be an enormous organisation of hundreds of millions of people that has lasted for some three millennia. However, even the Brahmins who are taken to be the creators and "spiritual police" of this organisation have never founded a pan-Indian organisation of their

119 One quotation from D. Zbavitel will suffice to illustrate the conviction about the Brahminical supremacy: "As spiritual leaders and ideologues, they presided over the whole society already in the archaic Vedic period and they have retained their status up to this day." Sómadéva, *Oceán příběhů*, 1:21.
120 Vavroušková, "Tradice a moderní společnost: hinduismus," 94.
121 Zbavitel, *Starověká Indie*, 275.

own. How could they have established and maintained their authority over the society then? Zbavitel claimed that they have done so by means of "ideological pressure" derived from the law of Karman.[122] This is a weak claim in the light of the arguments explained above. The prominent Czech Indologist himself admitted that "this ideological pressure" would not have sufficed by itself. In his opinion, the caste system has "much more convincing and effective mechanisms" including "strong organisation and social coercion, a single authority, and a punitive system."[123]

One would expect to get a detailed description of the strong organisation and the functioning of such authority. Instead, we are given very brief information about the existence of councils, *panchayats*, that could be described as caste or sub-caste committees in every village or municipal district. It is worth noting that Zbavitel's "sub-castes" refer to social groups known as *jatis*, counted in many thousands in today's India. Only in certain cases can we say that a particular *jati* connects itself with one of the four *varnas*.

In fact, the relationship between those two domestic categories is still an unresolved problem. Zbavitel simplified the matter considerably when he merely mentioned "sub-castes" and then went on to talk about "caste councils." It would be more apt to talk about the councils of individual *jatis*. However, the existence of *panchayats* does not in itself clarify how the caste system works in terms of the organisation of Hinduism. It is not clear how, if at all, the immense number of those local councils communicate with each other, not to open the question of development of this institution. Remarkably, the evidence introduced by Zbavitel undermines what he had stated before.

Towards the close of his chapter on castes, one learns that "the decision-making power in caste disputes does not lie with the Brahmins, as might be deduced from all that has been said about the unshakeable authority of Brahmins in Indian society from Antiquity up to the modern period."[124] A Brahmin's expert opinion or advice may be sought out if need be, but it is where his role ends, the decision is completely dependent upon the will of a particular *panchayat*. Zbavitel did not afford any explanation for this fundamental contradiction in his interpretation. *It is not just that there is no central organising authority of this allegedly religious*

122 Zbavitel, *Bozi, bráhmani, lidé*, 212.
123 Zbavitel, *Bozi, bráhmani, lidé*, 212.
124 Zbavitel, *Bozi, bráhmani, lidé*, 215.

organization of society in India; there is no unified doctrine either, and the supposed creators and supervisors of the caste system are practically powerless to enforce their precepts. At the end of the discussed chapter, Zbavitel, certainly surprised attentive readers with this comment on the matter of Hinduism as a religious organisation:

> Quite recently, orthodox Hindus have been trying to make up for *the lack of centralised religious organisation and authority over matters of faith and custom* by setting up committees consisting of scriptural scholars. These have mostly advisory but in some places also executive powers, working within a particular region (Gwalior, Mysore) or even a whole state (the Kashmiri Dharma Sabha). *However, these are modern "improvements" that are not supported by tradition and cannot be expected to become pan-Indian.*[125]

This is exactly the case: The central, all-encompassing organisation or authority has always been foreign to Indian traditions and modern efforts to create them have been unsuccessful thus far. One can only repeat again that the Brahmins themselves have never had a unified organisation nor do they have it now. In what way then could thousands of Brahmin groups have communicated across the whole of India and agreed on some common procedures? Further investigation also disproves the interpretation of Brahmins as Hindu priests. The Brahmin monopoly in spiritual matters, so frequently affirmed in scholarly literature, is not real. There is abundant evidence that Brahmins have had no monopoly on conducting rituals, neither in the past nor today.[126] A great number, if not the majority, of rituals are conducted by the members of households; some places of pilgrimage and Hindu temples, *mandirs*, are in the care of groups of ritual experts other than the Brahmins.

There is another argument against the sacerdotal role of Brahmins that is to be considered. Ancient texts as well as European testimonies tell us that Brahmins have often engaged in and still pursue occupations other than the supposed priestly vocation. Ivo Fišer and Kamil Zvelebil noted some examples of such evidence. The Buddhist *Jatakas* inform

---

125 Zbavitel, *Boží, bráhmani, lidé*, 216.
126 Vedic texts mention groups that preformed another type of ritual, different from the authors of the *Samhitas*, for example, references to the rituals of the Vratyas. See e.g. J. C. Heesterman, "Vratya and Sacrifice," *Indo-Iranian Journal* 6 (1962): 137. Till today, many rituals are conducted by other groups than the Brahmins, see e.g. C. J. Fuller, *The Camphor Flame: Popular Hinduism and Society in India* (Princeton: Princeton University Press, 2004), 66.

us that some Brahmins made their living as guardians of caravans, others by trading various merchandise, and others still by hunting in the woods.

Other stories tell of Brahmins working in agriculture; while some owned land and had it tilled by hired labourers, others walked behind the plough themselves, which the codes of law prohibited, and lived with their families in grave poverty. Even when pursuing different vocations, Brahmins would often engage in activities that their own lawmakers forbade: some dealt in alcohol, others made their living by peddling, hunting, or snake shows. One tale tells of a Brahmin who was a hired labourer working on a royal road to a park, which was considered a very menial work.[127]

In this respect, the Czech Indologists also mention the surprise of the German scholar Richard Fick who observed huge differences between "the proud priests and Pandits" of Varanasi and "the half-naked potato growers of Orissa" as both groups were Brahmins.[128] Today, the same surprise awaits Europeans on their first trip to India when they discover that many Brahmins manufacture shoes, pottery, or sell all kinds of commodities. After all, different texts such as the *Puranas* contain recommendations regarding occupations that are suitable for the Brahmins. For example, the *Bhagavata Purana* mentions agriculture or even gleaning leftover grains in the fields.[129] Therefore, neither historical nor contemporary evidence supports the idea that the Brahmins are some powerful priestly class of Indian society.

Who then have been and still are the Brahmins in India? This question can be answered, at least partially, by analysing another important idea in the European structure of interpreting Indian traditions. The Orientalists' story of religion in India maintains that Brahmins were challenged by ascetic groups of ancient times, especially the Buddhists.

127 Ivo Fišer and Kamil Zvelebil, *Země posvátných řek* [The country of sacred rivers] (Prague: Mladá fronta, 1959), 90.
128 Ibid., 91.
129 Bhag. 7.11.16, Bhaktivedanta Swami Prabhupada, *Srimad Bhagavatam, Seventh Canto*, 660–661.

Was Buddhism a Protest against the Brahminical Orthodoxy and the Castes?

Before tackling the question of the Buddhist protest against "priests," it is important to mention the ongoing debate of whether Buddhism is a religion or not. Czech scholars have not reached a consensus on this issue. Characteristically enough, *a controversy arises within a debate dealing with the Buddhist teaching in relation to the possibility of God's existence and the existence of soul.* Two representative works will illustrate two important milestones in the original production of Czech scholarship dealing with this topic: *Buddhismus [Buddhism]* by Vincenc Lesný (1948) and *Vznik a vývoj buddhismu v Indii [The Origin and Development of Buddhism in India]* by Vladimír Miltner (2001). Both these treatises exhibit considerable continuity in the argumentative structure. Right in the introduction to his book, Vincenc Lesný claimed that "Buddhism was not a completely new religious phenomenon," since it ensued from the Upanishadic teaching about the immortal essence of man. At the same time, however, his argument seems to suggest that ancient India had a concept of one sovereign God which the Buddhists abandoned: "Although the doctrine of the *Pali Canon* retained the deities of old times, the concept of god itself had become dispensable to it."[130] He went on to say that what others seek in God, the Buddhists found in the law of Karman, "which is exactly the reason why it is not quite correct to call Buddhism a completely atheist religion."[131] Discussing the concept of *vijnana* (translated often as consciousness), the Czech Indologist took a rather unconvincing shortcut to reach the conclusion that the oldest Buddhist teaching accepted the existence of eternal soul and that "apsychism" developed in the Buddhism of the later centuries.[132] Lesný also classified the old Buddhism as a national religion in opposition to Mahayana which he described as a global religion: If the *Udanam* says that a man should help his fellow man at every available opportunity and that he should live for others, "it hardly is in the spirit of the *Pali Canon* Buddhism. These words were probably uttered on the eve of a new era which transformed a national religion into a global one."[133]

130 Vincenc Lesný, *Buddhismus* [Buddhism] (Prague: Jaroslav Samec, 1948), 56.
131 Lesný, *Buddhismus*, 101.
132 Lesný, *Buddhismus*, 115–119.
133 Lesný, *Buddhismus*, 165.

In contrast to that, Vladimír Miltner claimed that the categories of Buddhist thought do not include any permanent self and that "the Buddha himself frequently, more or less tacitly, refused to concede the existence of such a permanent principle, just as he did not accept the idea of an eternal omnipotent god and creator of all living and non-living things."[134] The two scholars' conclusions differ in that Lesný found the ideas of an omnipotent God and a soul present in Buddhism, whereas, in accordance with the findings of more recent research, Miltner did not. However, this difference should not blind us to one important agreement between the two. *Both scholars considered the questions of God's existence and eternal soul as significant concerns in the teachings of Buddhism. It is in the connection with these concepts that they ponder whether Buddhism is a religion or not.* Both also highlighted the law of Karman as the basis of the Buddhist worldview, which should derive from *the Upanishads*.[135] Miltner said:

These terms (i.e., soul and God) were silently disregarded by the Buddha because they were quite dispensable to his philosophy and it is clear that he could do very well without them. 'A religion without a god,' if it is a religion at all, this approach makes the original Buddhism resemble the opinions of ancient Indian materialism from whose influence Buddhism was not completely free, at least not in the beginning. Above all, Buddhism emphasises the principle of inevitable and just retribution for every single deed. . . . This is probably the most important and the most distinctive characteristic of the Buddhist worldview . . .[136]

Was Buddhism a religion in Miltner's view or not? That remains unclear even at the end of his book, which presents three different claims. Moreover, the Czech Indologist inserted additional problematic statements into those claims. They can be summarised as follows: 1) First of all, Miltner said that Buddhism is a "broad spiritual movement" and "a peculiar religion without a god and without prayers."[137] Without providing

134 Miltner, *Vznik a vývoj buddhismu*, 206.
135 Resolving the questions about God and soul was also crucial to Zbyněk Fišer (better known as Egon Bondy). The Czech writer thought that refusing the existence of the two concepts was the very basis of Buddha's second noble truth. However, Fišer also interpreted the supposed Buddhist criticism of the Brahminical doctrine as a prototype of the Marxist dialectics. In Fišer's opinion, Buddha's teaching was "a dialectic development beyond the concept of religion in general." Compare Zbyněk Fišer, *Buddha* (Prague: Orbis, 1968), 37, 80–92.
136 Miltner, *Vznik a vývoj buddhismu*, 206.
137 Miltner, *Vznik a vývoj buddhismu*, 329.

a comprehensive explanation, he accepted Lesný's claim that the law of Karman "encapsulates the power that other religions seek in god." Subsequently, Miltner extoled "the immense merit of Buddhism" in spreading the teachings of *the Upanishads* amongst the common people.[138] However, he did not specify which Upanishadic doctrines he had in mind. Those could hardly be the teaching about the Atman and the *brahma*, which would be incompatible with the early Buddhism taught according to our current knowledge. Of course, *the Upanishads* teach about many other topics, for example, what constitutes *yajna* or how to beget a child. 2) Next we learn that Buddhism "cannot be defined or characterised as merely a religion, which is also the case with Hinduism out of which Buddhism developed and into which it eventually merged."[139] The Czech scholar held that a concise expression of the nature of Buddhism can be found in a frequently quoted verse stating that the Buddha discerned the cause behind the emergence of single entities and also explained their demise. 3) Finally, Miltner concluded that Buddhism can be defined "clearly and concisely" as one of the four most widespread spiritual movements of humankind, as "a profoundly humanist worldview philosophy."[140]

The first statement explains that Buddhism is a religion with some peculiar characteristics (it has no god nor prayers). However, what is it that makes it a religion? *The second statement says that defining Buddhism is probably as problematic as defining Hinduism, but nowhere is it made clear where the rub is.* The first statement would seem to agree with this, because just as in the case of Hinduism this is a claim of the type "phenomenon A lacks the defining elements x, y, z, but it is still a religion just as phenomenon B which is characterised by x, y, z."[141] The third statement uses the vague term "spiritual movement" and calls Buddhism a philosophy. The three suggested possibilities are so problematic that it is impossible to arrive at any conclusion. The inserted ideas do not provide more insights, quite the opposite, actually. Alongside this, one finds Lesný's nebulous claim about the power that other religions seek in God and the assertion that Buddhism spread the teachings of *the Upanishads*, although we do not know which ones specifically. Apart from that, the Buddha is described as a teacher who revealed causality and cessation of phenomena. How is it possible to prove that Buddhists

---

138 Miltner, *Vznik a vývoj buddhismu*, 330.
139 Miltner, *Vznik a vývoj buddhismu*, 331.
140 Miltner, *Vznik a vývoj buddhismu*, 331.
141 See Balagangadhara, *"The Heathen in His Blindness…"*, 11–20.

have sought in the analysis of causality what others looked for in the concept of God?

An important idea in the European interpretations of the development of Indian religions is *the model of protest against the Brahmin orthodoxy and competition between individual traditions*. Most frequently, this model is used in discussions relating to the development of ascetic traditions, Buddhism and Jainism in particular, dated approximately from the 6th century BC. Having studied all the available textual evidence, scholars isolated two important groups of ancient India: the Brahmins and *the Shramanas*. "Those who strive," a possible translation of the name of the latter group, were itinerant ascetics who freed themselves from social obligations and endeavoured to answer questions regarding the nature of man and the world, of life and death. Above all, they experimented with various psycho-physical exercises in which they sought knowledge, quietude, and insights into what the world is actually about.

> Heralded by the mystical speculations of *the Upanishads*, the contemporary atmosphere was marked by a general urge to explore and investigate mysteries such as the origin of the universe and the purpose of human existence, giving rise to great number of religious and philosophical schools. While Buddhist sources contain references to about 62 newly emerged sects, the Jain texts suggest that during the life of Mahavira there were as many as 363 of them.[142]

Czech scholars tend to associate the origins of many movements with a period of thought ferment that saw a reaction against "the soulless ritualism" of the Brahmins. It allegedly started off with the Upanishadic speculations (which are traditionally included in the Vedic corpus) and culminated in a complete schism. Three quotations will suffice to illustrate the explanation of Orientalists:

> *The Upanishads'* critical treatment of Brahmin fundamentalism paved the way for an intellectual quest that found expression in the śramaṇic teachings, Jainism, Buddhism, and other heterodox movements.[143]

---

142 Strnad et al., *Dějiny Indie*, 53.
143 Strnad et al., *Dějiny Indie*, 50.

The development and spread of Jainism, Buddhism, and other heterodox schools of thought that arose in protest against the complicated ritualism and inane sacrificialism of Brahmanism is far from indicating that they gained supremacy over the Brahmin orthodoxy or even ousted it.[144]

Since the 7th century B.C., non-orthodox, independent schools of spiritual thought began to emerge, taking the anti-Brahmin revolt even further—they both refused Brahmin social privileges and criticised the sacred texts, the Vedas themselves.[145]

The use of language is noteworthy in these quotes, because it implies that there used to be just one religion—Brahmanism—which has disintegrated further and further into new groups. These groups are thought to have fought against Brahmanism and supposedly engaged in mutual rivalry. Czech Indologists used words that indicate some revolutionary changes in the religious life of ancient India. Thus, one reads, for example, that "Buddha's teachings originated in a revolt against the Brahminical system."[146] *However, those changes are envisioned to have involved not only religion-related changes, but changes regarding the form of the society as a whole:*

Therefore, this competition among the three new religions in the following centuries has been, perhaps above all, a parallel struggle over the framework regarding the social organisation. At this point we can state that it was Hinduism that emerged victorious out of this contest. Over a thousand years later, it almost completely ousted Buddhism from India and relegated Jainism to the fringes of Indian society.[147]

The same interpretation is encountered in older Indologist scholarship. It also illustrates a peculiar treatment of evidence. Vincenc Lesný says that "the Buddha was decisively opposed to dividing human society into castes" which is said to have "radically differentiated the Buddha's

---

144 Strnad et al., *Dějiny Indie*, 57–58.
145 Knotková and Čapková, *Základy asijských náboženství*, 1:188–189.
146 Strnad et al., *Dějiny Indie*, 185.
147 Krása, Marková, and Zbavitel, *Indie a Indové*, 37. Likewise, Miltner thought that Buddhism was "a social revolution without much overstatement," and more specifically "a strong expression of the non-Aryan inhabitants and some Hindu lower classes" efforts to revolt against the rigid caste system and strict Vedic ritualism of Brahmanism.' See Miltner, *Vznik a vývoj buddhismu*, 143.

teachings from Brahmanism," a claim that he derives from the doctrine of Karman.[148] In this passage, Lesný maintained that in the Buddha's time common opinion concerning the consequences of all actions was already well-established by *the Upanishads*. He mentioned several examples from the *Pali Canon*, with accordance to this teaching illustrating how are the events of the present life the fruits of past deeds. However, it is not at all clear how and why "it logically follows"[149] that the Buddha was against the caste system. In contrast to that, it is worth noting that the law of Karman has been viewed as the ideological basis of the caste system even today. In fact, the explanation stating that everyone is born into a particular caste according to his former actions seems much more logical. However, as I have already discussed, the law of Karman was not universally accepted in the Buddha's time. Furthermore, in circumstances lacking the centrally maintained doctrinal authority, no teaching could have formed the basis of social organisation. Therefore, we cannot defend by its sole existence either the refusal or legitimisation of the organisation of ancient Indian society. *What became obvious is that the Czech Orientalist scholarship considers the law of cause and effect to be the cornerstone of both Hindu and Buddhist teachings.*

What kind of evidence exits of those truly unsettled times which supposedly saw the struggle of three religions over the shape of the ancient India's society? Was Buddhism indeed a "revolt" as Czech Indologists claimed? If that had been the case, one would expect the earliest surviving evidence, i.e. the *Pali Canon*, to contain severe criticism of the Brahmins, a critique of "the inane sacrificialism," a dismissal of Brahmins' role within the society, and a wholesale rejection of the caste system itself. One would also expect to find there a proposal of an alternative social model championed by "heterodox" movements.[150] However, Heesterman has pointed out that the surviving records offer a different picture:

> The question that occupies religious thought appears not to be: sacrifice or rejection of sacrifice, but rather what is the true sacrifice. Equally, the question does not turn on Brahmin superiority or its rejection, but on

148 Lesný, *Buddhismus*, 101. Cf. his claim that "Buddhism see all people as equals and thus Buddhism stands in stark contrast to Hinduism," Lesný, *Buddhismus*, 145.
149 Lesný, *Buddhismus*, 101.
150 Balagangadhara, *"The Heathen in His Blindness…"*, 208.

the point who is the true Brahmin. On these points both orthodox and heterodox thinkers seem to agree to a great extent.[151]

The first important question—that of what constitutes true *yajna*—must be left aside here. However, if the second part of Heesterman's thesis is valid, that is to say that the main point in the ancient Indian discourse was to determine the criteria of true Brahminhood, then it generates a strong argument against the generally propounded interpretation of the Buddhist and other "heterodox" groups. It would thus be extremely difficult to conceive of a dismissal of Brahmanism in a situation when the supposedly contending schools of thought take part in a debate about what makes Brahmin a true Brahmin. What kind of testimony do the *Pali* texts provide? One might as well start by quoting from the *Dhammapada* collection, which is still very popular amongst Theravadin Buddhists. The collection of verses devotes a whole passage to the question of who truly is a Brahmin. These verses make it clear that Brahmin is synonymous with a wise, or even a liberated individual:

> Seated stainless, concentrated, whose work is done, who's free of taint, who attained the highest aim, that one I call the Brahmin True. . . . In whom is no wrong doing by body, speech, or mind, in these three ways restrained, that one I call a Brahmin True. . . . I call him not a Brahmin though by womb-born mother's lineage, he's just supercilious if with sense of ownership, owing nothing and unattached: that one I call a Brahmin True.[152]

This is not some later ideological interpolation. The factual equation of an ascetic's path with that of a Brahmin's is directly mentioned in the Buddha's discourses, for example in *Majjima Nikaya* 39:

> And when you are asked, "What are you?", you claim that you are recluses. Since that is what you are designated and what you claim to be, you should train thus: *We will undertake and practice those things that make one*

---

151 J. C. Heesterman, "Brahmin, Ritual and Renouncer," *Wiener Zeitschrift für die Kunde Süd-und Ostasiens* 8 (1964): 27.

152 *Treasury of Truth: Illustrated Dhammapada*, translated by Weragoda Sarada Maha Thero (Taipei: Buddha Educational Foundation, 1993), 1519, 1538, 1556. Compare also verses from the part "Punishment" (10.142), or part "The Wise," or verses 17.234 and 21.294.

a recluse, that make one a brahmin, so that our designations may be true and our claims genuine . . .[153]

Instead of rejecting the alleged Brahminical sacrificialism, the Buddha suggested that the objective of his ascetic group and the Brahmins is the same. In this connection, Balagangadhara quoted another passage directly from the discourses. The *Sonadanda-sutta* shows how the Gautama Buddha asks a representative of a small group of Brahmins what kind of things one must possess in order to have the right to call himself Brahmin. The group's speaker Sonadanda names five criteria: a good paternal and maternal origin as far as seven generations back; he must internalise the verses of the *Samhitas* and other topics; he must be handsome; he must be immensely virtuous; and he must be a wise man.

The Buddha asks whether one can be rightfully called Brahmin if some of these criteria were omitted. Sonadanda gives him an affirmative reply, saying that handsomeness and colour of skin are not that important and can be disregarded. This way, they eventually arrive at two essential characteristics of Brahminhood: virtue and wisdom. When the Buddha asks if any of these two can be left out, Sonadanda gives him a negative answer. Where there is virtue, there is wisdom; where there is wisdom, there is virtuous conduct. The Buddha replies that he says likewise.[154]

One may, therefore, conclude that the oldest Buddhist documents do not condemn Brahmins but, in fact, offer testimony of acceptance of the ideal of a true Brahmin.[155] This would not in itself disprove the other claim made by Indologists that the ascetic traditions revolted against the caste system. Balagangadhara offered a possible counter-argument: In

---

153 *The Middle Length Discourses of the Buddha: A New Translation of the Majjhima Nikaya* (Boston: Wisdom Publicatons, 1995), 362.

154 Trevor Ling, *The Buddha's Philosophy of Man: Early Indian Buddhist Dialogues* (London: Everyman's Library, London 1981), 42–45, quoted in: Balagangadhara, "*The Heathen in His Blindness...*", 209–210.

155 In his translation of *Dhammapadam*, Karel Werner refers briefly to the Buddhist acceptance of the ideal Brahmin. However, he explained it as the Buddha's effort "to revive the spiritual dimension of the Brahminical civilisation" and "make the highest aim attainable by anyone without priestly mediation." See *Dhammapadam* (Prague: Odeon, 1992), 36. It is not clear at all what is the basis for Werner's claim that the Vedic ritual and the "Brahminical civilisation" had the same aim as the Buddha. The Orientalist narrative of Indian religion has remained the main framework in this Indological interpretation, as the reference to a priestly mediation testifies, together with the following description of the further development of Indian religion: "This approach lost ground in the subsequent centuries and Buddhism established itself as a separate religion, led by monastic communities of monks, holding a central position in India for several hundreds of years." *Dhammapadam*, 36.

the history of Europe, criticism of aristocracy was directly related to the efforts of promoting the ideal of human nobleness. What if the Buddhist engagement in the debate on true Brahminhood is similarly connected to the fight against the caste system controlled by Brahmins? The Indo-Belgian scholar refuted this objection in two steps. First, he pointed out the specific nature of the ascetic efforts directed outside the contemporary society, aiming at establishing at best loose communities of people who devoted themselves fully to the Buddha discovered path to awakening. *The Buddhist Sangha was not an alternative model for social organisation.*[156] The ascetics, men and women, lived outside society whereas other disciples of the Buddha lived in the so-called caste society.

Furthermore, the extant discourses need to be examined to see how the Buddha related to the genesis of the four groups in India's society. Is there evidence of his criticism of the social system? The *Aggannasutta* shows that there is none: The Kshatriyas, Brahmins, Vaishyas, Shudras as well as *Shramanas*, arose as separate groups "in a proper manner, in accordance with *dhamma.*" Interestingly, Brahmins are supposed to have been only the second group to be formed by way of a common resolution to give up wrongdoing such as stealing, lying, and the like. At the very beginning of the discourse, the Buddha states that virtues can be found amongst members of all the social groups, while extoling wise and virtuous people at the end. Clearly, the fact of the matter is that *the Buddha presupposes the existence of the social system of four varnas, considering it established in accordance with dharma and assuming that it will keep on existing in the future.*[157]

There is evidence of this in other passages of the *Pali Canon* for that matter. Consider, for example, Ananda's wish that the Buddha would choose to retire and die in one of the important cities of his time. Ananda, one of the most important disciples of Buddha suggested to his master that "There are many wealthy Kshatriyas, Brahmins, and farmers there, devoted to the Noble One who will duly honour the Tathagata's body."[158] Ananda would be evidently happy if Brahmins and members of other castes took care of the master's funeral ceremony. Would he even think so had the disciples of Buddha been engaged in strong opposition

---

156 Balagangadhara, "*The Heathen in His Blindness...*", 212.
157 Balagangadhara, "*The Heathen in His Blindness...*", 213–216.
158 According to the Czech translation of *Mahāparinibbāna-sutta*: *Velká rozprava o Buddhově úplné nibbáně* (Prague: DharmaGaia, 1995, 124. Translated from the *Páli* original text by Miroslav Rozehnal.

to the "caste system" for decades already? From all these arguments, we can conclude that the interpretation of Buddhism as a protest against Brahmins and the caste system is untenable.

To summarise, Czech academic works present Hinduism as one unified religion having its central sacred texts (*the Vedas, the Upanishads, the Manava-dharmashastra*), central doctrines (reincarnation, the law of Karman, *moksha* as the goal of life), and its priestly class of Brahmins. I showed how untenable, inconsistent, and vague are the Czech Indologists' claims about a "socio-religious organisation." Neither can we apply the terms sacred scriptures, doctrines, and priests to Indian traditions. The problem looms even larger in the case of Buddhism, inasmuch as the spectrum of opinions includes the paradoxical claim about "an atheistic religion," a hesitant nod to the conceptualisation of Buddhism as religion, a suspicion that Buddhism is something more than "mere religion," and its description as "a worldview philosophy." Despite the shared conviction of the Czech Orientalist production about the anti-caste agenda of the early Buddhism, the evidence shows otherwise. Buddhists did not reject Brahmins, they debated who was a real Brahmin, and their oldest texts do not bear any evidence of their supposed revolt against society under the control of Brahmin "orthodoxy."[159]

Most of Czech scholarship has been repeating the same basic structure of the story about religion in India for over eighty years. There are, of course, some differences in detail, accretion of new information, but the fundamental interpretative framework has remained the same. Moreover, one can show how different facts have been interpreted ad hoc, as for example Lesný's claim that the law of Karman is a proof of Buddhist protest against social inequality. It is noteworthy that the interpretation of Indian traditions as religious was virtually unchanged by Marxist dialectics which some Czech Indologists at least proclaimed they espoused,[160] and that the underlying structure of interpreting Indian traditions is identical in the works of Czech theologians in the second half of the 20th century.[161]

---

159 See more on the question in Martin Fárek, "Were *Shramana* and *Bhakti* Movements Against the Caste System?" in *Western Foundations of the Caste System*, ed. Martin Fárek et al. (Cham: Palgrave Macmillan, 2017), 127–172.

160 "No other false form of social consciousness, such as religion is, apart from Hinduism, has penetrated so perfectly all areas of the social consciousness and all the strata of India's society." Miltner, *Indie má jméno Bhárat*, 173.

161 Compare, for example, the passages dealing with Indian traditions in the following texts: Josef Kubalík, *Dějiny náboženství* [A history of religion] (Prague: Česká katolická charita, 1988),

Compared to the predominant descriptions of the Orientalist paradigm abroad, the picture painted by Czech scholarship of Indian "religions" does not fundamentally differ from that of other European Orientalists. Hinduism is to be a religion that is defined by the authority of *the Vedas*, the doctrine of reincarnation and the law of Karman, and by the fact that Brahmins, its priests, created and maintained the caste system. *Dharma* is described as a religious law and Vaishnavism and Shaivism are the two major sects.[162] In contrast to Czech scholarship, the global discussion is a great deal more concerned with delimiting the term Hinduism.[163]

While some researchers, albeit aware of the problematic nature of the description, cling to the essentialist definition of Hinduism, others have suggested a polythetic definition inspired by Wittgenstein's concept of language games and family resemblances. That is to say that the characteristic features that one example of a phenomenon picked up by such definition does not have, are present in another phenomenon of the group. In this approach, one category can include different phenomena, which do not share a single common characteristic. Consequently, it is not a problem if some traditions do not recognise *the Vedas* at all or are incognizant of them, because they share, for example, the concept of *dharma* with another tradition which, in turn, shares the teaching about the law of Karman with another one still, and so forth. As I argued elsewhere, the problem with this approach lies in the selection of what should be a prototypical example of Hinduism which sets the basis for further characterization. In fact, this prototypical Hinduism has the same defining features as one finds in the essentialist characteristics.[164] Another problem of this approach is that by correlating more or less arbitrarily chosen characteristics, one arrives at an absurdly wide and potentially infinite set. It is, therefore, impossible to characterize the phenomenon of study in this manner.

84–116; Jan Heller and Milan Mrázek, *Nástin religionistiky, Uvedení do vědy o náboženstvích* [A sketch of religious studies: An introduction into the science of religions] (Prague: Kalich, 2004), 127–128, 144–150. The two latter authors referred to works by D. Zbavitel, J. Filipský, J. Vacek, and other discussed Czech Indologists.

162 For a more detailed analysis, see Fárek, "Hinduismus: reálné náboženství nebo konstrukt koloniální vědy?," 227–242.

163 For example, Günther Dietz Sontheimer and Hermann Kulke, *Hinduism Reconsidered* (New Delhi: Manohar, 2001); Douglas R. Brooks, "The Thousand-Headed-Person: The Mystery of Hinduism and the Study of Religion in the AAR," *Journal of the American Academy of Religion* 62, no. 4 (1994): 1111–1126.

164 Fárek, "Hinduismus: reálné náboženství, nebo konstrukt koloniální vědy?," 232–234.

Another solution has been proposed by Heinrich von Stietencron. Having discussed the problems inherent in various essentialist characteristics of religion in India, the German Indologist concluded that this concept of Hinduism does not fulfil the criteria of a coherent system which could be a historical religion. In consequence, he proposed preserving Hinduism as an umbrella term denoting a culture, and reserve the term religion for its distinct great traditions: Vaishnavism, Shaivism, and Shaktism.[165]

Stietencron used the analogy with Abrahamic religions that do not have either a single founder, or one single sacred book, but share many other things, just as the great traditions of "Hinduism." However, this analogy is erroneous. The Abrahamic religions have one common foundation in the Jewish line of prophets, in the concept of monotheism, in eschatological thought, and so on and so forth. Nothing like this is true for Indian traditions. Another problem is that rather than resolving the characteristic features of Hinduism, Stietencron only shifted the very same approach to the debate one level lower. While the dominant explanation of Hinduism describes Vaishnavism, Shaivism, etc., as "sects" of one religion, the German Indologist considered them to be separate religions. What is the ground for their religious nature, though?

In accordance with the major interpretation, Stietencron's structure remains in essence the same. He talked about the original Vedic religion and Brahmin sacrificialism. The Buddhist and Jain groups were interpreted as "a period of reformation," a campaign against Brahmin elitism. The ascetic groups themselves became elitist and a new struggle against both Brahmins and ascetics started, claimed Stietencron. This is how monotheist traditions of Hinduism came about.[166] The model of heresy and fight against the clergy has remained intact as if we were observing a repeated history of Europe's religious schisms, but set in India.

Typically, Czech and global discussions keep trying to answer the question whether Buddhism is a religion, a philosophy, both, or a different thing altogether. There have been revealing analyses that explore the interpretation of Buddhism as a world religion and point towards

---

165 Heinrich von Stietencron, "Hinduism: On the Proper Use of a Deceptive Term," in *Hinduism Reconsidered*, 32–53.

166 See Hans Küng and Heinrich von Stietencron, *Křesťanství a hinduismus* [Christianity and Hinduism] (Prague: Vyšehrad, 1997), 41–45.

the origins of the problems inherent in these debates.[167] Czech and international scholarship keep repeating that Hinduism and Buddhism lack certain characteristics (such as a common founder, the church, a unified theology in the case of Hinduism, the concepts of God and soul in Buddhism), and yet they are religions. This betrays an inability to characterize them in positive terms: What are they? A negative characteristic would be a result of false logic, because by saying what something is not, it does not bring the discussion any step closer to understanding what a particular phenomenon is. The discussion is thus bound up with the general problem of understanding religion: Judaism, Christianity, and Islam share certain characteristics generally thought to constitute a typical religion, and whilst Hinduism, Buddhism, or Shintoism lack those completely, they are still considered religions.[168]

Seeing that we encounter such fundamental problems when attempting to characterize and explain the very subject of our study, it will be worthwhile to consider the theory and the metastructures of ideas that have given rise to those problems. What kind of metastructure is that? As a starting point, one can take the apparently negative findings derived from the way "Hinduism" and "Buddhism" have been construed. S. N. Balagangadhara asked a set of important questions in this connection. How exactly did Europeans become convinced of the religious nature of Indian traditions? What was the underlying evidence? Why do they consider *the Vedas, the Upanishads*, etc., to be central sacred texts? In what manner do they identify the above mentioned ideas as India's central doctrines? How did Europeans find that Brahmins were priests of unified Hinduism? What makes them think that ascetic traditions are religious and social protest movements? Before dealing with these questions, one has to consider the role of language and its relation to the building of theories.

---

167 See Philip C. Almond, *The British Discovery of Buddhism* (Cambridge: Cambridge University Press, 1988). The role of Western scholars in the genesis of the concept of unified Buddhism as a world religion is examined also by Tomoko Masuzawa, *The Invention of World Religions* (Chicago: University of Chicago Press, 2005), 121–146.
168 See analysis in Balagangadhara, "*The Heathen in His Blindness...*", 10–22.

Intermezzo: Language Usage, Theories, and Metastructure of Ideas

When studying European scholarship dealing with India's traditions, one encounters certain noteworthy terms. Let us reiterate the above mentioned descriptive keywords: revelation, scriptures, doctrines, priests, reform, worship, sects, God and gods, sacrifice, prayer, monks, conversion, etc. These terms are salient in both the positive interpretations (Brahmins are priests, *bhikkhus* are monks, Vishnu and Shiva are the main gods, Buddhists are a heterodox sect derived from Hinduism and eventually merged with it again) and in the attempts to say what traditions of India are not (Hinduism has no church, no Pope, nor does it know heresies). What kind of language is this? It is beyond doubt that this is the language of Christian theology. One might object that these words have long become part and parcel of scientific, non-religious usage. Are they not used in scientific theories that have been freed from their Christian connotations and are therefore universal? The general conviction is that since the age of Enlightenment and during the subsequent secularisation, humanities have been emancipated from the dogmatic confines of Christian thought. The question is whether secularisation has really brought about the desired independence from the language and theoretical framework of theology. Before Balagangadhara, other scholars have doubted this, for example, Piatigorski:

> In the latter context, approaches to Hinduism are bracketed within a framework of cultural, cognitive, and ideological encounters between the "West" and India. This of course is not simply a "neutral," curiosity bound, "context free," "scientific" endeavour. Rather, it is irrevocably anchored in a long-standing, ongoing process of projecting, mirroring, confronting, eluding, denying, asserting, and in short fabricating oneself and its other. As a part of this larger "plot" of understanding and constructing non-Western religions, approaches to Hinduism often take for granted that categories such as "god, rite, myth, belief, essence, cult, sacrifice, are worship" are universally valid. There is a tendency to explain that which is alien through a framework which itself is alien to the "object" that demands making sense of.[169]

---

169 Alexei Piatigorski, "Some Phenomenological Observations on the Study of Indian Religion," in *Indian Religion*, ed. R. Burghart and A. Cantlie (London: Curson Press, 1985), 215.

The approach adopted by Piatigorski did not result in a clear analysis of the framework of ideas, determining the questions and the spectrum of possible answers for the theories created within that framework. The use of language originally grounded in the theological paradigm requires a more thorough analysis than might be apparent at first. When Europeans tried to understand the traditional thought of India, the task of surmounting a linguistic barrier posed a particularly challenging problem. I do not mean searching for equivalent terms of natural language that denote everyday realities. If our ancestors wished to find out what a mango was, they only had to peel the ripe fruit and taste it. But how can one "taste" the meanings of words such as *dharma, atman, brahma, citta, buddhi* and many others? These terms result from the traditional way of Indian thinking about human beings, society, and the world. They are firmly anchored in a specific framework, or metastructure, of thought structures, and it is only that metastructure which endows them with meaning. In this sense, they are theoretical terms inasmuch as theological terms have a theoretical character in Europe.[170]

Balagangadhara emphasised that this is a meeting point of not merely two different languages, but two languages of different metastructures whose structures of ideas do behave, in some ways, similarly to theoretical explanations.[171] What words can then be used to translate terms from Indian theories into European languages? Inasmuch as Europeans have been after centuries of Christian theology understandably convinced of the universal validity of their understanding of cultures, or societies through the worldview expressed in religious categories, they have searched the local languages for equivalents of their own terms of reference. The Christian theological framework was specific in that it explicitly postulated the existence of religion as a quest for the only true God in all cultures (albeit mostly in a degenerated pagan form). When Europeans saw rituals, these must have been religious rituals. For example, in order to find the Indian term for worship, one would only have to ask then what do Indians call, say, making circles with a lit oil lamp in front of a statue of Ganesha. The established conceptual structure simply did not allow consideration that *puja* might be something other than a false or imperfect form of worship. A dictionary was thus gradually built that supposedly enabled Europeans to comprehend the Indian

---

170 S. N. Balagangadhara, "Translation, Interpretation and Culture," unpublished article, March 2012, 5.

171 Balagangadhara, "Translation, Interpretation and Culture."

people's understanding of their own traditions. In reality, this consisted of linking terms that cannot be equivalent with regard to their grounding in different frameworks of thought.[172]

The domestication of theological language, Biblical characters, and stories in European languages tends to be a given matter. Centuries of Christian thought have naturally influenced the language of our culture. However, this cultural commonplace can be highly problematic when applying naturalised terms of Christian thought to Indian traditions. This mostly leads to uncritical absorption of different concepts into a theological framework which endows them with meaning according to its own established ideas. To a significant degree, Indian otherness is not reflected upon in Europe, from the popular media to specialised scholarship. A few examples of this will suffice:

Mladá fronta DNES, a Czech daily newspaper, has published an article called *Why do Hindus consider the cow to be holy?* without pondering whether the term *holy* makes sense to Hindus. A few interviews carried out by the author with Hindus in New Delhi demonstrate that the respondents did not understand what the reporter was asking them. Surprised, the journalist elaborated on an explanation which had become popular amongst Indians with Western education: The cow was the nurturer of people, its milk will provide sustenance to many more people than the meat of the slaughtered animal, etc. Then, the "dogma" against the slaughter of cows was introduced. Although the proposed explanation is of an economic nature, the journalist concluded his article by saying "Cows are therefore holy in India."[173]

This illustrates the degree to which our natural language has been soaked with theological language. This absorption of Indian traditions into the Christian framework of thought is likewise evident in scholarship. For example, Lesný claimed that old Buddhism did not have a prayer "in which an ignited human soul sees the means of reaching a deity and identifying with it." Nevertheless, "spiritual concentration"

---

172 Tellingly enough, many missionaries and later colonial rulers either did not know any Indian languages at all or they knew very little of them. Therefore, they depended on translators and one can only speculate as to what formed the basis of their understanding and renderings. A record of contemporary speeches and disputations would afford striking evidence of cultural misunderstanding. See Donald F. Lach, *Asia in the Making of Europe*, vol. 1 (Chicago: University of Chicago Press, 1965); among Czech scholars, this problem was discussed, for example, by Jana Valtrová, *Středověká setkání s jinými* [The medieval encounters with the others] (Prague: Argo, 2011), 41–48.

173 "Proč je kráva pro hinduisty posvátná?" [Why is the cow holy for the Hindus?], *Mladá fronta dnes*, September 6, 2012, 12A.

which "takes the place of prayer" is said to have "the same purpose in Buddhism."[174] Some readers might be interested to find out in which Buddhist context Miltner used the following phrase: "The most heinous crimes and sins that inevitably resulted in eternal damnation."[175] This was used despite the fact that Miltner knew well that in Buddhism one cannot consider "eternal damnation" as a fate of any being. Scholars often compare Indian characters and motifs to the Christian ones. Manu is said to have been the "Indian Moses,"[176] Mara, a character of old Indian stories, is often likened to the New Testament devil as a tempter,[177] the Buddhist *Narakalokas* are compared to Purgatory.[178] Since the Middle Ages, European scholars have been discussing the Indian Holy Trinity, most often identified with Brahma, Vishnu, and Shiva.[179]

Furthermore, translations of Indian texts bear out the same problem of applying Christian categories. An example of interpreting the Vedic hymns in this way is the translation of verse 12.1.1 of the Atharvaveda: "satyaṃ bṛhād ṛtām ugraṃ dīkśā tapo brahma yajñaḥ pṛthivīm dhārayanti," which Oldřich Friš translated as "Noble truth, powerful order, piety, repentance, prayer, sacrifice sustain the earth."[180] However, study of Vedic rituals makes it clear that *diksha* is not "piety." It is a ritual qualification attained through a series of specific actions. For example, during the ritual of *Agnichayana*, the *yajamana* who commissions the ritual sits on a skin of a black antelope in the ritual arena, a turban wrapped around his head, he receives a stick, clenching his fists in a peculiar manner. He will stay at the site for the duration of twelve days, holding the staff and maintaining the position of his arms and hands as much as he can, abiding by certain restrictions. These concern primarily speech, abstention

---

174 Lesný, *Buddhismus*, 166.
175 Miltner, *Vznik a vývoj buddhismu*, 119.
176 In the Czech scholarship, see, for example, Fišer and Zvelebil, *Země posvátných řek*, 84.
177 Lesný, *Buddhismus*, 103. Western scholars create such comparison to this day. The claim that Mara is 'the Buddhist Satan' is, for example, in Jonathan A. Silk, *Riven by Lust: Incest and Schizm in Indian Buddhist Legend and Historiography* (Honolulu: University of Hawaii Press, 200, 62). It is also noteworthy that "schism" is a prominent idea of Silk's interpretations in this book.
178 Lesný, *Buddhismus*, 104.
179 See e.g. Thomas Maurice, *A Dissertation on the Oriental Trinities*, 1800, which is summarised in Trautmann, *The Aryans and British India*, 75. The search for the Holy Trinity in non-European cultures was not confined to India only. For example, Abel Rémusat, the first French Sinologist with high academic credentials, deduced from a text by Laozi that the Chinese philosopher knew of the Holy Trinity. See Oldřich Král, *Čínská filosofie: Pohled z dějin* [Chinese philosophy: A view from the history] (Lásenice: Maxima, 2005), 18.
180 *Védské hymny* [Vedic hymns], translated by Oldřich Friš, with the article by Petr Vavroušek (Prague: DharmaGaia, 2000), 78–79.

from sexual activity and certain types of food.[181] The term *brahma* presents a notorious challenge for translators, which apparently caused the Czech Indologist to fall back on the word *prayer* that fails to even come close to the actual meaning of the Indian word.

From time to time, some Czech scholars did note that the use of Christian theological terms did not help in understanding the Indian thought. For example, Karel Werner has drawn critical attention to the use of Christian concepts in Lesný's translation of the *Dhammapada* (1947). It is telling that this criticism was initiated by Nyanasatta Thera, a Czech Buddhist monk.[182] However, without sufficiently analysing the conceptual structures of the paradigm, these insights do not help us approach Indian otherness. Although Karel Werner introduced Nyanasatta's criticism, the Czech Orientalist himself used without explanation Christian concepts such as "saint," "transcendental," "redemption," etc.[183]

I already noted that Czech scholars often dwell on all that is absent in "Hinduism" or "Buddhism." Although such observations appear to suggest awareness that Indian traditions are fundamentally different from Christianity, I suggest that it is a rather implicitly theological way of thinking. For instance, Lesný conceptualised Buddhism by drawing a negative distinction from the Christian concept of deity, in a way betraying his Christian theological framework of thought: "In Buddhism of the *Pali Canon*, gods are not omnipotent, immutable, and eternal entities, creators of the world, the refuge of mankind."[184] Inasmuch as such negative characteristics fall short of actually clarifying the issue, introducing Indian terms into Czech is not of much help either. Rather than talking about the *devas* of Buddhist stories, which does not bring us any closer to understanding the Indian concept, it is necessary to explain the whole framework of ideas in which *deva* is a meaningful concept.

Since the problem of intercultural understanding is not primarily one of translation, it cannot be resolved on the level of language. It is a theoretical problem, which calls for the analysis of the whole metastructure of thought where individual terms obtain their respective meaning. In order to understand Indian traditions, we must first analyse our own fundamental ideas and identify the limitations that are imposed on us by our own paradigm. If we do not critically reflect upon our own

---

181 Staal, *Ritual and Mantras*, 72–73.
182 See Karel Werner's foreword to his translation of the same collection: *Dhammapadam*, 37.
183 Werner, *Dhammapadam*, 24, 35.
184 Lesný, *Buddhismus*, 101.

theoretical framework, we will necessarily arrive at the same problematic conclusions. Having discussed Czech interpretations of Indian traditions and the influence of theological language, I have reasons to believe that structures of Christian thinking remained important parts of the Orientalist paradigm. We can now search for answers to the question raised at the end of the previous subchapter. How did Europeans come to believe that Indian traditions are religious in nature?

Orientalists Continue with Theological Questions

S. N. Balagangadhara discussed many important topics and periods of encounters between Europe and India in his comprehensive volume *"The Heathen in His Blindness": Asia, the West, and the Dynamic of Religion*. However, there is one important period that Balagangadhara dealt with only marginally. It concerns the activities of the first British Orientalists, and thus the very origins of Indology as an academic discipline.[185] Consequently, the following discussion will focus on interpretations of Indian traditions found in the works of the British Orientalists John Zephaniah Holwell, Alexander Dow, William Jones, Henry Thomas Colebrooke, and Horace Hayman Wilson. The first three will be discussed in the light of arguments developed by Thomas Trautmann, Bruce Lincoln, and Urs App, highlighting the theological nature of the assumptions and goals of the founding fathers of Indology. Subsequently, I will demonstrate how this theologically grounded discourse continued in the works of H. H. Wilson, Monier Monier-Williams, Friedrich Max Müller, and other Orientalists of the 19th century. Their scholarship had a fundamental influence on European Oriental studies at the end of the 19th and the beginning of the 20th centuries, including Czech Indologists.

My discussion of the first British Orientalists' scholarship will mainly focus on their search for "primitive monotheism" in India, a crucial idea for interpreting *the Vedas* and other 'sacred texts' of India. Holwell, Dow, Jones, and others understood their many years of experiences in India as confirmation of the old Christian view of polytheism as degeneration from the original monotheism. The theological paradigm was the basis for classifying texts of various Indian traditions and creating a vision of

---

185 The book mentions mainly William Jones, see Balagangadhara, *"The Heathen in His Blindness...",* 94, 119, 122–123, 125, 138.

one religious tradition that had gradually degenerated and split up into various sects which corresponded to the scholars' Protestant understanding of the history of Christian Europe. We shall see what kind of role the British Orientalists assigned to the Brahmins in this contrived process.

The Biblical scheme of global history, or more precisely, the family tree model of Noah's progeny held a central importance in the thinking of the first Orientalists. It was on this basis that William Jones formulated his famous theory describing the relation of Indo-European languages. It is also worth noting that Jones tried to reduce the Puranic calculation of time to the much shorter Biblical chronology. These two topics will be dealt with later in the following two chapters that will discuss reconstruction of Indian history and analyse the origins of the theory of Aryan invasion of India.

Several scholars have drawn attention to the existence of a rich precolonial corpus containing explanations of Indian traditions that had developed long before the first British Orientalists came on the scene.[186] The corpus mainly consists of three types of literature: chronicles and cosmographies, works of missionaries, and travelogues. It is noteworthy that although the first British Orientalists were unaware of Jesuit works on India, they shared, for example, the same framework with them in terms of their questions and the range of possible answers. The work of the Jesuit missionary Roberto de Nobili (1577–1656) is a good example. However, before analysing the genesis of modern Oriental studies, it is necessary to re-examine the general characteristics of European approach to remote cultures which bears features typical of the theological paradigm from Antiquity to modern times.

Theories and Observations

What was the basic theoretical equipment used by Europeans to understand Indian traditions? What principles guided the way they structured their experience of a different culture? What kind of questions did they raise? There are two major considerations in this respect: the specific

---

186 See, for example, Raf Gelders, "Genealogy of Colonial Discourse: Hindu Traditions and the Limits of European Represetnations," *Comparative Studies in Society and History* 51, no. 3 (2009): 563–589; Will Sweetman, "The Prehistory of Orientalism: Colonialism and the Textual Basis for Bartholomaus Ziegenbalg's Account of Hinduism," *New Zeland Journal of Asian Studies* 6, no. 2 (2004): 12–38.

thought structure of the theological paradigm in relation to remote peoples and the influence of Christian thought on explaining and systematizing experience of Indian traditions.

First and foremost, Christian thought has always been firmly rooted in Biblical exegesis. According to that, the only merciful God, creator of all existence, maintains continuous contact with humanity. He uses various ways of calling upon people, especially by means of the revelation enshrined in the Bible as well as another book—that of the created world. According to Christian teaching, the advent of Jesus Christ was a fundamental turning point in history. Christians believe that God took upon himself the sins of the world and pointed the way to salvation for all mankind.[187] This is what his adherents keep on spreading. The Dictionary of Biblical Theology summarises the topic of divine communication with nations as follows:

> In this perspective, all nations on earth are under the wrath of God. The creator of universe gave all nations hints of His existence through the creation, and hints of His law through the conscience in every person. However, the pagans remained under the spell of their passions, because of their idolatry. They had the chance to be saved, if they would accept God's mercy through Gospel.[188]

Remote nations could be redeemed especially by the access to the true revelation—the acceptance of Jesus Christ as the foretold Messiah. This is where the emphasis on Christian mission comes from. However, what could be done with "pagans" who lived before Christ or have been barred by their geographical situation from receiving the gospel? It was speculated that "divine pedagogy" and "divine logos" were at work amongst the Greek and Roman pagans and later other nations as well. In the view of early Church fathers, at least some pagans of the past were virtuous

---

187 Discussing the significance of the story of Jesus of Nazareth, Lenka Karfíková noted: "With a little exaggeration, it is possible to argue that the whole of Christian theology started out as an attempt to explain how one contingent occurrence, i.e. the story of one man, can have such a revelatory and soteriological value. This founding concept of sacred occurrence which postulates a universal significance will be the paradigm of Christian self-determination and the Christian concept of deity." Lenka Karfíková, "Křesťanské pojetí božství" [The Christian concept of God], in *Bůh a bohové. Pojetí božství v náboženských tradicích světa* [God and gods: The concept of deity in the religious traditions of the world], ed. Radek Chlup (Prague: DharmaGaia, 2004), 60.

188 See entry "Nations" in Xavier Léon-Dufour et al., *The Dictionary of Biblical Theology* (London: Word Among Us Press, 1995).

or even holy men, especially philosophers like Socrates and Plato, poets like Homer or politicians like Pericles and Alexander the Great.[189] This resulted in the concept of *praeparatio evangelica*: Divine wisdom imbues various religions and philosophies with certain good traits that anticipate their full development in Christ's revelation. Another important component of this structure was the story of Genesis as a scheme of global history in which all nations received the true monotheist revelation from Noah and his sons. However, the original purity was prone to degeneration due to sinful human nature, and so Europeans took it for granted that they would encounter various forms of *the same* paganism in many parts of the world. Hardly anything could disrupt the universalising interpretative framework that presupposed the existence of religion amongst all nations. This interpretative framework was clearly delimited by the apologetic dichotomy of true versus false religion. For example, religion was thus characterised in the work of Isidor of Seville:

> Isidor reported that there were multiple religions in the 7th century world, divided into two categories: one involved the worship of idols and included the heathen or gentile peoples; the other was composed of Christians.[190]

If missionaries and merchants attempted to understand Indian traditions, the European repertoire of knowledge accumulated in literature since late Antiquity offered basically three possibilities: India either retains traces of the original monotheism brought there by Noah's offspring and kept alive by the influence of divine *logos*, or this monotheism had degenerated into idolatry. Furthermore, Christian tradition also associated India with Thomas the Apostle and the legends of Prester John's kingdom.[191] The possibilities of religious interpretations were thus exhausted, apart from the internal criticism of Nestorians and other "heretics"[192] and encounters with "old acquaintances," the Jews and Muslims of South Asia. What questions did Christian scholars and missionaries ask themselves within these boundaries? As will be seen later, they asked whether Brahmins knew the Holy Trinity, or which members of the Trinity they

---

189 See, for example, Boublík, *Teologie mimokřesťanských náboženství*, 23–25.
190 Margaret Hodgen, *Early Anthropology in the Sixteenth and Seventeenth Centuries* (Philadelphia: University of Pennsylvania Press, 1964), 58.
191 See *The Travels of Sir John Mandeville* (London: Macmillan, 1915). The famous travelogue was translated into many European languages, including the Czech translation in 1400.
192 Valtrová, *Středověká setkání s jinými*, 59–90.

knew; whether they knew the Ten Commandments and what law they followed; whether they worshipped the true god or false deities; and which of Noah's sons they originated from. Is it possible that they have retained true religion after the Flood? Margaret Hodgen draws attention to another important question raised by medieval and early modern Europeans: How did it come about that the original tradition from Adam to Noah disappeared and was supplanted by so many different rites, laws, and habits?[193] Their answers established the theory of originally pure monotheism, which should have been the basis of laws, rituals, and morality.

These questions gained a new significance in the 16th century. When the Protestant struggle with the Roman Church greatly revived the theme of paganism, early modern thinkers adopted the explanation from the apologetic model of ancient Christianity and directly equalled various traditions, both contemporary and past, with the gods of the ancient world. The cosmography of Sebastian Münster, first published in 1544, is an example of this. The fact that this book enjoyed great popularity in many European countries over the following century tells us a lot about the commonly shared ideas. Margaret Hodgen explained the German cosmographer's approach to different cultures:

> Unable, as were many devout Europeans of his time to conceive of rivals to Christianity, or of independently invented religious systems, Münster identified the strange and existing gods of the barbarians with those of the ancient Europeans, the Greeks and Romans, which in turn he viewed as later distortions of still earlier and original Christian truth.[194]

Because of the generally held belief in Genesis as a truthful description of global history, different traditions became only more or less degenerate forms of Christianity. The Christian conviction in the full revelation of truth in the Gospels leading to the knowledge of God formed European attitude to different cultures. On the one hand, different traditions were judged in terms of Christian theology, law, and ethics. On the other hand, Europeans did not suppose that they could learn anything from pagans in these important areas of human thought and conduct.

---

193 Margaret Hodgen, "Sebastian Muenster (1489–1552): A Sixteenth-Century Ethnographer," *Osiris* 11 (1954): 529.

194 Hodgen, "Sebastian Muenster," 522. Drawing on examples from the works of famous as well as forgotten authors, Hodgen showed that identifying historical figures or gods with Biblical characters was a widespread mode of interpretation.

The only exception was ethics and morality where the medieval genre of *exempla* provided some positive stereotypical descriptions of Brahmins. However, their spread was related to the specific medieval erudition expressed in chronicles and cosmographies. Rather than resulting from direct experience, the positive representation of Brahmins was inherited from Antiquity. If Europeans gained any experience of South Asia in the Middle Ages and in the early modern period, they would usually interpret it in the same way as this English traveller:

> Robert Knox was detained in Kandy between 1660 and 1680. He was a bright observer and provided a good description of the landscape and the local habits. This would lead one to suppose that his account of religion is also valid. He says that the religion of Ceylon was sheer idolatry, worshipping many gods and evil spirits even.[195]

Vincenc Lesný thus expressed the prevalent approach of European scholars to the cumulative accounts of Indian traditions: Europeans are supposed to be keen observers whose Christian faith does not deter them from giving truthful accounts of people whom they encounter. Having disagreed with the conviction, Balagangadhara noted that there is a difference between individual European experiences of India and the way they have been systematised and interpreted. This gave rise to experiential entities that have nothing in common with the Indian understanding of themselves.[196] The culture of the observer is always, in one way or another, reflected in his description of other people.

The reassuring belief in the validity of Western accounts of different cultures has been called into doubt before Balagangadhara's analyses by several thinkers, notably by Margaret Hodgen. She demonstrated how the theological thinking of the Middle Ages has shaped the categories used by Europeans to explain different cultures, with a centuries-long history of transmitting stereotypical characteristics that supposedly captured the nature of various peoples:

> During the thousand year interval between the decline of Rome and the discovery of the peoples of the New World, the active study of cultural diversities was in eclipse. If the facts of ethnology and ethnography were

---

195 Lesný, *Buddhismus*, 216.
196 Balagangadhara, *Reconceptualizaing India Studies*, 35–40.

noted at all, it was in the interest of religion: to lend substance to the slender Biblical account of the dispersion from the Ark; to prepare Crusaders and pilgrims to the Holy Land for the strange folk they were to meet there and on the way; or to put before the weaker brethren the moral inspiration of the supposedly exemplary peoples. . . . The occasional efforts of earlier cosmographers to respond to the problem of descriptive ethnology resulted in their employment of simple typologies couched within the narrow range of a small number of conventional adjectives. Each people—European, Asian, or African—was submitted to a descriptive formula, the shorter the better, which embodied prior judgements concerning their national virtue or iniquity.[197]

The medieval conception of different cultures engendered the specific idea of unchangeable types of people who perform the same rituals and maintain the same habits for centuries on end.[198] *The most varied practices of different cultures were understood as a result of differences between faiths.* Balagangadhara shows the consequences of this approach: European explanations structured the cumulative experience of Indian traditions as descriptions of physical appearance of people, their clothing, character, diet, architecture, and other elements of life along with fundamental judgements on religion and morality. Despite more and more details being added, the very same structure of describing different cultures has persisted until today:

> While this scientific orientation distinguishes our present-day anthropologist from his religious brother, what unites them is the idea that ethnography is on par with geography. To know a people and their culture is to have a descriptive acquaintance with them, in the same way that knowing the flora and fauna of a region requires a descriptive acquaintance.[199]

Modern theories have gradually replaced explicitly theological judgements on the religion and morality of encountered cultures. However, the belief that Europeans developed the correct or even the best theories for explaining them still remains influential. Even this basic attitude displays continuity in dealing with the otherness of Indian traditions in Europe.

---

197 Hodgen, "Sebastian Muenster (1489–1552): A Sixteenth-Century Ethnographer," 504.
198 Hodgen, *Early Anthropology in the Sixteenth and Seventeenth Centuries*, 54.
199 Balagangadhara, *"The Heathen in His Blindness..."*, 70.

Search for the "Primitive" Monotheism in India and Its Consequences

I have already pointed to a general answer to the question of how Europeans came to believe that there was religion in India. That belief was part and parcel of the Christian paradigm. Discussions of the 16th and 17th centuries that were preparing grounds for the Enlightenment thinking applied an older classification of religious traditions to all newly encountered cultures. Thus, four religions were identified: Judaism, Christianity, Islam, and paganism.[200] It was paganism that Europeans first started to differentiate into various subtypes, paving the way for the modern taxonomy of religion.

The conceptualisation of Indian traditions as religions was fundamentally formed by the works of the following British Orientalists: John Z. Holwell (1711–1798), Alexander Dow (1735–1779), Charles Wilkins (1749–1836), William Jones (1746–1794), Henry T. Colebrooke (1765–1837), and Horace H. Wilson (1786–1860). Almost all of them served in the East India Company. Alexander Dow was an officer in the colonial army. Charles Wilkins and William Jones were knighted in recognition of their contributions. They were also respected scholars who organised research in India.

Jones founded and presided over the Asiatic Society established in 1784. Colebrooke was the president of the Royal Asiatic Society founded in 1823. H. H. Wilson was the first to occupy the Boden Chair of Sanskrit at Oxford University. A list of their scholarly activities would take up many pages: translations of important texts from Persian and Sanskrit, discovery of the Indo-European family of languages, composition of the first Sanskrit-English dictionary, tentative dating of events of ancient Indian past, translations and compendia of legal literature, collection of manuscripts, and description of historical monuments. It is hardly surprising that their work is still considered the basis of modern Indology and other disciplines, including comparative linguistics. However, it was only recently that a few scholars pointed out the fundamental role of Christian theological paradigm in their interpretations of Indian traditions.

The whole topic can be summed up into the following interconnected arguments: The main Orientalists' project consisted in identifying Indian

---

200 Balagangadhara, *"The Heathen in His Blindness…"*, 70.

doctrines and therefore the collection and translation of texts regarded as religious. European theological thinking brought *the Vedas* into focus and construed them as evidence of the oldest religion of mankind in the wake of the Biblical Flood. As we shall soon see, this interpretation had in fact been developed at a time when Europeans had no knowledge of *the Vedas*, but the later Orientalists read them through the prism of this presupposed explanation. The first Orientalists took up the theological assumption of "primitive monotheism," the supposedly original religion of India which Holwell and Jones in particular understood as identical with their own deism.

Europeans thus constructed an evolutionary pattern, more precisely a pattern of the degeneration of Indian religion. These theological speculations exhibit an unequivocal continuity in the Orientalist works of Holwell, Dow, Jones, Colebrooke and Wilson up to Monier-Williams, and Friedrich Max Müller. In this perspective, Indian traditions seemed to offer fascinating answers to a number of questions. What did the original pure religion handed down by Noah's progeny look like? How did it degenerate? Do Indian "scriptures" confirm the stories of Genesis? Is it possible to use the Indian texts to trace the paths of Noah's progeny to different parts of the world?

Contemporary scholarship has clearly shown the influence of theological thinking in the interpretations of the first British Orientalists. Thomas Trautmann's *Aryans and British India* (1997) is often cited in this respect. *The precise extent and significance of the influence of Christian and the specifically deistic ideas of Holwell, Dow, Jones, and others on the resultant representation of Indian traditions are still disputed.* Trautmann cited passages from the Orientalists' works that prove a deistic interpretation of Indian traditions. According to the British scholars, the true Brahmin religion was a belief in one god and the apparent polytheism was merely a way of worshipping divine attributes.[201] However, there is every reason to infer that the British Orientalists only saw the original monotheism in the remote antiquity of India rather than in the Indian traditions of their own times. In this connection, let us start with J. Z. Holwell's *A Review of the Original Principles, Religious and Moral, of the Ancient Brahmins*. One has to bear in mind that Holwell was a rather odd Orientalist as he did not know Sanskrit and it is uncertain if and to what extent he learned any of the Indian vernaculars.

---

201 See, for example, Trautmann, *Aryans and British India*, 72.

Judging by the contents of his work, most of Holwell's writing about Indian sacred texts have been invented by him, although he did use some factual information. His story of Indian religion begins with a divine revelation to Brahma, the first created angelic being. After some time, it was necessary for one of the angels to descend to earth in human form and record in writing the original pure scripture that would have previously only been orally transmitted from Brahma. Holwell was also concerned with fallen angels. As time wore on, the original system of spiritual and worldly government was divided. The earth was ruled by descendants of one family and Brahmins were priests of a pure religion. Eventually, Brahmins were so blinded by greed for power that they changed the holy scriptures. They kept introducing new religious duties and finally sanctioned them by means of a faked sacred scripture:

> From the period that the *Anghotarrah Bhade* was published as the rule of the *Gentoo* faith and worship, superstition, the sure support of priestcraft, took fast possession of the people ... And in fact the people became in general mere machines, actuated and moved, as either the good or evil intentions of their household tyrant dictated.[202]

Those tyrants were perverse priests who set up a despotic regime. Holwell did not know the real *Vedas* but he claimed that they were a product of sacerdotal deception, based on some pieces of information collected by him. In the following decades, this idea of ancient Indian scriptural fake enjoyed great popularity in the learned circles of Britain. It is worth noting that Holwell repeated the old Christian notion of degenerated but originally pure religion and that his story is undoubtedly Biblical in its main structure and characters—creation of the world including angels, rebellion of some of them, the origin of evil, original sin, and the purpose of the revealed scripture. In spite of this, Trautmann claimed that at the end of his book Holwell "has completely rewritten Christianity with the help of Hinduism or, at any rate, some rough approximation of it."[203] The American scholar came to this conclusion because Holwell accepted the teaching of reincarnation and considered slaughter of animals as the cause of "apostasy from God." However, as we have seen, Holwell interpreted his pieces of knowledge of Indian

202 John Zephaniah Holwell, *A Review of the Original Principles, Religious and Moral, of the Ancient Brahmins* (London: Vernor, 1779), 17–18.
203 Trautmann, *Aryans and British India*, 71.

traditions in decidedly Biblical terms as he aspired to discover the original pure monotheism in the vein of Christian deists. Holwell wrote about an original Indian scripture "Chartah Bhade Shastah" which is most probably *Chatur Veda Shastra* in Holwell's reading of one of the modern languages of India. Holwell held that the ancient *Vedas* taught the same as Christian Gospel:

> But the above, we think, will suffice to prove, that the mission of Christ is the strongest confirmation of the authenticity and divine origin of the *Chartah Bhade Shastah* of Brahma; and that *they both* contain all *the great primitive truths* in their original purity that constituted *the first* and *universal religion.*[204]

Although Alexander Dow did not agree with Holwell in many things, as Trautmann noted, both Britons were of the opinion that Brahmins believed in one omnipotent God and that their polytheism was symbolic worship of divine attributes.[205] Let us leave aside the fact that Howell's and Dow's books had a great influence on Voltaire and that the whole discussion was influenced by Anquetil-Duperron's work.[206] Although these connections are significant, the present line of argument will only concern the British thinkers. British Orientalists pursued questions raised by Isaac Newton and Jacob Bryant, which is particularly noticeable in William Jones' work.

> It is my argument that Jones's proposal of the Indo-European language family is better understood when we recognize that the character of Jones's project was primarily ethnological, not linguistic; that his ethnology is of a kind that we may call Mosaic, that is, an ethnology whose frame is supplied by the story of the descent of Noah in the book of Genesis, attributed to Moses, in the Bible; that its proximate sources were the ethnological writings of Jacob Bryant and Sir Isaac Newton; and that Jones

---

204 Holwell, *A Review of the Original Principles, Religious and Moral, of the Ancient Brahmins*, 74.

205 Trautmann, *Aryans and British India*, 71–72. Their opinion was later shared by the East India Company official John Shore, who collected Persian translations of Sanskrit texts: "In fact it is pure Deism and has a wonderful resemblance to the doctrines of Plato. I doubt if any of his writings are more metaphysically abstract than some of the Hindoos." Quoted in Mukherjee, *Sir William Jones*, 78.

206 The Enlightenment Deists tended to embrace the thesis of degeneration of originally pure monotheism. For example, Baily and later Jones believed in the significance of discoveries in India for reconstructing the original religion of mankind. See Urs App, "William Jones's Ancient Theology," *Sino-Platonic Papers* 191 (July 2009): 47–52.

and the new Orientalism of the Calcutta Sanskritists need to be included in the narrative of the history of ethnology.[207]

Trautmann's work has brought several important insights. However, his term "Mosaic ethnology" is arguably misleading because Jones' investigations aimed primarily at discovering the original and pure monotheism of humanity. The efforts of Jones to describe the movements and geographical distribution of the nations of the world were an integral part of this project. Related to his effort to identify the movement of nations after the Biblical Flood, the reconstruction of the relationships between human groups and languages was only a means of achieving this goal. Nevertheless, Trautmann rightly pointed out the influence of Bryant and Newton. Both scholars advanced the belief in ancient wisdom that has been shrouded in mythological allegory.

Newton's *Chronology of Ancient Kingdoms*, published in 1728, adopts Euhemerist approach claiming that gods are deified heroes of yore. On this assumption, Newton attempted to identify a historical core of ancient myths and came up with biographical dates for supposedly historical figures.[208] The true goal of Newton's historical research was to discover remains of natural religion that appeared to corroborate his deist beliefs.[209] Newton's historical speculations were moulded by the theory of degeneration of this originally pure monotheism. While the line of Abraham's son Isaac retained some knowledge of it, the pure religion turned into worship of kings in Egypt, Assyria, and Babylon. When Newton considered Brahmins, he inserted them along with Chaldeans in his historical hypothesis between the original monotheist revelation and the religion of Persia. Newton regarded Brahmins, who were often misnamed "Abrahamans" by erroneous etymology, as descendants of Abraham by his second wife Keturah.[210]

Another source of Orientalists' ideas was the then highly regarded work of Jacob Bryant (1715–1804), especially his *Observations and Enquiries Relating to Various Parts of Ancient History* and *A New System or Analysis of*

---

207 Trautmann, *Aryans and British India*, 40–41.
208 See Bruce Lincoln, "Isaac Newton and Oriental Jones on Myth, Ancient History, and the Relative Prestige of Peoples," *History of Religions* 42, no. 1 (2002): 45.
209 Isaac Newton, *Chronology of Ancient Kingdoms Amended*, London 1728, quoted in Lincoln, "Isaac Newton and Oriental Jones," 5.
210 Lincoln, "Isaac Newton and Oriental Jones," 7–8.

Ancient Mythology.[211] Urs App has argued convincingly that William Jones took up Bryant's research objective to trace the original religion of mankind and its development both after and before the Biblical Flood.[212] In this research project, Indian traditions were used as evidence that would prove the historicity of Biblical stories and support the degeneration hypothesis of the decline of original monotheism. In his annual lecture "On the Gods of Greece, Italy, and India", Jones introduced his basic premise:

> From all this, if it be satisfactorily proved, we may infer a general union or affinity between the most distinguished inhabitants of the primitive world, at the time when they deviated, as they did too early deviate, from the rational adoration of the only true GOD.[213]

In this view, the practical need for translations and understanding of Indian texts, which British Orientalists understood as law, was an opportunity to investigate how the degeneration of original pure religion came about. When Jones, helped by the Pandits, was translating the *Manava-dharmashastra* (Manu's textbook of *dharma*), he compared its legendary author to the Greek lawmakers Solon and Lycurgus. After some etymological speculations, he suggested, somewhat tentatively, that Manu was, in fact, none other than Minos of Crete:

> If Minos, the son of Jupiter, whom the Cretans, from national vanity, might have made a native of their own island, was really the same person with Menu, the son of Brahma, we have the good fortune to restore, by means of *Indian* literature, the most celebrated system of heathen jurisprudence, and this work might have been entitled *The Laws of Minos*; but the paradox is too singular to be confidently asserted, and the geographical part of the book, with most of the allusions to natural history, must indubitably have been written after the *Hindu* race have settled to the south of *Himálaya*.[214]

211 Jones made a laudatory reference to Jacob Bryant already in his first lecture for the Asiatic Society of Bengal, entitled "On The Hindus." He regarded Bryant's analysis of ancient mythology as one of the main sources of knowledge about Asian nations' history. See Anna Maria Jones, *The Works of Sir William Jones in Six Volumes* (London: G. G. and J. Robinson, 1799), 1:20–21.

212 App, "William Jones's Ancient Theology."

213 Jones, *The Works of Sir William Jones in Six Volumes*, 1:230.

214 William Jones, *Institutes of the Hindu Law* (London: W. H. Allen, 1869), xv.

The system of Indian "pagan law" was harshly criticised by Jones as "a system of despotism and priestcraft . . . filled with strange conceits in metaphysics and natural philosophy, with idle superstitions, and with a scheme of theology most obscurely figurative, and consequently liable to dangerous misconception."[215] Nevertheless, Jones admitted that *Manava-dharmashastra* contains "a spirit of sublime devotion." In particular, he regarded the references to the *Gayatri mantra* as evidence that the author worshipped divine light.

As Urs App emphasized rightly, Jones continued his search for "the original religion of Indians" until his death. The last volume of the renowned Orientalist's collected works also contains parts of his essays and translations of *the Vedas* and *the Upanishads*, which were probably discovered in the estate of the dead by his friend John Shore, Lord Teignmouth. The preserved fragments testify that Jones endeavoured to discover evidence for the original pure monotheism of Indians. He chose to translate the *Ishopanishad*, rendering its famous first verse thus:

> By one Supreme Ruler is this Universe pervaded; even every world in the whole circle of nature.[216]

The other fragments include a statement comparing the Vedic passage to "The First Article of our Church"[217] and an analysis of the *Gayatri mantra* as a celebration of "the Being of beings."[218] In his introduction to the collected works, Lord Teignmouth observes that Jones wanted to "unveil the supposed mystery of the original Indian religion, a mission which he regrettably did not accomplish."[219]

Let us stop for a while in order to reflect upon these findings. British Orientalists who naturally had a long-lasting experience of India, and in Jones' case also a linguistic competence, looked for answers to the same questions as the generations of travellers and missionaries before them: What is Indian doctrine? Is it the primeval monotheism or a degraded polytheism?

These questions take for granted the universality of the European understanding of religion as a relationship with one God, creator of the

215 Jones, *Institutes of the Hindu Law*, xix.
216 Jones, *The Works of Sir William Jones in Six Volumes,* 6:423.
217 Jones, *The Works of Sir William Jones in Six Volumes,* 6:422.
218 Jones, *The Works of Sir William Jones in Six Volumes,* 6:417.
219 Jones, *The Works of Sir William Jones in Six Volumes,* 6:414.

world, and so forth. As we have already seen, Indian texts were used as research material in order to elucidate and complement the stories of Genesis. Serving in the colonial government, Orientalists encountered the 18th century traditions of India and equalled them with the Greek and Roman polytheism. This equation was based on the conviction about one originally pure religion that degenerated into various forms of the *same* paganism. This was also the starting point of speculations about historical events and linguistic families. Furthermore, *the Vedas* and *the Upanishads* were thought to preserve evidence of the oldest religion of India, and perhaps of all mankind. Formed by theological assumptions, the discussion continued among the subsequent generations of British orientalists. For example, Henry T. Colebrooke claimed:

> The real doctrine of the whole Indian scripture is the unity of the deity, in whom the universe is comprehended; and the seeming polytheism which it exhibits, offers the elements, and the stars, and planets, as gods. The three principal manifestations of the divinity, with other personified attributes and energies, and most of other gods of Hindu mythology, are, indeed mentioned. . . . But the worship of deified heroes is no part of that system; nor are the incarnations of deities.[220]

Horace H. Wilson developed the theologically based enquiry further. He accepted Jones' and Colebrooke's thesis of primitive monotheism in *the Vedas*. Because he in all probability could distinguish between what the Vedic ritual was like and the various forms of contemporary *puja*, he posed an apparently logical question. If the Vedic ritual represented the original monotheism, then *puja* must have been a result of a later stage in the degeneration of that religion into polytheism. Since then, the *Puranas* have been thought to document the decline of the originally pure religion, because many rituals of the *puja* type are described in these compendia. However, the supposed doctrines of Indian religion were assigned a central place in these speculations.

Wilson came up with the idea of three basic forms of Indian religion that he matched with their crucial changes; each form of this model also represents a historical period of religion in India. The oldest is the religion of *the Vedas*. It would surprise many readers that European knowledge of *the Vedas* was rather meagre in the 1840s, as Wilson himself

---

220 Henry Thomas Colebrooke, *Miscellaneus Essays* (London: W. H. Allen, 1837), 1:110–111.

admitted. He referred to Colebrook's general description containing few quotations, used a translation of a few passages by the Orientalist F. W. Ellis, F. A. Rosen's translation of the first book of the *Rigveda*, and Ram Mohan Roy's translation of *the Upanishads*. Relying on Colebrooke's belief that the Vedic religion was monotheistic and after considering the probable worship of heroes as propounded in the Euhemerist thesis, Wilson claimed:

> Still, however, it is true, that the prevailing character of the ritual of the Vedas is the worship of the personified elements; of Agni, or fire; Indra, the firmament; Váyu, the air; Varuña, the water; of Aditya, the sun; Soma, the moon; and other elementary and planetary personages. It is also true that the worship of the Vedas is, for the most part, domestic worship, consisting of prayers and oblations offered—in their own houses, not in temples—by individuals for individual good, and addressed to unreal presences, not to visible types. *In a word, the religion of the Vedas was not idolatry.*[221]

For Wilson, the second—mythological—stage of religious development consisted of worship of heroes. It is epitomized in the ancient Indian epics *Mahabharata* and *Ramayana*. The third stage is represented by *the Puranas*, which, in Wilson's thought, illustrate a rise of pantheism or identification of divinity with nature.[222] The third stage brought about the development of Indian sects mainly devoted to the worship of Vishnu and Shiva. This stage of Indian religion is characterized by a rise in the number of sects, which Wilson demonstrated by adducing examples of many sects described in the texts of the *Sarvadarshana-samgraha* and the *Shankara-digvijaya*.[223] All those sects are said to have emerged fairly recently. *Let us remember how Wilson created the three-stage scheme of degeneration of Indian religion, which M. Monier-Williams later revised into the well-known pattern of Vedism, Brahmanism, and Hinduism.*

Wilson's work is worth further consideration. His scheme of development, or rather degeneration, of Indian traditions, included the idea of ascetic groups' protest against Brahmin orthodoxy. Despite him admitting that "we have little or no knowledge of these systems"[224] or "heretical schools," he mentioned several names of these alleged reform groups.

---

221 Fitzedward Hall, *Works of the Late Horace Hayman Wilson*, 6:iii.
222 Hall, *Works of the Late Horace Hayman* Wilson, 6:iv–xiv.
223 Hall, *Works of the Late Horace Hayman Wilson,* 6:11–29.
224 Hall, *Works of the Late Horace Hayman Wilson,* 6:5.

Apart from more familiar Jainism and Buddhism, Wilson referred to "atheist" movements such as the Charvakas, Lokayatas, and Varhaspatyas. If these movements had wished only to advocate plurality of opinions, the Brahmins would not have found much fault with them:

> The founder of the Atheistical school, however, Vṛihaspati, attacks both the *Vedas* and the *Brahmans*, and asserts that the whole of the Hindu system is a contrivance of the Priesthood, to secure a means of livelihood for themselves, whilst the *Bauddhas* and *Jainas*, equally disregarding the *Vedas* and the *Brahmans*, the practice and opinions of the Hindus, invented a set of gods for themselves, and deposed the ancient pantheon: these aggressions provoked resentment: the writings of these sects are alluded to with every epithet of anger and contempt, and they are all anathematised as heretical and atheistical.[225]

Later research made Wilson change his speculations about a Brahmin counterattack that supposedly expelled Buddhists from India, assuming that it was more a process of assimilation. However, the Christian motif of a doctrinal schism that Wilson deduced from a few lines of the *Sarvadarshana-samgraha* collection remains. Western Indology has clung to the idea of the ascetic groups' fight against the supremacy of power-loving priests ever since.

The British Orientalist used these ideas as the basis for developing a critique of Indian texts and their dating. In his understanding, the *Puranas* were "pious frauds for temporary purposes." He maintained that it is easy to distinguish "authentic and primitive material" from "sectarian interpolations."[226] Orientalist hermeneutics thus obtained a principle that has been applied to this day—the older a text is, the more authentic evidence of the original religion it provides. Variations and changes typical for Indian storytelling art are usually viewed negatively form this point of degeneration hypothesis.

Wilson's work was continued by Monier Monier-Williams (1819–1899) and Friedrich Max Müller (1823–1900), who happened to be competing candidates for the Boden Chair of Sanskrit at Oxford. Monier-Williams was appointed to the Chair and later founded and presided over the university's Indian Institute that focussed on training officials of

---

225 Hall, *Works of the Late Horace Hayman Wilson,* 6:6.
226 Hall, *Works of the Late Horace Hayman Wilson,* 6:xi.

the British colonial administration. He received many honours, including knighthood. His Sanskrit-English dictionary is still in use. Friedrich Max Müller studied Sanskrit and other Asian languages under Franz Bopp's and Friedrich Schelling's supervision. He became Professor of Comparative Philology at Oxford and is still remembered for his translation of *Rigveda* and for initiating and editing the monumental series of the *Sacred Books of the East*. He is also considered to be one of the founders of comparative religious studies.

Monier-Williams took up the ideas of his teacher H. H. Wilson, but his main arguments exhibit traces of much older Enlightenment speculations relating to the origin of religion, applied to the Aryans as the authors of *the Vedas*:

> To trace the origin of religion among such a people requires no curious metaphysical hypotheses. It only requires asking what would be the natural working of their devotional instincts, unguided by direct revelation. Their material welfare depended on the influences of sky, air, light and sun . . .; and to these they naturally turned with awe and veneration.[227]

According to this British Orientalist, Indian religion underwent gradual changes after Aryans had settled in India; the worship of nature supposedly developed into theism, polytheism, anthropomorphism, and pantheism.[228] We see the growth of speculations about the origin of religion, characteristic of the second half of the 19th century, strongly present here. Nevertheless, Monier-Williams' portrayal of India's oldest religion is of special significance for our discussion:

> It was a belief which, according to the character and inclination of the worshipper, was now monotheism, now tritheism, now polytheism, now pantheism. *But it was not yet idolatry.*[229]

Monier-Williams' insistence on the absence of idolatry in the oldest religion of India reveals a real question, somewhat clouded by his confusing description of multifarious manifestations of religion in different worshippers. He pondered the same question that had been asked by travellers and missionaries for a long time before him and later by his

227 Monier Monier-Williams, *Religious Thought and Life in India* (London: John Murray, 1883), 1:4.
228 Monier-Williams, *Religious Thought and Life in India*, 1:11.
229 Monier-Williams, *Religious Thought and Life in India*, 1:11.

Orientalist predecessors: What was the original religion of the Indians? He answered it with the same idea: As it was not yet idolatry, it must have been a form of the true religion—primeval monotheism. He described Brahmanism as an excessive growth of ritual that found its critique in the philosophical thinking of *the Upanishads*, which he called "the special bible of this phase of Brahmanism."[230]

Upanishadic teaching was the supposed source of the idea of immortal soul and reincarnation as well as the concept of *brahma* comprising *sat, cit* and *ananda* (terms which are difficult to translate and can be tentatively rendered as "the true essence," "consciousness," and "bliss"). After this "philosophical stage," Monier-Williams inserted Wilson's mythological thesis, which is essentially Euhemerist: "Deified" heroes of epics, such as Vishnu's *avatar* Krishna, became major deities in the centre of worship. The last stage of Indian religion fully developed this worship of heroes. Although he calls this stage theist, Monier-Williams claimed that in India, forms of pantheism, theism, and polytheism are ever interwoven with each other.[231] The vague treatment of, allegedly, almost indistinguishable and interwoven "theisms" betrays not only his unclear thinking on the matter, but also his tacit endorsement of the idea of original natural religion.

Friedrich Max Müller also found the possibility of identifying the original religion of mankind in India very attractive:

> Interesting as the Vedas are to us, as historical documents, for they date from at least 1500 BC, and give us an insight into the origin and growth of religion unsurpassed by any other literature . . .[232]

The following passage displays Max Müller's opinion that *the Vedas* were an expression of primeval religion that came to ultimate fruition in his own faith:

> The time will come, I hope, when scholars in India will study the Veda, as we study it in Europe, namely as an historical record of the highest value in the history of religion; but even then I trust that in India the Veda will always retain its peculiar position as the oldest book which, for the first time, told the inhabitants of that country of a world beyond this world,

230 Monier-Williams, *Religious Thought and Life in India*, 1:26.
231 Monier-Williams, *Religious Thought and Life in India*, 54.
232 Friedrich Max Müller, *Biographical Essays* (London: Longmans, 1884), 40.

of a law beyond human laws, and of a Divine Being in whom we live, and move, and have our being.[233]

The Orientalist's letter, written to the Duke of Argyll in 1869, is a clear evidence of his belief that *the Vedas* are "the root of Indian religion." His complete translation of the *Rigveda* was a project that was to cast doubt on everything that post-dated *the Vedas*:

> Yet so much may be said with perfect truth, that if the religion of India could be brought back to that simple form which it exhibits in the Veda, a great reform would be achieved. Something would be lost, for some of the later metaphysical speculations on religion, and again the high and pure and almost Christian morality of Buddha, are things not to be found in the Veda. But, as far as the popular conceptions of the deity are concerned, the Vedic religion, though childish and crude, is free from all that is so hideous in the later Hindu Pantheon.[234]

Müller's classification of languages went hand in hand with his classification of religions whose ultimate aim was to prove development of religion as revelations of the true God that culminated in Christianity:

> In order to understand fully the position of Christianity in the history of the world, and its true place among the religions of mankind, we must compare it, not with Judaism only, but with the religious aspirations of the whole world, with all, in fact, that Christianity came either to destroy or to fulfil.[235]

The continuity of theological structure in the Orientalist thinking is thus well established by the foregoing analysis.[236]

The search for primeval religion in India continued as did the discussions about whether it was monotheism, polytheism, or henotheism, the latter being a concept introduced by Max Müller. For example, at the 3rd International Congress of History of Religion, G. A. Gierson, who has

---

233 Müller, *Biographical Essays*, 41.
234 Georgina Müller, *The Life and Letters of Right Honorable Friedrich Max Müller* (London: Longmans, Green, 1902), 1:382.
235 Friedrich Max Müller, *Chips from a German Workshop* (London: Longman and Green, 1868), 1:xxvii.
236 For further criticism of the F. M. Müller's theories, see e.g. Tomoko Masuzawa, *The Invention of World Religions*, 207–256.

since been forgotten, gave a lecture entitled "The Monotheistic Religion of Ancient India and Its Descendants."[237] The theme is also encountered in the work of Nicol Macnicol,[238] in James Hastings' long-used *Encyclopaedia of Religion and Ethics*,[239] and the list could be extended quite easily. The 19th century travelogues also testify to the general acceptance of the typology of Indian traditions as the result of degenerated religions:

> The religions of India may be classified as follows: I. BRAHMANISM, the religion of the Aryans, which found its earliest exposition in the hymns of the Vedas, and its development in the institutes of Manu. Originally it was monotheistic. . . . II. BUDDHISM, now the religion, in a degraded form, of one-third of the human race. . . . III. HINDUISM is the modern development in India of the religion of the Brahmans, modified by Buddhist teaching. And here again we find only degeneracy from the primitive standards. The Brahmans themselves have in many parts degenerated, and are corpulent, self-indulgent, immoral, worldly-minded men. Caste in all its tyranny prevails. Woman is immured in ignorance, and doomed to slavery.[240]

Although the popular work merged Monier-Williams' Vedism with Brahmanism, it echoes the same principles which amount to an identical scheme of Indian religion. The disintegration of the original monotheistic religion was followed by a movement of protestant dissension and later by further degeneration of both. This scheme calls forth another question. How did the "primitive monotheism" of the Indians happen to suffer such a decline? We have already heard the answer from J. Z. Holwell: The blame falls on the shoulders of power-obsessed priests who changed some content of the revealed scripture and eventually substituted it with their own fabrications. However, study of the past reveals that Holwell's claim is grounded in centuries old European representations of Brahmins.

---

237 G. A. Grierson, "The Monotheistic Religion of Ancient India and Its Descendant: The Modern Doctrine of Faith," in *Transactions of the Third International Congress of History of Religion*, Oxford 1908.

238 Nicol Macnicol, *Indian Theism from the Vedic to the Muhammadan Period* (London: Humphrey Milford, Oxford University Press, 1915).

239 James Hastings, *Encyclopaedia of Religion and Ethics*, 13 vols. (Edinburgh: T. and T. Clark, 1908–1926).

240 W. Urwick, *India 100 Years Ago: The Beauty of Old India Illustrated* (London: Bracken Books, 1985), x–xi (reprint of the 1st ed. by Religious Tract Society, 1885).

Raf Gelders has recently gathered substantial evidence revealing a remarkably vast body of European representations of Brahmins. He identified two basic types of representations between which the Christian representations of Brahmins oscillated since the Renaissance: from Brahmins as Proto-Christian saints to the most degenerated clergy.[241] The older, more positive representations derive from the ancient Greek and Roman reports about ascetics and Brahmins that the scholars of medieval Europe incorporated into the literary genre of exempla. While they criticised the contemporary state of Christendom's morality, remote India was a land of "saintly pagans" in European imagination. Since Eusebius' positive depiction of Brahmins, Christian writings can be shown to contain appreciation of their supposedly virtuous, ascetic and contemplative way of life. For instance, Peter Abélard claimed that Brahmins acquired knowledge of the Holy Trinity by natural reasoning like thinkers of Greek and Roman Antiquity.[242] Abelard's claim was taken up by Hugo of St. Victor who elaborated on the character of the Brahmin Dindimus adapted from a genre of tales about Alexander the Great. According to Vincent of Beauvais, Brahmins knew the Father and Holy Spirit of the Christian Trinity.[243] There are more similar examples.

There are exceptions to the generally positive medieval appraisal of Brahmins. M. Hodgen noted how travellers who did not receive formal education could have come to different conclusions, like Marco Polo:

> As for the Brahmins, Marco seemed to be entirely unaware of the heavy incrustation of fabulous material which for so long had obscured their real characteristics from European readers. To him, their chief excellence lay in their activities as merchants, rather than in their supposed renunciation of the world and its fleshpots. He mentioned their refusal to take the life of living things, their daily fasts, and their longevity. But disregarding widely publicized virtues, which may have seemed to him without foundation, he asserted that they were such 'cruel and perfidious Idolaters that it is very devilry.'[244]

241 Raf Gelders, "Ascetics and Crafty Priests," unpublished Ph.D. dissertation, Ghent University, 2010; Gelders, "Genealogy of Colonial Discourse," 563–589.
242 Petr Abélard, *Introductio ad Theologiam*, quoted in Gelders, *Ascetics and Crafty Priests*, 31–32.
243 Gelders, *Ascetics and Crafty Priests*, 43–45.
244 Hodgen, *Early Anthropology in the Sixteenth and Seventeenth Centuries*, 101–102.

It is noteworthy that Polo's opinion of Brahmins was conditioned by the same Christian frame of mind as the preceding examples: Instead of "saintly pagans" (who know God the Father by natural reason), he saw "cruel idolaters" (misled pagans). Although Polo anticipated negative interpretations prevailing since the 1550s, positive representations of Brahmins continued to occur in early modern writings, for example, in Johann Boemus' *Omnium Gentium Mores* (1520). Boemus extoled Brahmins' asceticism, bloodless worship of God, and other qualities.[245]

The appraisal of Brahmins underwent a radical change with the spread of Reformation. Protestants used the rediscovered knowledge of ancient authors, recovering the theme of idolatrous paganism in order to fight against the Roman Church's practices. Soon enough, the "invented" and "idolatrous" practices of the Catholic Church came to be criticised not only by likening them to ancient cults, but also by drawing comparisons with the increasing number of new accounts from India. Eyewitnesses of Indian rituals in Calicut and elsewhere brought descriptions of abominable idolatrous rituals, monstrous idols, and their officiants—the Brahmins. In a few decades, the Brahmins' positive image had been displaced by the idea of priests of false religion even though they had no part in this change themselves.[246]

In the following two centuries, European understanding of Brahmins would still oscillate between these two interpretations defined by Christian apologetics and by the sharpening of controversies in modern Christianity. Many missionaries, traders, travellers, and administrators of emerging colonies were drawn towards the negative image of priests who exploited their privileged status. For example, Francois Bernier, who stayed in India from 1656 to 1669, expressed this view thus:

> The Brahmins encourage and promote these gross errors and superstitions to which they are indebted for their wealth and consequence. As persons attached and consecrated to important mysteries, they are held in general veneration, and enriched by the alms of the people.[247]

A hundred years later, Holwell's and Dow's comments showed the persistent negative image of Brahmins among the British.[248] In their efforts

---

245 Gelders, "Genealogy of Colonial Discourse," 566–567.
246 Gelders, "Genealogy of Colonial Discourse," 571–582.
247 Bernier quoted in Mukherjee, *Sir William Jones*, 11.
248 Cf. Trautmann, *Aryans and British India*, 33, 72.

to identify the original pure monotheism in India, Orientalists had to face up to the question of where so many statues in the centre of diverse rituals came from. In the universalizing scheme of degeneration of religion, Brahmins were the culprits to be blamed for ruining the originally pure tenets, just like the clergy had spoiled the original message of the Church:

> The holy Tribe of Brahmins, who were chosen and appointed by Bramah himself, to preach *the word of God*, and labor the salvation of the delinquents; in process of time lost sight of their divine original, and in its place substituted new and strange doctrines; that had no tendency, but to the establishing their own power.[249]

The predominant image of Brahmins in European literature was, therefore, negative in the early modern period. Nevertheless, there were few exceptions. A Jesuit missionary Roberto Nobili (1577–1656) was a remarkable personality who was highly successful in his missionary endeavours in Madurai, South India. He achieved fluency both in spoken and written Tamil and acquired good knowledge of Sanskrit. Let us briefly consider our two topics in his work: the search for monotheism in India and interpretation of Brahmins. It is evident that Nobili knew Indian texts much better than many Orientalists of the 19th century. He wrote about Indian grammar, poetry, logic, astronomy, medicine, law, and other topics.[250] In spite of that, his theological paradigm allowed for the same range of answers as has been the case with later Orientalists.

Nobili was interested in a discipline of Indian sciences that he calls "scientia de Deo seu Theologia."[251] He was referring to the *darshans*, schools of Indian philosophy, which he described in some detail. In the primary texts of *the Upanishads* he found the Christian concept of the one true God as well as the Holy Trinity. According to Nobili, the term *brahma* "did not denote a 'specific and false god,' but rather 'God in general' (non significat deum aliquem determinatum et falsum, sed Deum in communi); it was used to designate the one true immaterial God, at least as far as it was possible for him to be known through the natural light of reason."[252] Drawing an analogy with the early Church

249 Holwell, *A Review of the Original Principles, Religious and Moral, of the Ancient Bramins*, 20.
250 See Halbfass, *India and Europe*, 39–40.
251 Halbfass, *India and Europe*, 40.
252 Halbfass, *India and Europe*, 40.

Fathers' accounts of ancient Greek and Roman philosophers, he argued that Brahmins were wise men rather than priests.[253] It is noteworthy that even this apparently unconventional interpretation was defined within the scope of the Christian apologetic debates of the Antiquity.

It is time to summarise the findings that we have arrived at by answering the question of how European representations of Indian traditions, shared by the Czech Orientalists, have taken shape. We have seen how the first British Orientalists adopted the theological questions of their predecessors and how they developed them, from Holwell's speculations about the original revealed scripture of India, mangled and falsified by Brahmins, to Jones' quest for the original monotheism of India in *the Vedas* and *the Upanishads*, including the Indians' supposed "early departure" from monotheism to polytheism. This was the starting point of the degeneration hypothesis of Indian traditions. I have shown how this idea was developed by H. H. Wilson and Monier-Williams into the three historical stages of Indian religion: from monotheist Vedism to the extravagant ritualism of Brahmanism to Hinduism. Few short passages from two Indian texts were sufficient for Horace H. Wilson to speculate about anti-Brahminical rebellion of the ascetic movements. Here, the European experience of Protestantism and the idea of conflicting schismatic sects shaped the view of Indian traditions.

We have also seen how Wilson used Holwell's fantasies about faked scriptures to interpret *the Puranas*. Although the Vedic collections were thus "cleared" of Holwell's allegation, there is a good reason to believe that the evidence of both *the Vedas* and *Puranas* was tailored in order to fit the original idea of Brahminical fraud. Since none of Holwell's British contemporaries had any knowledge of Sanskrit or access to the actual texts, Holwell could claim that there had been earlier texts than the extant Vedic collections. As soon as Jones and other British scholars had acquired some understanding of Sanskrit and accessed the Vedic collections, they found that there was no earlier "holy scripture." On the other hand, they discovered *the Puranas* containing descriptions of *puja*, which must have been idol worship in their eyes, and other strange practices. Wilson shifted Holwell's ideas from hypothetical to actual texts: *The Vedas* were the oldest evidence of monotheism whereas *the Puranas* were forgeries. The fictitious distinction between genuine and counterfeit

---

253 Halbfass, *India and Europe*, 41.

sacred texts shaped the hermeneutics of emergent Indology that classifies texts hierarchically according to their presumed originality.

It is noteworthy that *linguistic competence did not bring about any substantial changes in the questions or outcomes of the first British Orientalists' research*. J. Z. Holwell and A. Dow did not know Sanskrit, whereas William Jones, Henry T. Colebrooke, and others did. In spite of that, they all viewed Indian traditions through the thought structure of the same theological paradigm. They all saw in the oldest Indian texts evidence of mankind's original monotheism. Jesuit Roberto Nobili, who had substantial knowledge of Sanskrit, entertained basically the same idea. This speaks for the determining role of theory, or web of ideas, in the selection, interpretation, and evaluation of data.

Within this explanation, one question naturally arose: Who was responsible for the degeneration of the "primitive" monotheism? The answer was anticipated by the Protestant-Catholic controversies in which the argument against degenerate clergy gained force by reference to "similar abominations" in India. The power-hungry priests were to be blamed for the decline of Indian religion. It is worth noting that the exceptionally sympathetic appraisement of Brahmins by Nobili stemmed from the apologetic interpretation developed by the Church Fathers as well as the Jesuit missionary principle of accommodation, which stirred serious disputes within the Catholic Church. All the themes mentioned so far were fitted into the framework of global chronicle: At the time of the first Orientalists, this consisted of the Biblical scheme of the post-diluvian dispersal of nations, enshrined within a short chronology of human history. This brings us to the next topic: the role of European historiography in understanding the Indian past.

Religion, Historiography, and Indian Past

*Effacing the otherness is possible if and only if there is a framework,
which does not allow an otherness. A universal human history
is the framework, which makes it possible
to deny the other to religion.*
S. N. Balagangadhara

*What role has the European conceptualisation of religion played in the study
of India's past?* A fundamental one in at least three respects: 1. Despite
gradual secularisation, theological thinking with central focus on religion shaped modern historiographical theory and practice, which can be
seen in the reconstruction of Indian history. 2. The constructs of Indian
religions, such as Hinduism and Buddhism, seemed to explain many
problems that puzzled European thinkers. 3. The European, and particularly British, concept of Indian history and the description of indigenous
traditions as religious have been accepted by generations of Indian intellectuals who have been trying to come to terms with them until today.

In their full extent and significance, these three topics are beyond the
scope of this chapter which only aims at broadly outlining them, leaving many related issues aside. It concerns primarily the first two topics,
whereas the third theme will only be discussed in terms of what kind of
problems are involved. First, an outline will be given of how European historiography was formed primarily by theological thinking. Most
importantly, the general belief that European historical scholarship has
become independent from its theological roots since the Enlightenment
will be challenged. Secondly, the influence of theological thinking on

the modern reconstructions of Indian history will be demonstrated with several examples. The manner in which European religious assumptions have impeded our access to Indian (non-Muslim) ways of thinking and dealing with the past will become evident. In conclusion, an answer will be offered to the frequently debated question of whether there was historical thinking in India prior to the advent of Muslim scholarship. A possible direction of future research will also be suggested.

The Legacy of Christian Thought in Historiography

It is a truism to say that Christian theology played a major part in the formation of European historiography. For example, Jacques Le Goff wrote:

> Christianity has been seen as constituting a break, a revolution in historical mentality. . . . A historical religion anchored in history, Christianity is supposed to have lent a decisive impetus to history in the West. Guy Lardreau and Georges Duby have again emphasized the link between Christianity and the development of history in the West. Lardreau recalls Marc Bloch's remark, "Christianity is a historian's religion," and he adds, "I am quite simply convinced that we practice history because we are Christians." To which Georges Duby responds: "You are right: there is a Christian way of thinking, which is history. What is history in China, in India, in black Africa?"[254]

Let us have a closer look at what exactly this decisive impetus involved. The influence of theological thinking on the inception and development of modern historiography has been examined among others by Herbert Butterfield and Amos Funkenstein. Along with other insights, their observations are reviewed in the following summary discussion in order to clarify the fundamental influence that theological thinking has had on historical thought in Europe.

What did Christian theology bequeath to European historiography? In enumerating features of this legacy, it is important to keep in mind that they are all interconnected concepts that form a highly specific structure of interpretative framework employed to make sense of past events.

---

[254] Jacques Le Goff, *History and Memory*, translated by Steven Rendall and Elizabeth Claman (New York: Columbia University Press, 1992), 142.

Furthermore, the emerging framework of Christian historical thinking was fundamentally grounded in Christian responses to the Roman intelligentsia's criticism, which bore close resemblance to their criticism of the Jews. The result was a concept of history, radically different from the "pagan" tradition of historiography that had preceded it and ran parallel to it for some time. What did Christian apologetics contribute in terms of comprehending the past?

It was, above all, the *universalising framework of the global chronicle* that arose from Christian interpretation of the Hebrew Bible. Christian thinking transformed the history of Jewish tribes who expected the fulfilment of prophesies issued by their prominent ancestors into the history of the whole human race that was to expect the advent of their only saviour—Jesus Christ. *The detailed temporal imagination characteristic of the Jewish prophets was supplemented with the imminent expectation of Christ's second coming and the end of the world became the basis for a linear concept of time* that was supposed to evolve from the creation of the universe, through the turning point of Christ's advent until its foretold ending.

> The fascination with historical time and its structure was the most important contribution of the apocalyptic mentality to the Western sense of history. The apocalyptician grasped all of history as a structured, well-articulated meaningful unity. His detailed account of the future drama of the end, down to days, hours, and precise actors, was drawn from the background of his perception of the whole of history as a dramatic struggle between the forces of good and evil.[255]

The clearly structured drama encapsulated in the universalising framework of the global chronicle was described as a list of events on a single linear timeline. Therefore, the Church Fathers devoted much time to connecting events and chronologies of various regions into a single universal chronology. In the 4th century, Eusebius of Caesarea wrote the *Chronicle* and the *Ecclesiastical History* that influenced the following centuries of Christian historical thinking.[256] As it is well known, these works

---

255 Amos Funkenstein, *Perceptions of Jewish History* (Berkeley 1993), 77; quoted in Samuel Moyn, "Amos Funkenstein on the Theological Origins of Historicism," *Journal of the History of Ideas* 64, no. 2 (October 2003): 643–644.

256 Around 229 AD, Sextus Julius Africanus was apparently the first to attempt the composition of a universal Christian chronicle from Adam to his own times. The five books of his *Chronographiai* were used by Eusebius.

were an apologetic argument used in discussions with Roman intellectuals who questioned Christians' claim to the antiquity of their own tradition. According to Josef Dobiáš, it was

> necessary to ground the new Christian society in the given environment . . . by vindicating it. This involved producing evidence that Christian tradition can well compete with or even ultimately far surpass the antiquity of pagan tradition. The endeavour to prove this primacy instigated one of the supreme achievements of historical science ever—*the creation of a coherent chronological system.*[257]

The Jews also defended themselves against Roman criticism by trying to prove the antiquity of their tradition; Flavius Josephus is a name that readily comes to mind. However, Christian thinking re-interpreted Jewish history in its own way. Among other things, it resulted in linking the framework of the universal chronicle to a unifying chronology. Eusebius' chronological skeleton of universal history was such a momentous achievement that the historian Johann Heinrich Gelzer declared at the end of the 19th century that it still was the basis of all chronological work.[258] As it is well known, Augustine's, Jerome's, Isidore's and Bede's works were all patterned on Eusebius' books. All these important theologians supplemented and elaborated the universal chronology of events.

Yet, identifying events and dating them was not the main goal. It was also important to interpret them. Christianity also adopted the originally Jewish idea of history as a process of gradual development and revelation of its meaning. Theologians like Eusebius, Socrates Scholasticus, Evagrius Ponticus, Sozomen, and Theodret of Antioch believed in free will and "therefore, unlike Graeco-Roman historians, they didn't think that fortuitous fate (*fatum*) played any role in history. In their view, the world is ruled by Logos or Divine Reason, in other words, Providence, which shapes the structure of all nature and history. Thus, it was possible to analyse history and consider the inner logic of the constituent chains of events."[259] Providence was a force that surpassed the free will of men and human decisions. Even surrendering to passions was interpreted as conscious or frequently unconscious realisations of God's intention:

---

257 Josef Dobiáš, *Dějepisectví starověké* [The historiography of the ancients] (Prague: Historický klub, 1948), 300.

258 Dobiáš, *Dějepisectví starověké*, 301.

259 Le Goff, *History and Memory*, 143.

Once Augustine had pointed out the ultimate meaning and goal of mankind's history, history ceased to consist of human intentions, deeds, and gradual realisation of God's unfathomable plans in which human beings are, after all, mere tools despite a considerable amount of liberty that issues from the exercise of free will.[260]

This idea was also introduced into Christian theology from Jewish thought that understood even weakness of the Jewish nation as

a proof of God's immense power. God's power manifests itself by using the biggest empires—Assyria, Babylon, and Egypt—as "rods of his wrath" . . . to purify Israel; yet these world powers are unaware of it . . . and they attribute their success to their own strength. Here, perhaps, was the earliest, the original version of "the cunning of God" or "the cunning of reason": by following their own blind urge for power, the nations of the world unknowingly serve a higher design.[261]

The early Church Fathers thought that God directly intervened in human history by punishing sins and heresies, rewarding faithful believers. Orosius' interpretation of events in the Roman Empire is an example of this. The conflagration of a Roman library caused by lightning is said to have been the punishment for the slaughter of senators ordered by Commodus. The city and the emperors were supposedly punished for prosecuting Christians. Nero's Rome saw a plague and a rebellion in Britain. Another plague ravaged the empire after Marcus Aurelius' attack on Christians. Trajan was punished with childlessness for prosecuting the Church. There was an earthquake when Constantine took an interest in Arianism. On the other hand, his acceptance of true Christianity led to splendid victories. Another example of rewarding a faithful believer is the subjugation of Persians and Goths by the emperor Theodosius.[262] These and similar interpretations would last long into the modern times, until the visible hand of Providence gradually became invisible in modern historical thinking.

260 Dobiáš, *Dějepisectví starověké*, 314.
261 Amos Funkenstein, *Theology and the Scientific Imagination from the Middle Ages to the Seventeenth Century* (Princeton: Princeton University Press, 1986), 245.
262 Orosius, *Seven Books of History Against the Pagans*, translated with an Introduction and Notes by A. T. Fear (Liverpool: Liverpool University Press, 2010), 89.

In the search for the intentions of Divine Providence and its interpretations, the main focus was on the development and condition of Christian communities. First depicted by Eusebius as a struggle between good and evil, and further developed by Augustine in his monumental work, *the Ecclesiastical history represented the unifying idea of all past events.* It was a "history of triumph and spread of the faith, an exact analogy to what history of global civilisation, culture, or progress is to us today . . ., independent of geographical borders, a truly universal history transcending all state entities."[263]

However, rather than a mere "analogy," which may be accidental, it was the source and pattern of later secularised endeavours to explain the history of civilisation and culture.

Let us further consider the theme of the gradual development of the meaning of history as a progress towards the triumph of the true faith. The patristic tradition conceived of history as a struggle between God's community and the community of the Devil's followers, or, in other words, as a struggle between Christianity and paganism. Religion, our central topic, played the main role not only in theological thinking and argumentation concerning history, but was also a fundamental characteristic of entire human groups, nations, and cultures. In this view, history is a global arena of conflict between the adherents of true and false religion, i.e. between Christians and pagans:

> Eusebius knew only too well that he was writing a new kind of history. The Christians were a nation in his view. Thus he was writing national history. But his nation had a transcendental origin. Though it had appeared on earth in Augustus' time, it was born in heaven "with the first dispensation concerning the Christ himself" (1.1.8). Such a nation was not fighting ordinary wars. Its struggles were persecutions and heresies. Behind the Christian nation there was Christ, just as the devil was behind its enemies. The ecclesiastical history was bound to be different from ordinary history, because it was a history of the struggle against the devil, who tried to pollute the purity of the Christian Church as guaranteed by the apostolic succession.[264]

---

263 Dobiáš, *Dějepisectví starověké*, 303.
264 Arnoldo Momigliano, "Pagan and Christian Historiography in the Fourth Century A.D," in *The Conflict between Paganism and Christianity in the Fourth Century*, ed. Arnoldo Momigliano (Oxford: The Clarendon Press, 1963), 79.

Another characteristic feature is the specific periodization of history and the character of each period. In its own way, Christian theological thinking integrated the biblical idea of different ages that structured Jewish history. Eusebius discussed six ages: from the Creation to the Flood, from Noah to Abraham, from Abraham to David, from David's reign to the Babylonian captivity, and thence to the advent of Jesus Christ. The last age commenced after Christ. *Theology thus developed both a new periodization of history and the idea about a historical role of different empires and human groups, nations.* This periodization of history, developed by the early Church Fathers, offered a new view of the past for several reasons. First and foremost, it gave a more specific picture of divine intentions and the gradual revelation of meaning in universal history. *There emerges an idea of eras of specific character that differ from each other fundamentally and will never occur again.* The foundations of this concept were laid down by Augustine, shifting the focus from the apocalyptic calculation of the end of the world to the description of the different periods. According to him, the individual days of creation correspond to the different ages of the world in their character rather than their length or number of years. Just as Genesis relates that on each day of creation something different happened, the same is true of each corresponding age.[265] This periodization of history introduced into the concept of history both a specific structure that was radically different from the previous cyclical concept of time and the idea of a unique nature of each era.

Defence against the accusation that Christians were responsible for the decline of the Roman Empire and subsequently for Alaric's sacking of Rome in 410 as well turned the argument against the critics. At the same time, Rome became an instrument of Providence. Eusebius claimed that the Roman Empire was destined to be a means of spreading the true faith and ultimately becoming the God's Kingdom on the earth.[266] The question of who was entitled to wisdom, knowledge, and rule of the world thus gradually became a great issue in the European medieval thinking.

> In profane history the theme was that of the transfer of power. The world in every age had one heart; the rest of the universe lived according to its rhythm and impulse alone. The succession of the empires, based on Oro-

---

265 Funkenstein, *Theology and the Scientific Imagination from the Middle Ages to the Seventeenth Century*, 260–261.
266 Funkenstein, *Theology and the Scientific Imagination from the Middle Ages to the Seventeenth Century*, 256–257.

sius' exegesis of the dream of Daniel, from the Babylonians to the Medes and Persians, then to the Macedonians, and after them to the Greeks and the Romans, was the guiding thread of the medieval philosophy of history. It proceeded at the double level, that of power and that of civilization. The transfer of power, the *translatio imperii*, was above all a transfer of knowledge and culture, a *translatio studii*.[267]

In the 12th century, Otto of Freising considered the Holy Roman Empire the denouement of *translatio imperii*, while Chrétien de Troyes thought the same of France, and Richard of Bury of England in the 14th century. It is noteworthy that these and other chroniclers shared the idea of a gradual transfer of wisdom and power from the East further and further to the West. Richard of Bury used an allegory of Minerva visiting different nations. She was supposed to have started her journey long ago in India, and having travelled among many different nations, "she has just arrived happily in Britain, the most illustrious of the isles, the microcosm of the universe."[268]

The European Middle Ages naturally preserved the concept of *translatio imperii* and the whole framework of theological thinking about the past with all the above mentioned characteristics. This medieval thinking afforded special importance to the exegetic principle of accommodation as noted by Amos Funkenstein. This concept was expressed in the words "the scripture speaks the language of man," originally an interpretative principle of Jewish legal thought. It is also found in Augustine as he explained why God used to require ritual sacrifices from the chosen people and why he did not require them any longer. Like Jewish exegetes, Augustine attributes to God's dealings with mankind answers adjusted to specific times and people.[269]

Funkenstein demonstrated that the idea of accommodation was developed into great historical speculation according to which God gave people of a specific period only what corresponded to the intellectual, moral, and even political level of their development. For instance, according to Joachim of Fiore, the law given to the people of Israel was "good for their times," but the problem was that the Jews refused to change with

267 Jacques Le Goff, *Medieval Civilization 400–1500* (Oxford: Blackwell Publishers, 1992), 171.
268 Le Goff, *Medieval Civilization 400–1500*, 172.
269 Funkenstein, *Theology and the Scientific Imagination from the Middle Ages to the Seventeenth Century*, 223.

time. Similarly, Hugo of Saint Victor maintained that sacraments were introduced in the course of time according to the changing conditions of mankind.[270] The idea of historical progression was thus developed by means of specific argumentation that concerned the relation of Providence to human race:

> Attempts to link the divine plan of salvation with the intrinsic evolution of humanity through the mediation of a divine pedagogy comprised the backbone of Christian philosophies of history since the second century. They ascribed, at least on the level of theological interpretation, a different *qualitas temporum* to different periods of history. In so doing they aided in the formation of categories of historical reasoning that have been used since the 17th century.[271]

Of course, much more could be said about the development of European historical thought from Antiquity to the Middle Ages, therefore I am providing readers with references to specialised scholarship here.[272] When we turn our attention to the later development of theological thinking about the past, we see three major themes at least. Firstly, it is the rise of the Protestant concept of history; secondly, the development of critical methods of analysing historical sources;[273] and thirdly, the arrival of the Enlightenment and thus of Modern thought. Albeit important, the first two topics will not be considered here.

On the other hand, the heritage of theological thinking in the modern historiography since the times of Enlightenment is of crucial importance here. *Although historians are more or less aware of the theological origins of secularised historiography, they are much less attentive to the problem that secularisation has not brought about as significant changes in the structure of ideas or in historical practice as it is generally thought.* The point at issue is well illustrated by František Kutnar and Jaroslav Marek, two prominent

---

270 Funkenstein, *Theology and the Scientific Imagination from the Middle Ages to the Seventeenth Century*, 225–227.
271 Funkenstein, *Theology and the Scientific Imagination from the Middle Ages to the Seventeenth Century*, 222.
272 Glenn F. Chesnut, *The First Christian Histories: Eusepius, Socrates, Sozomen, Theodret and Evagrius* (Macon: Mercer University Press, 1986); Deborah M. Deliyannis, *Historiography in the Middle Ages* (Leiden: Brill, 2003).
273 Examples include Lorenzo Valla's well-known criticism of the so called *Donation of Constantine* in the 15th century, Pasquier's and others' criticism of the purported Trojan origin of the Franks in the 16th century, and Mabillon's systematic criticism focused on the authenticity of historical documents in the 17th century.

Czech scholars of historiography, who claimed that medieval and modern historiography share "some similar features in the conception of historical development or in elements of the philosophy of history."[274] This involved "transcending the particularism of Antiquity's view of history" by creating a single universalising framework in which history progresses to one ultimate goal.

Ideas such as meaning of history and completion of historical development have since been reappearing in various forms of historical thinking and have been also subsumed into contemporary historiography, *albeit its religious background has almost disappeared.*[275]

I argue that, in fact, much of the "religious background" has been preserved in the structure of ideas concerning the past. The secularisation of Christian thinking has had a specific result. The characteristic structures of theological thinking about the past have been retained despite them being gradually severed from their original framework in which they made sense. The framework of universal global history has persisted along with the linear concept of time and the practice of integrating more and more chronologies of various cultures into the single linear chronology of the universalising framework. It is not clear what makes this universalising framework of the global chronicle so desirable, considering that it transforms the plurality of many cultures' memories into mere appendages of the history of Europe.

"Transcending the particularism of Antiquity's view of history" consisted in transforming the diverse traditions of the ancient world into one paganism which integrated the past of various communities into God's plan that they unconsciously fulfilled. One ought to keep in mind that rather than a collaboratively created past, the universalising framework meant the history of the Church's campaign against paganism. Historical truth was thus clearly defined as God's revelation that was pitched against myths and sagas surrounding the worship of false deities. The early Church Fathers used various ways to prove that their interpretation of history was true, as opposed to "unreliable pagan" works.[276]

---

274 František Kutnar and Jaroslav Marek, *Přehledné dějiny českého a slovenského dějepisectví* [Synoptical history of the Czech and Slovak historiography] (Prague: Nakladatelství Lidové noviny, 1997), 16–17.
275 Kutnar and Marek, *Přehledné dějiny českého a slovenského dějepisectví*, 17.
276 See e.g. Orosius, *Seven Books of History Against the Pagans*, 14.

European historiography turned any distinct and independent concept of the past into a mere fable containing a historical core at best. This antithetical distinction between true and false history has continued in secularised historiography, along with the theological idea of history progressing towards its climax. The original climax, Christ's second coming, has been gradually abandoned and replaced by a vision of just government and happy life on earth, originally only concomitant with Christ's second coming. Enlightenment thinkers are known to have considered their own time to be the climax of history that commenced the rule of reason securing the desired happiness of mankind.

I argue against the widespread opinion that Enlightenment thinking, especially since Giambattista Vico and Pierre Bayle, freed European historiography from the theological framework and inaugurated the era of a rational and scientific discipline. For example, František Kutnar and Jaroslav Marek wrote about the Enlightenment:

> Its fundamental historic significance lies in the fact that interpretations of society and human history got rid of elements of theological and transcendentally oriented thinking. Once and for all, religious dogmas lost their role in solving the relation of man to the world and history became a human act that can only be comprehended by rationally analysing the realities of this world, rather than by speculating about unfathomable powers concealed behind empirical experience.[277]

Have religious dogmas lost their role in understanding the relation of humans to the world? Is it really the case that European thinkers have, since the Enlightenment, stopped "speculating about unfathomable powers concealed behind empirical experience?" Let us consider relevant evidence. If the historians of historiography repeatedly refer to Vico as a thinker who marks the emancipation of historiography from theological presuppositions, let us confront this claim with Funkenstein's analysis:

> Vico sought after a better way to save the "history of the gentes" from being altogether devoid of divine providence. Direct providence, he maintained, governs the history of the chosen people, Jews and then Chris-

---

277 Kutnar and Marek, *Přehledné dějiny českého a slovenského dějepisectví*, 135.

tians; but the indirect providence governs the affairs of nations by the very laws that govern the enfoldment of human societies.[278]

Let us remember that Vico was mainly considering the development of human societies in the context of contemporary discussions about political organisation. To put it simply, Vico also saw history as a struggle between refined individuals and societies with inferior people governed by their passions. He claimed that while the rough and inferior usually prevail, the society eventually rises gradually to a better level. However, theological considerations of the role of religion still played a major part in Vico's thought. If Vico considers the development of society as a progress from a primitive, or even bestial state to a cultivated society, the idea of religion played a fundamental role in this process. He tried to show how fundamental this role was:

> Divine providence initiated the process by which the fierce and violent were brought from their outlaw state to humanity... It did so by awakening in them a confused idea of some divinity, which they in their ignorance attributed to that to which it did not belong. Thus through the terror of this imagined divinity, they began to put themselves in some order.[279]

Funkenstein argued that Vico thus endowed Xenophanes' criticism of Greek traditions with a new meaning of fundamental historical importance. According to Vico, the driving force of history was the human faculty to imagine gods. However false these ideas may be, they were all ultimately inspired by a true quest for divinity since the faculty itself is given to mankind by Providence.[280] These considerations must lead to a definite conclusion: There is a true religion and a true image of God that all people should aim for. What is *not* theological about these cogitations?

Bayle's opinions still arouse so much debate and are interpreted so differently that it would be impossible to treat them adequately in brief.[281]

---

278 Funkenstein, *Theology and the Scientific Imagination from the Middle Ages to the Seventeenth Century*, 279.

279 Giambattista Vico, *De Unio Principio*, quoted in Funkenstein, *Theology and the Scientific Imagination from the Middle Ages to the Seventeenth Century*, 283.

280 Funkenstein, *Theology and the Scientific Imagination from the Middle Ages to the Seventeenth Century*, 289.

281 "According to just the 20th century interpretations, Bayle might have been a positivist, an atheist, a deist, a sceptic, a fideist, a Socinian, a liberal Calvinist, a conservative Calvinist, a libertine, a Judaizing Christian, a Judeo-Christian, or even a secret Jew, a Manichean, an

Nevertheless, even a cursory glance at his work will show that he was concerned with issues such as theodicy and other theological questions. Be that as it may, we can deal briefly with another great representative of the Enlightenment. How did Voltaire approach theological thinking in the conception of history? Among other things, he is commended for his *Essay on the Manners and Spirit of Nations* on account of which many considered him the founder of modern philosophy of history. Kutnar and Marek described this work and *The Age of Louis XIV* as "Remarkable for its brilliant insight, sense of great historical correlations, and clear discerning style."[282] The Czech historians also extolled Voltaire for his effort to write a history of culture rather than overviews of mostly political events. Furthermore, Voltaire was praised for his appreciation of Asian cultures, Chinese in particular, which he integrated into the universal history of humanity. What are the "brilliant insights" concerning the past that Voltaire offered?

The French philosopher focused on the issue of original religion and reiterated earlier ideas of people who were too preoccupied with survival to elevate their minds to God, their creator. He talked about the religion of "primitives" who have a very "crude" form of worship or none at all. In his view, inhabitants of certain parts of Africa, North America, and marine islands represent the surviving type of a primitive man. These "primitives" have only acquired knowledge of God by instinct. According to Voltaire, however, true knowledge of God requires "either reason or revelation." He thinks that Cicero and other ancient philosophers recognised the existence of "the Highest and Omnipotent God."[283] Voltaire also considered the religions of the Chaldeans, the Egyptians, the Greeks, and the Jews. He wrote about India and China as well. All of Voltaire's commentary exhibits his firm conviction that humans have been created, that human races have been located in various parts of the Earth by Providence itself, and that ideally, human communities develop from a "primitive" state characterised by a religion of fear and the effort to win the favour of "minacious deities" towards a full realisation of one God, who is the creator, the omnipotent, etc. What is *not* theological about this account of human history?

---

existentialist." Edward N. Zalta et al., *Stanford Ecyclopedia of Philosophy* [online] http://plato.stanford.edu/entries/bayle/.

282 Kutnar and Marek, *Přehledné dějiny českého a slovenského dějepisectví*, 138.

283 Francois M. A. Voltaire, *The Philosophy of History, or a Philosophical and Historical Dissertation* (London: Thomas North, 1829), 19–27.

To this day, European thinking has been shaped by the structures of theological thinking that has shaped historical theory. Since Antiquity, concrete examples of historiographical work have exhibited painstaking treatment of documents, comparison of differing accounts, and reconstruction of individual facts. However, as Balagangadhara noted, any amount of facts cannot prove or disprove the underlying theological paradigm.[284] The process of secularisation has preserved this relationship between partial criticism of sources and the far-reaching interpretations of them. Enlightenment scholars followed the paradigm given by the traditional theological framework of their respective church teaching, like Catholics František Martin Pelcl or Gelasius Dobner in Czech lands, or that of deism, like Voltaire. They were able to criticise the erroneousness of Catholic legends, to question the doctrine of the Three Estates, and likewise. However, despite gradual secularisation, Christian thinking has preserved its basic structures in considering history as a meaningful and goal-directed process that involves all of humanity.

The historiography of Romanticism is often interpreted as a reaction against the Enlightenment approach to history and, in a way, its antithesis. For example, much attention has been given to the difference in evaluating the Middle Ages between representatives of the Enlightenment and Romanticism. Moreover, modern European nationalism became a topic of great importance among historians of the Romantic period. Although these are certainly significant themes, one must also deal with the continuity of the 19th century historiography with preceding thought. *Basically, further development of historiography involved three trends: continuing denominational historiography, new great philosophies of history, and finally, historians' increasing resignation from pursuing any grand theory of history. Nevertheless, the former relationship between the evolving critique of sources and the theoretical structures has been preserved:* Any amount of critically verified and reassessed data could neither corroborate nor disprove broader theoretical interpretations.[285]

---

284 Balagangadhara, "What do Indians need: A History or the Past" [article online], http://xyz4000.wordpress.com/2012/02/16/whatdoindiansneedahistoryorthepastsnbalagangadhara/.
285 In the 20th century, this problem of the Western historical thinking was pointed out by Popper; see Karl Popper, *The Poverty of Historicism* (London: Routledge, 2002). Popper focused on questioning the assumptions on grounds of which the great theories of history would predict events, especially those of Karl Marx. Popper's criticism was motivated by his interest in differentiating between real science and pseudoscience. His well-known criterion in this effort was falsifiability, i.e. the possibility that a theory can be disproved by an observation. In this respect, great historical theories are unscientific because they are capable to interpret any event in the line of their ideas, and it is difficult to say which event would be a falsifier of their claims.

Precisely during the time when European historical thinking was gradually abandoning belief in the literal validity of Genesis and other Biblical stories and theology ceased to be the explicit theoretical framework of new schools of historical thought, most historians resorted to increasingly elaborate critique of sources and consequent accumulation of facts, abandoning attempts at building a new theoretical framework. True, the 19th century had its great theoreticians of history, such as Hegel, Comte, Marx, and others. However, the victorious historical positivism made many historians view the possibility of a new fundamental theory of history with scepticism, to say the least. One can generalise that they mostly did not consider theory to be relevant to their specific questions. The ideas of Hegel and other great thinkers were relegated to philosophy of history that only interested a small number of the members from the quickly increasing community of European historians. The situation in the United States was even more extreme, Leopold von Ranke's research method was adopted as the most significant contribution of European historiography. These problems of 19th century historiography have been noted, for example by Herbert Butterfield:

> But the study of the varied attempts to make a scientific use of historical data is possibly one of the more neglected aspects of the history of historiography. And if the 19th century carried to a high degree the microscopic examination of evidence and the critical use of sources, there has not always been the same conscious attempt to develop the scientific method in respect to our wider constructions and interpretations.[286]

While Butterfield gives a fairly mild assessment of the situation, many historians' abrogation of theory was a matter of programmatic decision.[287]

The divorce of methods and particular questions from their original framework of ideas and the eschewal of theory of any kind by most historians were not without consequences. Jaroslav Marek characterised the situation at the end of the 19th century thus:

> Historical science became synonymous with autotelic accumulation of antiquarian knowledge that is devoid of any meaning. Reduced to facts

---

286 Herbert Butterfield, *Man on His Past: The Study of the History of Historical Scholarship* (Cambridge: Cambridge University Press, 1955), 43.

287 Peter Novick, *That Noble Dream, The "Objectivity Question" and the American Historical Profession* (Cambridge: Cambridge University Press, 1988), 37–38.

and techniques, the primitive methodology of historiography and its inability to explain the meaning of what had been discovered was blatant
especially in comparison with the state of natural sciences. From the 1850s,
the research outcomes of natural sciences formed the basis for developing
philosophical interpretations of reality, however one-sided and impetuous
those might have been. In comparison with the natural scientist, the historian gave the impression of a mere collector who accumulated material
that would require further scientific interpretation. As soon as historiography came into contact with ideas of a philosophical nature—as it had
to when its extending the pool of facts had turned out to be sterile—it
became evident that historiography had an insufficient theoretical basis.
In fact, such a basis did not exist.[288]

Is it really the case that there did not exist any theoretical basis? It is
true that many historians had no *explicitly* formulated theory of history.
However, on what basis did they choose the events and personalities
that they focused on? On what basis did they order facts into causal connections? On what basis did they interpret them? If they did not rely on
any explicitly formulated theory, is it possible to find a theory that was
implicitly present in their work?

A closer examination of historical practice reveals that it still derived
from theological, albeit gradually secularised, ideas. The frame of the
universal global chronicle integrating events in various parts of the world
on a single chronological axis has been preserved. A new research field
emerged, called world history, in which it is necessary to interpret the
history of individual nations, frequently identified with the history of
states. In the interpretations of national and global histories, *the secularised idea of historical progress, i.e. humanity's march towards a desired goal*, has
remained central. Today, historians speak of teleology or metanarrative.
Mary Fulbrook discussed the dependence of three versions of this "great
narrative" on the previous theological thinking:

The classic metanarratives in Western Europe in the 19th and earlier 20th
centuries were couched in terms of some notion of progress, whether that
of the Unfolding of World Spirit Realizing Itself (the Hegelian version),
or its materialist inversion in terms of Class Struggles and Human Eman-

288 Jaroslav Marek, *O historismu a dějepisectví* [About historicism and historical science] (Prague:
Academia, 1992), 174–175.

cipation towards Pure Communism (the Marxist version), or the Onward March towards Liberty and Democracy (the Whig version) ... In different ways, they are all essentially secularised versions of the Judeo-Christian master narrative: from the Fall, through the dark satanic struggles between Good and Evil, to the ultimate Redemption and Final Judgement. They presuppose grand patterns in history, which will eventually (whether or not it has yet been achieved) culminate in something much better than what has gone before. In some senses they all share the 19th century faith in evolutionary progress towards some ultimate goal, or *telos*, of all human history.[289]

Jerzy Topolski described the secularisation of the idea of historical progress in similar words, adding that despite its 19th century transformation the idea of progress "has not lost its essence."[290] What is the essence of the idea of progress? The theological thinking and imagination summarised above. Another way of speaking about the idea of progress is to discuss evolution. Topolski noted how "historiography consolidated itself in the myth of evolutionism, one of the so called fundamental (or organising) myths." As it is well known, Darwinism played a substantial role in the process. Further thorough analysis of evolutionism would require considering the separation of Darwin's ideas from its original principles, which resulted in the materialist interpretation of evolution along with the influential idealist conceptions of evolution current in the second half of the 19th century.[291] Those had a rich history, one of their antecedents being in the Enlightenment four-stage scheme of social development, conceived as progress from utter savagery towards European civilisation.

It must be noted that Fulbrook's and Topolski's language is slightly confusing because terms such as "great narrative," "master narrative," and "fundamental or organising myth" do not capture what actually happened. To deal with the past, Christian thinking developed a whole specific framework whose structure was described above. Naturally, the framework was theological. In the practice of believing historians, it was

---

289 Mary Fulbrook, *Historical Theory* (London: Routledge, 2008), 59.
290 Jerzy Topolski, "Pojem úpadku v dějinách a hospodářských dějinách" [The concept of decline in history and economical history], in *Kritéria a ukazatele nerovnoměrného vývoje v evropských dějinách* [The criteria and signifiers of the uneven development in the European history], ed. Luďa Klusáková (Prague: FF UK, 1997), 65.
291 See Peter J. Bowler, *The Invention of Progress: The Victorians and the Past* (London: B. Blackwell, 1989).

a structure determining their concrete ideas that preceded modern theories. By *determining* I mean both the shaping and restrictive functions of the framework in which certain questions are raised and solved in a specific manner, whereas other questions are not raised at all since they do not make sense or are hardly conceivable in terms of this framework. The secularisation of theological thinking brought about a change in that the explicitly recognised theological framework became an implicit and largely unreflected upon background of modern historiography. Topolski was aware of this problem:

> In historiography, the fundamental myths (quasi-theories or metaphors) make up *a supra-theoretical network that is deeply ingrained in historians' thinking and reflected in their texts. Such a network usually works automatically in the form of a belief.* The evolutionary myth involves a deeply rooted (albeit frequently ostensibly rejected) belief in historical progress. This gives rise to positive evaluations of facts or processes such as "progress," "growth," or "flourishing" and negative evaluations called "decline," "breakdown," "collapse," or "fall," etc.[292]

Topolski's "supra-theoretical network" is a different expression for what I mean by structures of thought creating one large framework, the metastructure. Its characteristic features can be seen in works of Karl Marx, Émile Durkheim, and Max Weber, the thought fathers of the three principal schools of European and American historiography—the Marxist historiography, the Annales School, and the American Modernization Theory. Neither the criticism of historicism nor the deconstruction of Postmodernists (Hayden White, Frank Ankersmit, and others) have succeeded in changing the influence of secularised theological thinking in the historiography of the 20th and the beginning of the 21st centuries.

A few examples will suffice to illustrate how the basic structures of the original theological framework have persisted in historiography to this day. Philosophers and historians alike have searched for the meaning of specific events in relation to the variously formulated idea of progress (e.g. the Great French Revolution and the American Revolution as fundamental turning points in the history of humanity on its way to the long-desired freedom), discussed the role of nations in history (e.g. the Czech controversy over the meaning of Czech history), and looked for

292 Topolski, "Pojem úpadku v dějinách a hospodářských dějinách," 66.

the meaning of human history as such. Arnold Toynbee was a historian who attempted to delineate fundamental civilizations and their development throughout history. Toynbee searched for laws and regularities in human history. He distinguished two levels of thinking about history: "the study of reality" relating to "human affairs" and a "higher dimension" of history which he called "metahistory." For Toynbee, this higher dimension is linked with the idea of progress. It is telling that Toynbee quoted Saint Augustine's *De Civitate Dei* as an example of work on the "higher dimension" of history.[293]

Global history and its periodization is still effectively identified with the history of Europe and its expansion overseas. A cursory look at the contemporary textbooks of history shows this fact well: They divide global history into Prehistory, Antiquity, the Middle Ages, and Modernity whose turning points as well as most factual events come from the history of "Greater Europe" (see Blaut's comment below). Other vast cultural areas, such as India and China, make a short appearance in Antiquity, they are marginally mentioned in the Middle Ages, and become the stage of European colonisation in Modernity as a matter of course. And the project of global, or general, history represents one of the significant trends as well as problems of contemporary historiography:

> The great problem is that of global general history, of the secular tendency to a history that would be not only universal and synthetic—an old enterprise that extends from ancient Christianity to the German historicism of the 19th century and to the countless universal histories produced by the popularization of history in the 20th century—but also integral and complete, as La Popeliniére put it, or global, total, as Lucien Febvre and Marc Bloch's *Annales* maintained.[294]

In other words, the secularised theological thinking maintains an exclusive control over interpreting the past of various cultures and traditions of the world. The basic features of European historiography were

---

293 Arnold Toynbee, *The Study of History*, quoted in Topolski, "Pojem úpadku v dějinách a hospodářských dějinách," 67.
294 Le Goff, *History and Memory*, 211. The project of global history has given rise to a new specialised journal in 2006. See the manifesto in the first issue: Patrick O'Brien, "Historiographical Traditions and Modern Imperatives for the Restoration of Global History," *Journal of Global History* 1, no. 1 (2006): 3–39.

formed by Christian thinking and this is still the case today, however difficult it may be to realise the impact of this paradigm of European historical thinking due to secularisation and the self-aggrandising myth of heroic objective science.[295] What impact has that had on the study of Indian past?

History of India Written by Europeans

A special characteristic of the European awareness of India and other remote countries was its changelessness lasting for centuries, from Antiquity to early modern times. The empire of Francs gradually arose out of the ruins of the Western Roman Empire whereas the Byzantine Empire, the direct heir of the eastern part of the Roman Empire, was sealed off and deprived of much of its territory by the Caliphate. The horizon of Christian Europe had been drawn by its greatest political rivals for several centuries, initially by the united Caliphate and subsequently by its successor states. The struggle with the powers under the banner of Islam had for centuries been the focal point of Christian perceptions and aspirations concerning the knowledge about distant cultures. Informations about cultures beyond this horizon had by and large been inherited from Antiquity and consisted of fragments by Classical authors that were being rearranged and realigned in medieval encyclopaedias and chronicles. Such was the image of India, including the positive image of Brahmins described in the first chapter.

It seems that it didn't cross chroniclers' minds that ancient authors' accounts were no longer au courant after the lapse of several centuries. Accounts of Nestorian communities were compounded by unrealistic tales about mighty Christian rulers who might be convenient allies in the fight against Muslim dynasties. The tales of Prester John's kingdom are the best example of such knowledge. Therefore, the image of India was a mixture of fantasies about monstrous people and wishful belief in powerful Christian kingdoms, spiced up with a real experience of luxury exotic goods. Only a small number of missionaries and merchants had first-hand acquaintance with India.[296]

---

295 The Enlightenment model of heroic science and the idea of progress have been analysed, for example, by Joyce Appleby, Lynn Hunt, and Margaret Jacob, *Telling the Truth about History* (New York: W. W. Norton, 1995).
296 Valtrová, *Středověká setkání s jinými*, 73–83.

By gradually gaining military and technological superiority, especially on the sea, the Portuguese and later other Europeans came to have much more intensive contact with India. Apart from Malabar Christians, who were not as numerous as expected, and the strong presence of Islam, Europeans came across local traditions. Endeavouring to convert Indian peoples, missionaries had been discovering India' peculiar customs and remarkable learning. The key point at issue was to determine what religion it was. The answer first offered by Jesuits and subsequently by Protestant missionaries was overwhelmingly the same: It is some form of paganism. The formation of Christianity during Antiquity still had the fundamental role of the interpretative framework within which Europeans tried to understand their experience with other cultures.

> The 16th through 18th century travel reports began to build up a series of images and pictures of other cultures in two distinct, if interrelated ways: on the one hand, a description of cults, religious practices and beliefs; on the other, interpreting and explicating the former by reference to 'similar' phenomena involving the Ancients.[297]

The long defunct traditions and cults of ancient Greece and Rome were as if they had come back to life in the eyes of the 16th and 17th century Europeans. The strange and unknown traditions of India were promptly interpreted as another form of the same Ancient paganism, as another form of the same false religion. What impact has this heritage of Christian theological thinking had on reconstructing Indian past? Leaving aside the works of missionaries, travellers, and direct predecessors of the first British orientalists, we shall focus on the work of William Jones and later Orientalists. In construing Indian past, Jones was bothered with several questions inherent in the contemporary theological discussions. Does at least something within the "Hindu" religion continue to be a form of primeval monotheism, as argued e.g. by Dow and Holwell? In any case, Jones was convinced that he had a unique opportunity to observe survivals of a long disappeared ancient world:

> Of the Indian Religion and Philosophy ... it will be sufficient in this dissertation to assume, what might be proved beyond controversy, that we now live among the adorers of those very deities, who were worshipped

---

297 Balagangadhara, *"The Heathen in His Blindness..."*, 101.

under different names in old *Greece* and *Italy*, and among the professors of those philosophical tenets, which the *Ionick* and *Attick* writers illustrated with all the beauties of their melodic language.[298]

In view of the evident antiquity of Sanskrit literature, the question arose of how these sources reflected the earliest history of humanity as recorded in the Bible. If Indian traditions were indeed that old, there was a fascinating possibility that they would fill details in the Biblical accounts. Firmly convinced of the truthfulness of Biblical stories, starting with Genesis, Jones matched them with motifs from Indian stories. In the epics and the Puranic texts, he saw evidence of Indians' memories relating to the creation of the world, the deluge and the migrations of human race, i.e. Noah's offspring:

> We have, therefore, determined another interesting epoch, by fixing the age of Krishna near the *three thousandth* year from the present time; and, as the three first *Avatars*, or descents of Vishnu, relate no less clearly to an Universal Deluge, in which eight persons only were saved, than the fourth and fifth do to the punishment of impiety and the humiliation of the proud, we may for the present assume, that the second, or silver, age of the Hindus was subsequent to the dispersion from Babel . . .[299]

Jones believed that the Indians used to have a sense for precise chronology and preservation of historical data, although it had been obscured and veiled in allegory. Evidently, he tried to prove that Puranic stories about the *avatars* of Vishnu were allegorical remnants of true memories of events described in the Bible. He related the first three *avatars* to the Flood, the fourth and fifth one to Nimrod, the Rama *avatar* with the settlement of Noah's sons, and so on. He considered the *Bhagavata Purana* story about the rescue of Manu and other sages by the fish *avatar* to be clear evidence of the deluge and thought that Manu was none other than Noah. Nevertheless, he explained other Indian stories about a global deluge as local events.

---

298 Jones, *The Works of Sir William Jones in Six Volumes*, 1:28. The British Orientalist developed the idea in one of his subsequent lectures for the Asiatic Society of Bengal, in which he identified Ganesha with Roman Janus, Satyavrata Manu with Saturn (based on Bochart's opinion that stories about Saturn derive from the story of Noah), and so on; see "On the Gods of Greece, Italy and India," in Jones, *The Works of Sir William Jones in Six Volumes*, 1:229–280.

299 Jones, *The Works of Sir William Jones in Six Volumes*, 1:29.

Jones thus arrived at "independent evidence" in favour of his own periodization of history consisting of the diluvial period, the age of patriarchs, the age of Moses, and the age of prophets. He was also convinced that the enormous lengths of Indian ages and cycles had a historical core and by reducing them, he endeavoured to calculate the "correct" chronology of important events. Although Jones' periodization does not correspond to Augustine's six ages, it has the same foundation in the Biblical narrative as the framework of the universal chronicle of humanity. It had the same purpose as theological historiography—to advocate the precisely calculated beginning of the world. Jones clung to the date that had been fixed by the Archbishop Ussher to 4004 BC and was recognised by the Anglican Church at the time.[300]

S. N. Mukherjee has noted that Jones' main intention was to advocate Biblical narratives in the face of growing criticism. His speculations about the Indian "evidence" in favour of the historicity of Biblical stories were to be "of solid importance in an age when some intelligent and virtuous persons are inclined to doubt the authenticity of the accounts delivered by Moses concerning the primitive world."[301]

It is noteworthy that the structure of the Biblical story about the deluge and the dispersal of Noah's sons on the earth formed the basis for Jones' famous discovery of the Indo-European family. The Biblical narrative describing the confusion of tongues and the genealogies of Noah's offspring informed Jones' family tree model of linguistic groups and their propagation. The following chapter will deal with this matter in more detail.

Although lauded for his love and knowledge of Indian traditions, Jones took an approach that was clearly shaped by the framework of theological thinking: *The local narratives of native peoples' past, including the Indian conception of time, were changed to fit the Biblical framework. Apparently, it didn't occur to Jones that Indian thinking and narratives had a significance on their own, independent of European culture.* In his eyes, their only value consisted in proving the truthfulness of the Bible, including specific figures (Manu as Noah, etc.), events (the Creation, the Flood, the dispersal of Noah's sons) and the whole concept of time transformed into a linear timeline and recalculated in terms of the Biblical ages. Everything that did not fit the framework of the Biblical story, for instance the enormous

---

300 For more details about this topic, see Trautmann, *Aryans and British India*, 57–59.
301 Rightly stressed quote of Jones in: Mukherjee, *Sir William Jones*, 100.

time span of Puranic ages, was dismissed by Jones as allegory or fable.[302] It was a total denial of Indian otherness, reshaping autochthonous ideas to fit the Biblical pattern.

Many of Jones' half-forgotten successors, such as Thomas Maurice, continued in the same vein. Thomas Trautmann presented an apt description of his work:

> The whole structure and much of the substance of these works is from Jones, but without his genius. Maurice accepts the antiquity of Hinduism and *its role as the key to ancient paganism and as independent proof of the Biblical narrative*, but attacks those parts of it, especially the doctrine of the four ages of cyclical time, that conflict.[303]

New trends of secularised European thought gradually desisted from explicitly advocating the Biblical narrative in interpretations of India's past. The topic of religion as a constituent of culture remained. For instance, the controversy concerning the role of religion in Indian history was the burden of James Mill's critique of William Jones and other Orientalist, as will be shown towards the end of this chapter.

Let us note an important coincidence in the development of European historiography in the 19th century. Precisely during the time of its secularisation, when Christian theological background became less and less explicit, more and more emphasis was put on collecting, classifying, and comparing sources, there was much less effort to rethink theoretical interpretations of data thus obtained. This trend is also perceptible in British India. In the course of the 19th century, many enthusiasts were busy collecting, deciphering, and translating Indian manuscripts, discovering archaeological sites, and sometimes recording local oral traditions. Several generations of Europeans were engaged in this endeavour, continuing the work of the 18th century Orientalists. As Horace H. Wilson, Elphinstone, William H. Hunter, A. V. Williams, Vincent A. Smith, and others had been reconstructing the ancient history of India, they made some ground-breaking discoveries. Those include the dating of Chandragupta Maurya's reign, proposed already by William Jones, James Prinsep's decipherment of the Brahmi script, or the discovery of the Buddha's remains by Alexander Cunningham,

---

302 Jones, *Institutes of Hindu Law*, xii.
303 Trautmann, *Aryans and British India,* 75.

the founder of Indian archaeology.[304] The admirable painstaking work of several generations yielded an enormous amount of manuscripts, monument documentations and other results, many of which still await closer research.[305]

Yet, this impressive accumulation of facts and celebration of specific achievements in dating significant figures and events of ancient Indian history conceal the assumptions and nature of the European project. Is it not striking that 19th century researchers did basically the same intellectual work as early Church Fathers? They recorded and reconstructed various local memories of past events and connected them in one universal chronology. For example, while Vincent A. Smith concluded that the existence of many of the Mahabharata's heroes could not be substantiated by any available sources, he tried to determine the place of the kings of the Puranic lists in Indian history. Smith and others compared those lists with Buddhist and Jain sources in order to create the chronology of all India and relate it to the global chronology:

> In order to be available for the purpose of history, events must be susceptible of arrangement in definite chronological order, and capable of being dated approximately, if not exactly. Facts to which dates cannot be assigned, although they may be invaluable for the purposes of ethnology, philology, and other sciences, are of no use to the historian.[306]

Although focused on discovering facts, the trend did not mean that the construction of India's past was unimportant to the grand unifying ideas of history. On the contrary, major theorists of the 19th century used the reconstructed past of India as an argument or an illustration in solving their European problems. The conceptualisation of Indian religions played an important part in this. In his interpretation of history, Hegel argued that Indian thinking had never developed into a real philosophy because of religion. He relegated Indian thinking as well as other traditions of "Oriental" thought to an antechamber of philosophy at best. How he arrived at this conclusion will be specified below.

---

304 An engaging, but uncritical overview of the British reconstruction of India's past can be found in John Keay, *India Discovered: The Recovery of a Lost Civilisation* (London: HarperCollins, 2001).

305 According to a conservative estimation, some 160 000 Sanskrit works have been preserved; see George L. Hart, *A Rapid Sanskrit Method* (New Delhi: Motilal Banarsidass, 1989), viii.

306 Vincent Smith, *The Early History of India* (London: Oxford University Press, 1914), 27. In other words, what cannot be dated has no historical existence.

It must be emphasised that Hegel's thoughts were anchored in the belief in the universality of religion and that he was unconcerned with his factual ignorance of Indian thinking. The European exploration of the Indian schools of philosophy (*darshanas*) was in its infancy. Hegel's chapter on Indian thought in his *Lectures on the History of Philosophy* is based mainly on Colebrooke's article 'On the Philosophy of the Hindus.'[307] It is noteworthy how the German philosopher commenced his essay on Indian thought by criticising ancient Indian chronology:

> Nothing can be more confused, nothing more imperfect than the chronology of the Indians; no people which attained to culture in astronomy, mathematics, etc., is as incapable for history; in it they have neither stability nor coherence. It was believed that such was to be had in the time of Wikramaditya, who was supposed to have lived about 50 BC, and under whose reign the poet Kalidasa, the author of Sacontala, lived. But further research discovered half a dozen Wikramadityas and careful investigation has placed this epoch in our 11th century. The Indians have lines of kings and enormous quantity of names, but everything is vague.[308]

By criticising Indian chronology and the "inaccuracy of all figures," Hegel stood up against European admirers of Indian wisdom. In his view, Indian philosophy was identical with religion at a certain stage of development, which had a serious impact on Indian traditions in his conception of human development. They ended up on the lowest degree of development, like the whole of "Orient" for that matter. *Hegel's rather unclear argumentation postulated a direct relationship between the state of consciousness, the supposed Indian religion, and the political regime of "Oriental despotism."* As it is well known, Hegel developed his conception of human history as the progress of human spirit towards freedom. In his opinion, freedom of thought is directly linked to personal freedom, which is also understood politically.[309] The German philosopher directly related personal and political freedom as "being for itself" to overcoming religious fear. Oriental traditions are said to recognise only the "master-slave state" which reflects unsurpassed fear and dependence. The Orientals'

---

307 Henry T. Colebrooke, "On the Philosophy of the Hindus, Part I," *Transactions of the Royal Asiatic Society of Great Britain and Ireland* 1 (1824): 19–43.
308 Georg W. F. Hegel, *Lectures on the History of Philosophy* (London: Kegan Paul, Trench, Trübner, 1892), 1:126.
309 Hegel, *Lectures on the History of Philosophy*, 1:96.

consciousness is thought to vacillate between two extremes: It either considers its individuality to be accidental, an awareness of the finite merely as the finite, or it may become "the infinite, which is however mere abstraction."[310] Hegel interpreted Indian traditions as a religion caught up between these two extremes:

> In religion we even find self-immersion in the deepest sensuality represented as the service of God, and then there follows in the East a flight to the emptiest abstraction as to what is infinite, as also the exaltation attained through the renunciation of everything, and this is specially so amongst the Indians, who torture themselves and enter into the most profound abstraction. The Indians look straight before them for ten years at a time, are fed by those around, and are destitute of other spiritual content than that of knowing what is abstract, which content therefore is entirely finite. This, then, is not the soil of freedom.[311]

The popular equation is heard to this day: Primitive religion and primitive thinking equals despotism and lack of freedom. In contrasting human freedom with "Oriental despotism," Hegel builds up on earlier discussions of a theological nature. Those merged three old ideas: the role of degenerate clergy, the influence of climate on the character of people, and Aristotle's ideas about the despotic form of government (exalting the Greek freedom as opposed to the tyranny of the Persian Empire in the 4th century BC). Since the Renaissance, the accusation of "despotic government" in contrast with European states had been levelled first at the Ottoman Empire and later at the Mughal Empire in India as well as other regions of Asia.[312]

The most controversial constituent of the "despotism thesis" is the influence of climate. As it is well known, the impact of climate on human thought was emphasised by Montesquieu. Montesquieu attributed the differences that he seemed to discern between Indian and Chinese thinking to the influence of India's hot climate. He claimed that tranquillity and nirvana were the natural goals of mental activity where great heat drains one's energy. He also wrote about laziness that

---

310 Hegel, *Lectures on the History of Philosophy*, 1:97.
311 Hegel, *Lectures on the History of Philosophy*, 1:97.
312 In this respect, S. N. Mukherjee pointed out the critique of the Mughal system of land tenure and government in general written by Thomas Roe, the English ambassador at the court of Jahangir. See Mukherjee, *Sir William Jones*, 9.

he thought had given rise to such thinking in India. Voltaire object-
ed to Montesquieu's speculations arguing that the climate in Italy, for
instance, had not changed substantially over the last two thousand
years even though the society had been fundamentally transformed.[313]
Charles Grant, an official of the East India Company, whose works had
a considerable impact on later British policies in India, also thought
that the influence of climate on the character of India's inhabitants
was overrated. On the other hand, he attached great weight to another
widely accepted component of the despotism thesis—the influence of
religion controlled by degenerate clergy. Relying on Halhed's translation of the *Manava-dharmashastra*, he claimed that Hindu laws sustained
immorality and injustice:

> Nothing is more plain, than that this whole fabric is the work of a crafty
> and imperious priesthood, who feigned a divine revelation and appoint-
> ment, to invest their own order, in perpetuity, with the most absolute
> empire over the civil state of the Hindoos, as well as over their minds.[314]

Ideas about a static Indian, and Oriental society in general, controlled
by despotic government of priesthood had a very wide currency among
European scholars at the beginning of the 19th century. It is a telling
fact that these stereotypical ideas are found in lectures penned by historians who worked in Czech lands in the first half of the 19th century. For
example, German President, a teacher at the Piarist grammar school in
Litomyšl and later a professor of history at the University of Vienna, lec-
tured about "the inhibitive role of the clergy in Oriental despotic regimes
because, in his view, the restriction on learning outside the priestly class,
along with the influence of the climate, lethargic mind-set, and despotic
government resulted in the sciences failing to flourish in Oriental societies, as they did among the Greeks."[315]
Arthur Zempliner traced the origins of some of Marx's ideas in
these Enlightenment speculations: "The discovery of a certain corre-
lation between the geographical environment of the Orient and the

---

313 Arthur Zempliner, *Čínská filosofie v novověké evropské filosofii* [Chinese philosophy in the modern
     European philosophy] (Prague: Academia, 1966), 104.
314 Charles Grant, *Observations on the State of Society among the Asiatic Subjects of Great Britain, Par-
     ticularly with Respect to Morals; and on the Means of Improving It*, 1796, 83.
315 Milan Skřivánek, *K osvícenskému pojetí a výuce dějepisu ve světle rukopisů piaristické koleje v Lito-
     myšli* [To the Enlightenment concept and teaching of history in the light of manuscripts from
     the Piarist college in Litomyšl] (Pardubice: Univerzita Pardubice, 2008), 61.

political system of 'Eastern despotism' suggested a path that led via Herder and Hegel to Marx's discovery of the so called 'Asiatic mode of production'."[316]

Marx's thoughts on the "Asiatic mode of production" and "Oriental despotism" appear, for example, in Egon Bondy's introduction to his *Indian Philosophy* including a mention of priests: "On the other hand, the mass of agricultural workers was dominated by a despotic state—whether controlled by an autocrat or a coterie of bureaucrats and priests."[317] Using Marx's hypothesis, Bondy characterised the specificity of Indian thought: "We must realise that the specific social and human conditions of the so called Asiatic mode of production have modified and left a definite mark on the history of the philosophy that developed on the territory of this socio-historical formation."[318] It is quite amazing to see how one can develop interpretations of economy and society from the theological speculations about the decline of religion and the degeneration of priests in Orient.

As explained above, the framework of the universalising Christian chronicle has been secularised into global or "general" history. This makes up both a universalising framework of interpretation and various fields of historical studies. We still teach periodization of global history in the good belief that every period has a special spirit, or *Zeitgeist*, that is only comprehensible in the context of that period. This structure has been applied to Indian past and generations of historians of India have learnt and adopted the same approach from the British. Although some contemporary researchers are aware of particular problems, they usually end up with the same solutions that they have previously questioned.

Let us consider two examples illustrating the debate about periodization of Indian history. Today, scholars tend to acknowledge that the original British periodization, created in the 19th century and used for a long time, was actually defined by the religious allegiance of major ruling dynasties. Thus, historians wrote about Hindu, Muslim, and European (i.e. Christian) periods of Indian past.[319]

316 Zempliner, *Čínská filosofie v novověké evropské filosofii*, 105–106.

317 Bondy was a writer's name of a Czech dissenting Marxist thinker and poet, his own name was Zbyněk Fišer. The quotation is from: Egon Bondy, *Indická filosofie* [Indian philosophy] (Prague: Vokno, 1991), 9.

318 Bondy, *Indická filosofie*, 9.

319 See *The Imperial Gazetteer of India: The Indian Empire* (Oxford: Clarendon Press 1909), 2: xxii–xxx.

The division into these periods resulted from the ideas of religious, and therefore also cultural progress that the ideologists of the British Empire defined as development from primitive religion towards its highest form—British Protestantism. Jaroslav Strnad has noted that in the work of many influential authors, the terms "Antiquity," "Middle Ages," and "Modernity"—eventually applied to the history of India—stand for the very same chronological periods characterized in religious terms. They have been "renamed primarily in order to get rid of their problematic religious and national connotations."[320] In this point of argument, Strnad turned to another related topic. How could a mere change of the names have eliminated the problematic connotations? Or more precisely, how could renaming a concept affect its connection to the whole structure of the theological ideas which makes it possible to speak of specific epochs that illustrate the development of human history? However, the authors of *Dějiny Indie* do not revisit this topic and retain the periodization in the structure of the text.

Similarly, the Slovakian Orientalist, Dušan Deák, was aware of the problem of using European periodization when he paraphrased Ronald Inden's objection: "Is it adequate to apply, for example, the ideas of Antiquity, the Middle Ages, and Modernity along with the notions of inspiring antiquity, the dark ages of ecclesiastical supremacy, the Reformation and the beginnings of modern world of science and experiment to the past of Asia?"[321] And just like Strnad and other Czech Indologists, Deák used the European periodization, marking off the end of Indian Middle Ages with the death of Aurangzeb in 1707. The reason he gave for using the periodization whose suitability for comprehending India's past he formerly questioned is its "common usage in Slovakia."[322]

The old idea of *translatio imperii* (transfer of rule) became an argument used by the British Empire's ideologists who saw the workings of Divine Providence or a necessary result of humanity's development and progress in the subjugation of India and other parts of the world. *Translatio imperii* operated in the general education of the Anglo-American world as late as the first half of the 20th century and determined a specific view of history which J. M. Blaut called "historical tunnel vision" or simply "tunnel history":

---

320 Strnad et al., *Dějiny Indie*, 17.
321 Deák, *Indický svätci medzi minulosťou a prítomnosťou*, 13.
322 Deák, *Indický svätci medzi minulosťou a prítomnosťou*, 22.

The older form of tunnel history simply ignored the non-European world: typical textbooks and historical atlases devoted very few pages to areas outside the Greater Europe (that is, Europe and countries of European settlement overseas, plus, for ancient history and the Crusades, the Near East), until one came to the year 1492. Non-Europe (Africa, Asia east of the Bible Lands, Latin America, Oceania) received significant notice only as the venue of European colonial activities, and most of what was said about this region was essentially the history of empire. Not only was the great bulk of attention devoted to Greater Europe in these older text-books and historical atlases, but world history was described as flowing steadily westward with the passage of time, from the Bible Lands to eastern Mediterranean Europe, to north-western Europe.[323]

Although imperial history is no longer as significant as it would have been a hundred years ago, our secondary school textbooks unfortunately tend to conform to what Blaut describes as the tunnel vision of history. And those who are interested in India's past, encounter the above mentioned problems of European interpretations. Today, we do not seek Mercury in the Buddha, nor do we identify Puranic characters with Biblical figures or reduce the enormous sections of Indian ages to a few centuries or millennia of Biblical chronology. However, we still fail to enquire into what those narratives meant to Indians themselves. How did they understand them and what has made them last in manifold versions in the contemporary Indian culture? Instead of such research questions, we look for a historical core in Indian narratives, delegating them either to history of literature or worse, to the realm of fairy tales.

The Truth of History Versus the Truth of Stories

Research which aims at proper understanding of how different is the traditional Indian treatment of the past from ours is obfuscated by continuing disagreement as to whether Indians had or had not any historical consciousness prior to the introduction of Muslim and European historiographies. Before suggesting a research that would seriously consider Indian narratives to be *an autonomous and distinct treatment of the past independent of European thinking*, it is necessary to shed light on a problem

---

323 James M. Blaut, *The Colonizer's Model of the World* (New York: Guilford Press, 1993), 5.

inherent in the said controversy. It stems from the fact that the use of term "historical consciousness" is quite fuzzy. This fuzziness involves the fact that the scope of the debate is constrained by the framework of thought which allows for two possible solutions only. It does not enable us to comprehend the specificity of Indian thinking about the past. As argued so far, European historiography is a very specific way of thinking about past events, fundamentally depending on the Christian theological thought.

This understanding of historical consciousness was shared by both parties in the controversy. Thus, it is only possible to approach the past either as "history proper," rooted in the theological foundations of historiography, or as a "myth." While certain traits of this binary polarity had already been introduced by Plato and other Greek philosophers, it got its particular meaning in Christian thought: We either know real history or merely myths and fables. This framework does not allow for other possibilities and myths and fables are always branded as invented, and therefore untrue. This strict distinction leads us back to early Christian thought:

> An old apologetic theme of Christian literature is the comparison between the reliable, continuous biblical tradition from the beginning of the world as against the pagan historical accounts that are fragmentary and the further away in time, the more mythical.[324]

The European construction of India's history started with this approach. However, it was preceded by Muslim historiographers on whom the research of India's history from the 10th to the 18th century relies to a great extent. With their theological beliefs, Christian and Muslim thinking about the past evidently have much in common,[325] making them construe "true" historical thought in opposition to mythical thinking:

> The distinctions between myth and history is already notable in Muslim writers on India's history such as Firishtah, which is only to remind us that there is a deeper past to this constituting of history, one in which belief in the Biblical God and non-belief in the gods of others play roles in con-

---

324 Funkenstein, *Theology and the Scientific Imagination*, 208, footnote no. 20.
325 For an overview of older Muslim interpretations of Indian traditions, see Hilman Latief, "Comparative Religion in Medieval Muslim Literature," *American Journal of Islamic Social Sciences* 23, no. 4 (2006): 28–62.

stituting a realm of paganism and mythology as opposed to the realm of eventful and factual history.[326]

Indeed, Muslim scholars were the first to mention the ahistoricity of the Indians, starting with Al-Biruni. Muslim historiography was followed up by French and British Orientalists who translated historical treatises mostly from Persian. Consequently, the first European histories of India took the Muslim invasions of India as their starting point.[327] When Europeans learned Sanskrit and began to realise the character of many traditional stories, they agreed with their Muslim predecessors. For example, Henry T. Colebrooke remarked: "Unfortunately, writers have seldom given the dates of their compositions; and the Hindu's love of fable and distaste for sombre narrative have been as unfriendly to the biography of authors as to the history of princes."[328] In this view, Europeans had to discover the ancient past of the Indians, and although local historiography of the so-called pre-Muslim period was factually non-existent, they succeeded in reconstructing the history of the subcontinent by studying manuscripts, inscriptions, and archaeological material.

Soon enough, however, there were efforts to find some historical consciousness among the Indians and the argument as to whether they had it or not began. One such effort was Horace H. Wilson's reconstruction of India's history in which he disagreed with James Mill's criticism of the Indians. Mill claimed that Indians had been unable to develop history because they had never stepped beyond the stage of myths and fables. As opposed to the picture of Indian religion presented by the first Orientalists who considered it a degenerated but originally pure deism, Mill claimed that Indian religion had always existed in a highly primitive form only. Although he did not know any Indian languages nor has he ever been to India, he used European accounts and especially the works of the first Orientalists to paint a black picture of a primitive Indian society dominated by a superstitious religion created by the Brahmins. Nevertheless, he shared the Orientalists' opinion that the Indian religion consisted in the worship of personified natural forces, the same as once practiced by "pagan" Greeks:

---

326 Trautmann, *Aryans and British India*, 226.
327 See, for instance, Alexander Dow, *A History of Hindoostan, translated from the Persian* (London: J. Walker, 1812); Charles Stewart, *The History of Bengal* (London: Black, Parry, 1813).
328 Henry T. Colebrooke, "On Ancient Monuments, Containing Sanscrit Inscriptions," *Asiatic Researches* 9 (1807): 399.

The Hindus never contemplated the universe as a connected and perfect system, governed by general laws, and directed to benevolent ends; and it follows, as a necessary consequence, that their religion is no other than that primary worship, which is addressed to the designing and invisible beings who preside over the powers of nature, according to their arbitrary will, and act only for some private and selfish gratification.[329]

Yet this discussion is to Mill an answer to a much larger problem. How much did Indians comprehend of the Christian God, the Creator of our universe?

If all the unrevealed knowledge which we possess respecting God, the immediate object of none of our senses, be derived from his works, they whose ideas of the works are in the highest degree absurd, mean, and degrading, cannot, whatever may be the language which they employ, have elevated the ideas of the author of those works. . . . The only question, therefore, is, what are the ideas which the Hindus have reached concerning the wisdom and beauty of the universe. To this the answer is clear and incontrovertible. No people, how rude and ignorant soever, who have been so far advanced as to leave us memorials of their thoughts in writing, have ever drawn a more gross and disgusting picture of the universe than what is presented in the writings of the Hindus.[330]

According to Mill, the Indians did not advance at all on the evolutionary scale of nations due to the way their thinking had been shaped by their religion. It is noteworthy that Mill set down the contemporary European conception of rationality as a necessary condition for development of a historical consciousness. Thus, in fact, Mill opined that the lack of European theological treatment of history was responsible for the Indians' intellectual immaturity:

But the human mind must have certain degree of culture, before the value of such a memorial is perceived. . . . Exaggeration, therefore, is more fitted to his desires than exactness; and poetry than history. Swelled by fiction, and set off with the embellishments of fancy, the scene lays hold of his imagination, and kindles his passions. All rude nations, even those

329 James Mill, *History of British India, with Notes and Continuation by Horace Hayman Wilson* (London: James Madden, 1840), 1:386–387.
330 Mill, *History of British India*, 1:384–385.

to whom the use of letters has long been familiar, neglect history, and are gratified with the productions of the mythologists and poets. It is allowed on all hands that no historical composition existed in the literature of the Hindus; they had not reached that point of intellectual maturity, at which the value of a record of the past for the guidance of the future begins to be understood.[331]

In contrast, Horace H. Wilson argued that it is possible to glean historical data from the Puranic lists of royal dynasties as well as from the surviving inscriptions and coins, allowing one to speak of Indian historiography before the influence of Muslim historical scholarship. His optimism was also aroused by the discovery of Kalhana's *Rajatarangini*, an 11th century Kashmiri chronicle, which he found in 1821. Inscriptions form Orissa, described by Andrew Stirling in 1825, also seemed promising. In addition, Wilson encouraged James Tod to publish his research on the history of the Rajputs.[332] The British Orientalist expressed his views in the fifth edition of Mill's *History of British India*, which he was invited to augment and supplement with his commentary.[333]

While Jones and Wilson took the old Indian epics and *the Puranas* as credible sources of historical knowledge shrouded in myth, later researchers were increasingly sceptical of the historical value of these texts. However, even today, historians and Orientalists continue to speculate, for example, that the historical core of the *Mahabharata* consists of events that *the Vedas* describe as the Battle of the Ten Kings.[334] While a critical analysis of the Puranic genealogies of the ruling dynasties provided some useful information, European scholars had to set it against the surviving inscriptions and correct it in accordance with them. As J. F. Fleet, among others, pointed out that the further back into the past those lists go, the more controversial and contradictory they appear. The surviving genealogies of significant families and the superiors of *mathas* (centres of ascetic communities) are a similar case.[335] Therefore, Fleet wrote at the beginning of the 20th century:

---

331 Mill, *History of British India*, 2:66–67.
332 David Kopf, "The Wonder That Was Orientalism: In Defense of H. H. Wilson's Defence of Hinduism," in *Bengal Vaisnavism, Orientalism, Society, and the Arts*, ed. Joseph T. O'Connell (Ann Arbor: Michigan State University, 1985), 77.
333 Mill, *History of British India*, 2:66–69.
334 Strnad et al., *Dějiny Indie*, 44.
335 For example, see J. F. Fleet on historical sources in India in *The Imperial Gazetteer of India: The Indian Empire*, 2:1–15.

It is, indeed, very questionable whether the ancient Hindus ever possessed the true historical sense, in the shape of the faculty of putting together genuine history on broad and critical lines. As we shall see, they could write short historical compositions, concise and to the point, but limited in extent. But no evidence of the possession by them of the faculty of dealing with history on general lines has survived to us in the shape of any genuine historical work, deliberately written by them as such, and also accurate and reliable.[336]

Until today, European and Indian scholars have been discussing the reasons why ancient Indians did not have any historical consciousness at all. Leaving aside the stereotypes attributed to all Orientals, such as "predilection for myths, fables, and fantasy" and "aversion to serious narrative," European researches have blamed the alleged stagnation in the society's development on the domestic religion and its caste system. The religious thought of India is said to have considered time to be a marginal subject, relating the teaching of reincarnation to a cyclic conception of time. Three quotations will suffice to illustrate these opinions. A. B. Keith wrote about the traditional schools of Indian thought:

The names of some great authorities may be preserved, as in the case of schools of philosophy, but nothing whatever with any taint of actuality is recorded regarded their personalities, and we are left to grope for dates. This indifference to chronology is seen everywhere in India, and must be definitely connected, in the ultimate issue, with the quite secondary character ascribed to time by the philosophies.[337]

Similarly, Dušan Zbavitel pointed to the ancient Indian concept of enormously long epochs as well as to the ideas relating to reincarnation. According to Zbavitel, preoccupations of Western historiography were of no consequence:

In this view, every single individual life story has a sense and an order of its own, and what we tend to understand as historical development is perceived in a different light. The main focus of European historiography—human society, changes in its economic, political and social relations and

---

336 Fleet, *The Imperial Gazetteer of India*, 5–6.
337 A. B. Keith, *A History of Sanskrit Literature* (London: Oxford University Press, 1920), 147.

institutions, or, say, the influence of powerful individualities—merely constitutes a frame of an individual's actions, largely unimportant from the perspective of the individual's rebirths. Such an understanding can hardly leave much room for historiography proper or sustain any claims advancing its importance.[338]

To this day, Louis Dumont's opinions are highly influential and frequently quoted, claiming that progress in India was impeded by religion and especially by the caste system, leading to many centuries of stagnation. He said that religion controlled the economic and the political spheres, and under the rigid caste system the "hierarchical man" had neither the conditions nor the reasons to develop historical thinking.[339]
In contrast to the averred absence of local historiographical corpus until the 11th century, some advocates of autochthonous historical consciousness have argued, starting with H. H. Wilson, that the surviving epics and *Puranas* can be shown to contain a historical core. To this day, the European concept of historical consciousness tends to be identified with the genealogical lists and panegyrics of different rulers' lives and deeds.[340] *In fact, rather than an argument in favour of a traditional Indian historical consciousness, it only advocates the possibility to reconstruct a narrative structure of the past from the surviving literature as we are used to in European historiography.* Other scholars, e.g. Albrecht Wezler, pointed out the existence of specifically Indian theories of time and clear Sanskrit terminology that enables detailed distinctions between various *tempora*.[341] While Wezler attempted to prove the existence of a "specifically Indian" historical consciousness, he made the following revealing comment:

But if one looks into the problem of India's alleged total lack of a sense of history, etc., one cannot but notice that *with regard to any culture it is not the lack of historiography but its existence that first of all calls for an explanation*; as long as it is not possible to define the general cultural conditions necessarily leading to the beginnings of historiography as such, it is absolute-

338 Zbavitel, *Staroveka Indie*, 9.
339 Dumont's opinions have been repeated by respected historians; see e.g. Le Goff, *History and Memory*, 132–133.
340 See e.g. Michael Witzel, "On Indian Historical Writing. The Role of Vamsavalis," *Journal of the Japanese Association for South Asian Studies* 2 (1990): 1–57.
341 Albrecht Wezler, "Towards a Reconstruction of Indian Cultural History: Observations and Reflections on 18th and 19th Century Indology," *Studien zur Indologie und Iranistik* 18 (1993): 305–329.

ly pointless to continue the discussion about the possible reasons of the Indians' presumed lack of a sense of history.[342]

I cannot agree more that it is the existence of our European historiography that requires explanation. The first part of this chapter is an attempt at sketching such an explanation. It appears that we still rely on the thought structures of Jewish and especially Christian treatment of the past as well as their temporal imagination. The cultural circumstances that gave rise to this approach to time were very specific, not "general." Since Jewish, Christian, and later Muslim considerations of the past share some common theological features, the Indians could not have had any knowledge of them for a long time. One cannot but agree that this insight makes the discussions aimed at the explanation of the lack of Indian historiography or its marginality before the arrival of Muslim dynasties irrelevant.

Nevertheless, A. Wezler himself did not develop his argument in this direction and joined those who searched for historiography in India. Why? Closer reading of Wezler's article shows that the whole discussion is obscured by vague ideas about history, historiography, and historical consciousness. It is true that we possess reliable records of time counting in ancient India, lists of important rulers, lines of succession of Vedic teachers, Upanishadic thinkers, etc. There are the Buddhist works such as the *Mahavamsa* and the *Dipavamsa*, and there is much information in the still largely unresearched Jain corpus. Indubitably, ancient Indians postulated the difference between the past, the present, and the future. It is likewise beyond doubt that they had various ways of dealing with memories of past events and personages. However, all this does not prove that they developed historical thinking of the European type, which is still grounded in theological metastructure.

The problem is that researchers continue to equate historical consciousness and its concomitant historiography with any treatment of memories and conceptualisation of time in Indian thought. The whole debate is thus caught up in the European distinction of historical thinking as opposed to myth. *Trying to solve this problem within this framework, researchers consequently fall short of appreciating the difference of Indian culture.* The debate is still influenced by the idea that civilised nations have had to develop historiography. This is what must have given rise

---

342 Wezler, "Towards a Reconstruction of Indian Cultural History," 322.

to numerous essays and articles by Indian authors who tried to advocate the idea of an original, albeit somehow indeterminate Indian historical consciousness.[343] Why shouldn't we simply accept the abundant evidence suggesting that the ancient traditions of India did not develop historical consciousness and their treatment of the past differed significantly from ours?

This problem may become a promising path towards a better understanding of mutual otherness. *On the one hand, we shall ask how and why historiography developed in European culture; on the other hand, we shall explore the distinctive Indian treatment of narratives about past events.* Since the two cultures have largely failed to understand each other in this respect, it constitutes an excellent topic of comparative research.

An objection can be raised now: How is it that the Indians did not grasp European historiography considering that so many prominent and less well-known Indian historians have been writing historical books for generations by now? Do I intend to deny the existence of a rich modern Indian historiography or to belittle it? Indeed, I do not. The problem is that the argument based on the existence of modern Indian historiography fails to tackle two difficulties. Firstly, Said's insight was already discussed, concerning the education of Europeanised intellectuals who taught at British-founded universities (Calcutta, Mumbai, Chennai) and secondary schools in the colonial times. Secondly, it has also been remarked that there has been, with few exceptions, scarcely any contact or understanding between this new intelligentsia and the traditional scholars.

Therefore, if we wish to understand Indian traditional thinking in this regard, we cannot rely on Indians educated at Oxford and Cambridge or at the universities in India that have been shaped by Western patterns to this day. The traditional treatment of the past can be explored by researching the role of the narratives that the conquerors spoke of with so much scorn, from Al-Biruni to James Mill. From the 11th to the 19th century, traditional stories arose independently of Western influences, for example, by J. F. Fleet's record of the *Rajavalikathe* in Kannada, written around the beginning of the 19th century, or the somewhat earlier Tamil text *Kongudesa Rajakkal*.[344] To this day, traditional storytellers and singers enjoy great popularity in India and similar compositions are still

---

343 A representative example is Ranjan Ghosh, "India, *Itihasa*, and Interhistoriographical Discourse," *History and Theory* 46 (2004): 210–217.

344 Fleet, *The Imperial Gazetteer of India*, 6.

being produced. However, if they are studied at all, they only happen to be the subject of ethnological or anthropological research.

And there is another difficulty. Whether Indian intellectuals understood European thought since the 19th century to the present day or not is a significant research question in itself. To what extent and how exactly have Indians grasped the theoretical grounds of Western historiography? A cursory glance at recent Indian scholarship shows that they certainly have adopted methods such as source critique, painstaking and detailed collection of data (such as inscriptions), archaeological analysis of numerous monuments, etc. from the British.[345] However, as soon as we look at Indians' attempts at theoretical interpretations, we come across difficulties in their understanding of the European ideas.

For instance, talking to a colleague in Karnataka who is a lecturer on European history, I found out that he considered the Pope a principal agent in instigating the Great French Revolution. Likewise, it transpires that Indian intellectuals know a good deal about Protestantism but exhibit a total lack of understanding when discussing the principles of the Reformation in any greater depth. In a central discussion at the conference Rethinking Religion in India (New Delhi, 2009), the author was surprised to see how some major advocates of secularisation and respected Delhi-based intellectuals failed to understand the basic premises that European secularisation had built on. But for the time being, let us return to the main line of argument.

Why has the past, the precise dating, and the chronology of events within the framework of the global chronicle been so important to Christianity? An answer to this question was suggested by Schopenhauer, claiming that Christianity is history by its very nature. It is envisaged as "a series of events, a collection of facts, a statement of the actions and sufferings of individuals: it is this history which constitutes dogma and the belief in it is salvation."[346]

Amos Funkenstein has come up with a more thorough and detailed explanation regarding the importance of knowledge of how things happened. Christianity has two books that one is required to read: the Bible and the events happening in our world. Not only are these events explained as manifestations of God's will as we have seen in Orosius'

---

345 For a very thorough and detailed description of this kind see, for instance, Shrinivas V. Padigar, *Vishnu Cult in Karnataka* (Mysore: Directorate of Archaeology and Museums, 1996).
346 Arthur Schopenhauer, "The Christian System," in *Essays of Arthur Schopenhauer* (New York: A. L. Burt, 1893), 272.

work, for instance. Early Christian thought instigated a meticulous search for parallels between the events of the Jewish Bible, the Gospels, and the subsequent times. The sacrifice of Isaac prefigured the sacrifice of Jesus Christ, Jacob's twelve sons prefigured the twelve Apostles, and the like:

> Though traces of such symbolic reading (or re-enacting) of history can be found in the Jewish, biblical, apocalyptic, or even Midrashic tradition, it became central to the Christian self-understanding to a measure unknown before. The typological reading of history was not reading of texts and the 'decoding' of their symbols, but of history itself. It treated the events themselves—to use the fortunate phrase of Iunilius Africanus— as a "prophecy through things" rather than words. . . . Its prominence in the Christian horizon may also be due to the fact that not only Christ's words, but his very life, person, body, and death acquired central, sacral meaning.[347]

It was fundamental for believing Christians that the events described in the Bible had really happened. The historicity of Biblical narratives is the founding stone of the doctrine, and as we see, their specific interpretation developed by the early apologetics was a central formative moment of theological thought. Biblical parallelism is also evident among Protestant churches, the first generation of American Puritans being a good example of this. And one should not forget the influence of Millennialist expectations and the general belief that it is possible to deduce the future from past events because they are divine signs. Although the theologies of traditional and later newer churches differ in many respects, the historicity of the Biblical narrative and of Jesus Christ's life has remained of crucial importance.

When confronted with the otherness of Indian narratives, William Jones declared: "Either the first eleven chapters of Genesis . . . are true, or the whole fabric of our national religion is false; a conclusion, which none of us, I trust, would wish to be drawn."[348] As we see, Jones considered the historicity of Biblical stories the alpha and omega of his religion. He thought its validity depended on whether these events had occurred in the way described by the Bible and the subsequent exegetic tradition.

---

347 Funkenstein, *Theology and the Scientific Imagination from the Middle Ages to the Seventeenth Century*, 250.
348 Jones, "On the Gods of Greece, Italy, and India," 233.

There was no other way but to distort Indian narratives in order to make them fit the Biblical model prevalent in the Europe of Jones' time. Paradoxically, this historical approach eventually led to Biblical criticism, which Jones had tried to avoid by distorting Indian narratives, and the events that had gone unchallenged for centuries were called into question. As it is well known, the ensuing debates involved the figure of Jesus himself and there is a varied range of theological opinions on the matter today (let us just remind ourselves of the "three searches for the historical Jesus"). However, the very existence of these debates and their importance in European thinking proves the importance of the link between specific events (i.e. that they happened) and the truth value of the whole religious message (i.e. that it is true).

Schopenhauer was also possibly the first to point out the fundamental otherness of Indian traditions in this respect:

> Buddhism, for instance, have, it is true, historical appendages, the life, namely of their founders: this, however, is not a part or parcel of the dogma. . . . The Lalitavistara . . . contains the life of Sakya-muni . . . but this is something which is quite separate and different from the dogma. . . . The dogma is by no means one with the career of its founder. . . . The Lalitavistara is not, then, a Gospel in the Christian sense of the word; it is not the joyful message of an act of redemption; it is the career of him who has shown how each one may redeem himself.[349]

With respect to the analysis in the preceding chapters, it may be confusing that Schopenhauer spoke of Buddhist "dogma." The context makes it clear, however, that he simply meant "teachings." Let us focus on the difference between Christianity and Indian traditions that the German philosopher tried to capture. Whereas Christian thought accords a central importance to the factuality of Jesus Christ's life and other events, no such link has developed in Indian traditions. Whether the Buddha lived or not is irrelevant to the truth value of the practices that are supposed to lead to the ultimate insight (*samadhi*). The validity of teaching and mainly practice derives from the experience of a living teacher and his disciples.

Inspiration can be drawn from an infinite number of various stories that are often mutually unrelated or even contradicting each other from

---

349 Schopenhauer, "The Christian System," 272.

our point of view. *While Europeans thought of the Puranic concept of time, the tales of the Mahabharata or the Ramayana epics, or the Buddhist narratives as a challenge to their own worldview, Indians utterly failed to understand the issue.* As Europeans were surprised to find again and again, Indians appeared to treat their stories differently. They did not perceive them as valid statements on the nature of the world (dogma) nor did they view European translations of the Biblical narratives into Indian languages and their dissemination on the subcontinent as rival enterprises. As far as the author knows, the best analysis of the difference between Christian and "Hindu" approach to the historicity of their narratives has been offered by Balagangadhara. First, he introduced a part of a dialogue between a German author and his "Hindu" acquaintance on the island of Bali. It is worth citing in full here:

> One day I asked him if he believed that the history of Prince Rama—one of the holy books of the Hindus—is true. Without hesitation, he answered it with "Yes." "So you believe that the Prince Rama lived somewhere and somewhen?" "I do not know if he lived," he said. "Then it is a story?" "Yes, it is a story." "Then someone wrote this story—I mean: a human being wrote it?" "Certainly some human being wrote it," he said. "Then some human being could have also invented it," I answered and felt triumphant, when I thought that I had convinced him. But he said: "It is quite possible that somebody invented this story. But true it is, in any case." "Then it is the case that Prince Rama did not live on this earth?" "What is it that you want to know?" he asked. "Do you want to know whether the story is true, or merely whether it occurred?" "The Christians believe that their God Jesus Christ was also on earth," I said, "In the New Testament, it has been so described by human beings. But the Christians believe that this is the description of the reality. Their God was also really on Earth." My Balinese friend thought it over and said: "I had been already so informed. I do not understand why it is important that your God was on earth, but it does strike me that the Europeans are not pious."[350]

One can hear similar responses both from the people of Bali, of the Indian Subcontinent, and of Sri Lanka. Balagangadhara analysed the conversation: The story of Rama is true to the "Hindu," even though

---

350 Peter Bichsel, *Der Leser, Das Erzählen: Frankfurter Poetik Vorlesungen* (Darmstadt und Neuwied: Hermann Luchterhnd Verlag, 1982), 13–14; quoted in Balagangadhara, *"The Heathen in His Blindness...",* 367–368.

somebody could have invented it and wrote it down. At the same time, the "Hindu" is not sure if Rama has ever lived at all, and what is more, it is of no concern to him. Whether Rama lived or not does not affect the truthfulness of the narrative. The "Hindu" thus differentiates between a true story, which Europeans consider to be his sacred book, and the question of whether this narrative records past events. To sum up, he says in fact that the issue of *Ramayana's* historicity is in no way related to its truthfulness.[351]

We face a dilemma: On the one hand, various Indian narratives which we tend to relegate to mythology appear to be somehow related to the past. On the other hand, their validity does not depend on whether the specific events passed down in the stories really occurred. Furthermore, there is evidence of painstakingly recorded genealogies, not only of royal families, important teachers, etc. One can therefore speak of memories of events that occurred in previous generations as well as stories whose function is much less clear to us.

These two ways of thinking go hand in hand in India to this day, as the research conducted by Bernard Cohn shows, for instance. He picked up the treatment of the past in various groups of the North Indian village of Senapur to demonstrate that memories of past events, including the genealogies of group lineages, were passed on in a narrative form there. For example, the Thakur *jati* preserves the stories of the *Ramayana* and creatively expands them with memories of events that happened under the British rule.

Thus, for example, in a scene of a theatre performance when Rama courts Sita, a character of a king from Manchester comes on stage, a caricature highly reminiscent of a railway official.[352] Moreover, the Thakurs preserve very accurate memories of their own lineage that goes back to 16th century Rajputs. While these genealogies mainly describe land tenure in individual families, they also preserve memories of significant events. It is noteworthy that the villagers frequently held very lively conversations about events that had taken place several generations ago, as Cohn found after long enquiry. Cohn identified these two types of treatment of the past in all the other twenty remaining *jatis* in the village although they naturally differed in content from the stories of Thakurs.[353]

---

351 Balagangadhara, *"The Heathen in His Blindness..."*, 368.
352 Bernard Cohn, "The Pasts of an Indian Village," in *Time: Histories and Ethnologies*, ed. Diane O. Hughes and Thomas R. Trautmann (Ann Arbor: University of Michigan Press, 1998), 23.
353 Cohn, "The Pasts of an Indian Village," 24–25.

Cohn's classification is problematic in that he called the second type of past "historical." If we wish to avoid vagueness, or distortion of the Indian understanding, the second type cannot be called historical inasmuch as the inhabitants of the village do not think in the framework of European historical thought. Cohn's research only shows that Indians preserve memories of their ancestors, rulers, and various other important figures' names, including their actions. However, it confirms a major difference from our history: Indians have taken very little interest in a long-term precise chronology and they have never ordered various events in a unified chronology of pan-Indian, not to say global, dimensions. They have not tried to find the purpose of history in those memories. Nor can we talk of a single group or organisation that would have achieved such a central position in memories of India which would even remotely resemble the place of the church in Western historiography. At the same time, there is a continuous tradition of various narratives that mingle with memories of past events.

Rather than accumulating more data and incorporating them into projects of global history, the real challenge in understanding the Indian concept and treatment of the past consists in researching the *functions of stories, of preservation of memories of various events (occurrences, genealogies), and the relationship between them.* It will be necessary to look for answers to questions like the following: What constitutes the truthfulness of narratives in Indian culture as opposed to the status of historical factuality in European historiography? In what way do traditional narratives become linked up with memories of past events? How do they relate to one another? Only after at least some of these questions have been addressed in a promising way, can we begin to ask if Western thinking could draw some inspiration from those traditional Indian ways of dealing with the past.

Changing Interpretations of the Aryans[354]

The Aryan invasion of India is recorded in no written document, and it cannot yet be traced archaeologically, but it is nevertheless firmly established as a historical fact on the basis of comparative philology.
Thomas Burrow

The prevailing story is that the beginning of Indian history is marked by a major watershed brought about by the arrival of a new people in the northern part of the subcontinent. According to this theory, the Aryan tribes arrived in the Indus Valley basin sometime in the middle of the second millennium BC, subjugating or ousting the older Dravidian and Munda populations. This is supposed to have ushered in a new era of Indian history characterised among others by the development of the Vedic religion. The theory interpreted and integrated several discoveries of European Oriental Studies: the Indo-European language family, the demonstrable distinctiveness of the Dravidian languages, which are different from the Indo-European, and last but not least, archaeological findings, especially the discovery of civilisation in the Indus Valley basin. It will be necessary to consider what kind of questions the

354 Some of the arguments in this chapter have been introduced at the conference "Náboženství a politika" [Religion and politics], organised by the Department for the Study of Religions, Faculty of Arts and Philosophy, Pardubice, on October 3, 2006. The author wishes to acknowledge some fundamental insights that arised from conversations with Marianne Keppens (Ghent University) at the first two conferences in the series *Rethinking Religion in India*, New Delhi, 2008 and 2009. Discussions with Dilip Chakrabarti (Cambridge University) were also important.

invasion theory addressed and in what way. What were the assumptions of the theory? What kind of evidence and arguments can be posed in its favour or against it?

While the Aryan Invasion Theory provoked considerable and sometimes heated discussions in global scholarship, Czech literature hardly reflects this debate at all. In principle, Czech Indology restates the old, sometimes slightly modified template of the Indo-European Aryan invasion of India, as if it were an unshakeable fact. To show this, it will suffice to compare a claim made in the pre-war book *Indie a Indové* by V. Lesný to a passage from a book of the same title published by three Czech Indologists sixty years later:

> A long time ago, the ancestors of the contemporary Indians arrived in India from Europe and their culture was Aryan. However, this Aryan culture that has since unified and ennobled India only cast a thin veil on the lower aboriginal classes of inhabitants whose non-Aryan influence has continued to permeate the society.[355]

> The Aryans, i.e. the Noble or the Exalted ones. After long journey through the vast territories of Western Asia, their vanguard reached North-western India and destroyed the rapidly declining Indus Valley Civilisation (or gave it a *coup de grâce*). Being pushed by further migrant waves of their nomadic kin who came in their wake, they flooded the extensive lowlands of today's Punjab.[356]

The sole mention of a competing theory can be found in the relevant passage of *Dějiny Indie* by Jan Filipský who nevertheless belittles it, noting that "a small, but very vociferous faction has emerged, opposing the Aryan invasion theory"[357] without introducing a single argument put forward by the opponents. The Czech Indologist merely noted that they refused the validity of reconstructing the Indo-European proto-language, maintaining that the homeland of the so-called Indo-Iranian languages is Southern Asia.[358] Unfortunately, he did not introduce any detailed overview of the arguments and speculations developed by the

---

355 Lesný, *Indie a Indové*, 7.
356 Krása, Marková, and Zbavitel, *Indie a Indové*, 27. Similarly Miltner, *Vznik a vývoj buddhismu*, 14–17, and Vavroušková, "Tradice a moderní společnost: hinduismus," 94.
357 Strnad et al., *Dějiny Indie*, 39.
358 Strnad et al., *Dějiny Indie*, 39.

invasion theory opponents. Such treatment of a different theory is not acceptable. In assessing the validity and merits of any theory, one ought to consider value of its ideas rather than the number of people who propose this or that argument. It is not true either that all the opponents of the Aryan invasion or migration theory refused the concept of Proto-Indo-European language. While the bibliography of *Dějiny Indie* refers to a few major English treatises that sum up the counter-arguments on the topic, the text itself does not include a single one of them, besides the one mentioned above.

I will focus our discussion on the origins and transformations of the Aryan invasion theory. While Filipský ascribed the invasion theory to Mortimer Wheeler in the wake of the post-war debate on the topic,[359] the idea is, in fact, a much older speculation. I will argue that Christian thought created the basis for the much later rise of the 19th century linguistic and anthropological research, while the 20th century saw interpretations of archaeological discoveries according to a ready-made theoretical model. It is worth noting that many opponents of the Aryan invasion theory share some of the principles implicit in the invasion paradigm, i.e. the idea of a close relationship between language, religion, and ethnicity. Let me summarize some of the important points prevalent in the current debate.

The by now classical Aryan invasion theory says that between 2000 and 1500 BC nomadic tribes started moving from the original Indo-European homeland, defined by a common language from which Sanskrit and Old Persian stemmed. Another common feature was their religion, the worship of gods and goddesses of whom the earliest evidence is found in the Vedic collections. The older version of the theory maintained that the Aryans destroyed the Indus Valley Civilisation (or gave it the final death blow according to the above cited Indologists). More recent versions of the theory talk more cautiously of a gradual advance in several waves. The Aryans are supposed to have subjugated the local Dravidian population and set up the social system of the four *varnas* in which the conquered Dravidians ended up on the lowest rank of the hierarchy. These powerful conquerors penetrated further along the Ganges until they reached the Vindhya Range in the south. This vast geographical expansion is dated approximately to the years of 800–550 BC. Rather than further direct expansion, the spread of Aryan influence into

---

359 Strnad et al., *Dějiny Indie*, 38–39.

South India was culturally mediated. In the north, the Aryans supposedly merged with the subjugated people; the most pure lines of blood were kept by Brahmins.[360] The Aryans are considered bearers of major cultural stimuli, including the development of language, religion, social organisation, and technological innovation (e.g. the use of horse-drawn two-wheeled war chariots).

There is a loose group of at least three different arguments that disagree with the Aryan Invasion Theory (AIT). The first thesis advocates an autochthonous and much more ancient origin of Vedic rituals, identifying Vedic culture with Indus Valley Civilisation.[361] The second opinion, the Outside of India Theory (OIT), argues explicitly for both an autochthonous origin of the Aryans and Aryan migration westwards.[362] This idea is defended by many Indian researchers and some popularizing authors today, but two hundred years ago, it was promoted by Friedrich Schlegel and was highly popular among German intelligentsia for a long time. The third thesis considers the Indian origin of the Aryans plausible, albeit very tentatively. This group of researchers mainly aims at a critical reassessment of the principles on which the AIT has been founded.[363] Put forward by Colin Renfrew, a specific line of the debate is a thesis that the Aryans began to spread from Anatolia as early as the seventh millennium BC during the Neolithic Revolution.[364] Renfrew expounded on this "hypothesis A" together with discussing a "hypothesis B," which actually propounds the arrival of the Aryans in India at the time of the Indus Valley Civilisation's decline.[365]

What are the arguments used by the advocates of these various theories? First of all, it will be necessary to unravel this web of interconnected problems and arguments. I will go along three steps that will present the Aryan discussion from the point of view of different disciplines. At the same time, as we reach deeper into the origins of the contemporary

360 See e.g. T. Burrow, "The Early Aryans," in *A Cultural History of India*, ed. Arthur L. Basham (New Delhi: Oxford University Press, 1975), 20–29.

361 See e.g. S. P. Gupta, "The Indus-Sarasvati Civilisation. Beginnings and Developments," in *The Aryan Debate*, ed. Thomas Trautmann (New Delhi: Oxford University Press, 2007), 157–204.

362 Georg Feuerstein, Subhash Kak and David Frawley, *In Search of the Cradle of Civilization* (New Delhi: Motilal Banarsidass, 1999).

363 These arguments were put forward by B. B. Lal, Jim G. Shaffer, Hans H. Hock, Kenneth A. R. Kennedy, and others. They will be summarized in the next section.

364 Colin Renfrew, *Archaeology and Language: The Puzzle of Indo-European Origins* (Cambridge: Cambridge University Press, 1988).

365 Colin Renfrew, "Archaeology and Language," in *The Aryan Debate*, ed. Thomas R. Trautmann, 205–229.

debate, it will gradually become clearer what the archaeologists, anthropologists, and linguists based their ideas on. These will be the theses argued for in the consequential steps:

1) Archaeological findings have been interpreted on the basis of linguistic and racial theories' conclusions for a long time. Today's archaeologists and anthropologists distance themselves from projecting these suppositions on archaeological findings due to a continually increasing body of evidence that does not support the AIT.

2) Authors such as Poliakov, Arvidsson, and Trautmann have instigated discussions concerning the relationship between racial theories and linguistic evidence of the Aryans' identity. The physiological characteristics ascribed to the Aryans have been rejected by now.

3) The analysis will focus on the theological origins of ideas concerning the historical movements of human groups and the spread of languages. It appears that European theological thinking about the past of humankind gave rise to the idea of a people of a specific religion invading India. The idea was later compounded with linguistic findings. Another connected problem is how the invasion theory emerged as an explanation for India's social organisation, which Europeans call the caste system.

The arguments used in the above discussions include attempts at deciphering the scripture that has been preserved on the seals found in the Indus Valley Civilisation sites and deducing the positions of heavenly bodies from the surviving Vedic corpus in order to date its composition more precisely. Both are very dubious endeavours and will not be considered further here.[366] Some discussions involving the Aryans are decidedly politicised, an aspect of the discussion which will not be examined here either.

---

366 The problems arising from efforts to decipher the Indus Valley Civilisation script as a record of a Dravidian language or Sanskrit, or even Sumerian in some older scholarship, were reviewed by Kamil Zvelebil, "Decipherments of the Indus Script," in *The Aryan Debate*, ed. Thomas R. Trautmann, 254–273, including further bibliography on the topic. The difficulties and ambiguities involved in interpreting the astronomical references of the Vedic corpus are summarised in Hans Henrich Hock, "Philology and the Historical Interpretations of the Vedic Texts," in *The Indo-Aryan Controversy*, ed. Edwin Bryant and Laurie L. Patton (London: Routledge, 2005), 295–303.

What Did Archaeology Prove?

The search for the remains of Aryan tribes on the AIT basis consists in three tasks: identifying the original homeland of the Indo-European-speaking tribes, documenting their gradual migration to India in archaeological material, and determining which sites in Southern Asia are of Aryan provenance. The discovery of the Indus Valley Civilisation in the 1920s was fundamental in necessitating the revision of the then accepted version of AIT. The Aryans had long been described as bearers of a higher civilisation, which supposedly enabled them to subjugate the "savage" Dravidians. However, who created the Indus Valley Civilisation, then? If it had not been the Aryans, there were several problems to be resolved. It would be necessary to move the accepted chronology of the Rigveda whose composition had been dated to the 12th century BC, as suggested by Max Müller. Furthermore, the picture of the Aryan society as reconstructed from *the Vedas* did not testify to an urban civilisation of the authors. If it had been the Dravidians who created the Indus Valley Civilisation, one ought to expect some archaeological evidence that would document the Aryan invasion, fights with the Dravidians, and the conquest of extensive territories in the northwest of Southern Asia. What are the outcomes of the existing findings and their interpretations?

Speculations about the Indo-European homeland range from more or less serious scientific surmises to curious ideas, including Bal Gangadhar Tilak's well known claim that placed the Aryan homeland beyond the polar circle. The Indian archaeologist B. K. Thapar summarises the discussions up to 1970, saying that the precise localisation of the homeland that have received the attention of one or more researchers vary from 30° to 70° of north latitude and 5° to 95° of east longitude! Cited to this day, those researchers considered the Danube Delta, the Baltic states, the Scandinavia, the south of Ukraine, the southern regions of the Volga valley, the south of Siberia, the steppes of Central Asia, and other regions.[367] Since then, there have been other proposals, including the above mentioned Anatolia and discounting the rival theory of the autochthonous Indian origin of the Aryans. Even today, AIT scholars

---

367 B. K. Thapar, "The Aryans: A Reappraisal of the Problem," in *India's Contributions to World Thought and Culture*, ed. L. Chandra et al. (Madras: Vivekananda Rock Memorial Commitee, 1970), 147–164.

cannot agree on the location of the Aryan homeland and the geographical range of their surmises remains immense.[368]

It must be emphasised that archaeology was a latecomer in the formation of the AIT and archaeologists interpreted their findings according to the presupposed linguistic and racial theory as late as the 1950s. This was closely reflected in the efforts to identify the material remains of the Aryans on the Indian subcontinent. Kenneth Kennedy noted that these attempts apparently started in 1905. At that time, Theodor Bloch was conducting research in Lauria Nandangarh in today's Bihar. He thought that the sketch of a female figure on a golden leaf depicted the Vedic goddess Prithvi and that the location is an Aryan burial site.[369] However, archaeology only came to the limelight after the discovery of the Indus Valley Civilisation, which posed the problems alluded to above.

Very influential in his time, the archaeologist Gordon Childe attempted to interpret the first findings of Marshall and his team without waiting for the results of more long-term research. As early as 1926, Childe proposed three possible explanations of the newly discovered civilisation: "The civilisation was entirely Aryan, or it was gradually penetrated by Aryan elements, or the Aryans were merely destroyers of that culture."[370] *The basic problem is that Childe postulated the well-known hypothesis of the Aryans being the destroyers of the Indus Valley Civilisation long before this became an archaeological problem. Furthermore, the discovery could never become a counter-evidence against the accepted AIT.* The idea of an invasion was primary and the question of integrating the new findings with it was merely subsidiary. When some years afterwards M. S. Vats recorded differences in burial rites and motifs on ceramics that were revealed in his findings in Cemetery H at Harappa, Childe thought it confirmed his third surmise; Cemetery H was Aryan, in his opinion.[371] The association of the Aryans with Cemetery H was popularised by Mortimer Wheeler after World War II.

The British archaeologist connected Childe's and Vats' claims with his other findings. Before discussing those, it will be necessary to

368 Kenneth A. R. Kennedy, "Have Aryans Been Identified in the Prehistoric Skeletal Record from South Asia?," in *The Indo Aryans of Ancient South Asia*, ed. George Erdosy (New Delhi: Munshiram Manoharlal, 1997), 41; Trautmann: *The Aryan Debate*, xxxviii–xxxix.

369 Kennedy, "Have Aryans Been Identified in the Prehistoric Skeletal Record from South Asia?," 41.

370 Gordon V. Childe, *The Aryans: A Study of Indo-European Origins* (London: Kegan Paul, Trench, Trübner, 1926), 34.

371 Gordon V. Childe, *New Light on the Most Ancient East* (New York: D. Appleton-Century Company, 1934).

briefly mention the diffusionist paradigm that inspired Wheeler. By now a half-forgotten principle of archaeological studies, there was a widespread belief after World War II that the creators of the Indus Valley Civilisation were not of local origin and that they came from the West. The diffusionist model of culture, spreading from one source precluded considering that an advanced culture may have developed in India without Western influence. The idea was shared by scholars who may not have been aware of each other's work, as the case of the Czech scholar Bedřich Hrozný shows.

At the time when Wheeler published his famous article giving evidence of fortifications at Harappa (1947), Hrozný was working on the fourth edition of his own model of spread and interaction of Indo-European and Semitic peoples. The Czech scholar's theory is a noteworthy example of analysis that continued to derive civilisation from its supposed cradle in Mesopotamia. Hrozný opined that the Indus Valley Civilisation was created by "Proto-Indians," a mixed people of Hittites, Hurrits, and "Proto-Aryans" who took possession of the Indus valley sometime around 2400 BC. He arrives at this conclusion by a highly conjectural comparison of Indus Valley Civilisation script with the deciphered tables of the Sumerians, Babylonians, and Hittites, including speculations about theonyms and a "syncretic religion of the Proto-Indians."[372] It is noteworthy that Hrozný attributed responsibility for the demise of the Indus Valley Civilisation to a *Dravidian invasion*:

> The two cities and the entire Proto-Indian culture were destroyed around 2000 BC as a result of an invasion by a foreign people into the northwest of India. The rich and magnificent Proto-Indian metropolises, centres of Indian and southwest Asian caravans, were wiped out and their populace was mercilessly slaughtered as the findings of human remains bear out. After the turn of the millennium, the cities remained uninhabited. In all probability, the barbarian people who destroyed this oldest Indian culture could only have been the *Dravidians* whose scanty remains have been preserved in the *Brahui* people inhabiting the mountainous region of Balochistan. Where these Dravidians came from is uncertain, although they too might have come from the northwest.[373]

---

372 Bedřich Hrozný, *Nejstarší dějiny přední Asie, Indie a Kréty* [Ancient history of western Asia, India and Crete] (Prague: Melantrich, 1945), 193–194.
373 Hrozný, *Nejstarší dějiny přední Asie, Indie a Kréty*, 194–195.

Only then there should have been the second wave of Aryan migration, the bearers of the Vedic ritual. Remarkably, the state of scholarship in the wake of World War II allowed Hrozný to attribute the downfall of the Indus Valley Civilisation to the Dravidians rather than the Aryans. The Czech scholar inserted the putative barbarian marauders in between two waves of Indo-European invaders. It is clear that *the idea of invasion as a fundamental factor of cultural change was a default premise that could lead to contradictory conclusions with the use of the same evidence.* Moreover, although Hrozný spoke of findings of human remain which supposedly proved the massacre of the two cities' populace in the Indus Valley, he never gave any specific reference to support this claim. The bibliography and index of his treatise do not seem to show that he was aware of Wheeler's discoveries at Harappa and Mohenjo-daro. It is unclear where he derived this conclusion from.

Nevertheless, Bedřich Hrozný and Mortimer Wheeler shared the same diffusionist thesis. As late as the mid-1960s, Wheeler ascribed the genesis of the Indus Valley Civilisation to Mesopotamian models. Although the British archaeologist had to acknowledge by dint of many new findings that the Indus Valley Civilisation had "its individual technology and script" and "rather distinctive character," he would still claim that it was "well led and inspired by a great and mature idea," specifically the civilisations of Mesopotamia and Egypt. Wheeler thus explicitly refuted the possibility of a gradual autochthonous development by stating that although Indus Valley Civilization was no mere colony of the West, it must have been inspired by its idea of civilization.[374]

It should be noted that Mortimer Wheeler was also an officer in the British Army, which inclined him to search for a certain type of evidence. When he discovered fortifications in one part of Harappa in 1946, and subsequently a group of skeletal remains at Mohenjo-daro that appeared to bear marks of violence, he considered those to be clear evidence of fights of the cities' defenders against the Aryans.[375] Wheeler also consulted Sanskrit scholars who confirmed Vedic allusions to the destruction of city dwellings. The British archaeologist concluded that he had succeeded in proving the Aryan invasion with his findings.

---

374 Mortimer Wheeler, *Civilization of the Indus Valley and Beyond* (London: Thames and Hudson, 1966), 61–62.
375 Mortimer Wheeler, "Harappa 1946: The Defences and Cemetary R37," *Ancient India* 3 (1947): 58–130.

In the 1950s, Stuart Piggott supported Wheeler's conclusions while researching sites in Sindh and Balochistan for signs of political and social turmoil that would correspond to the supposed date of the Aryan invasion and the demise of the Indus Valley Civilisation.[376] Although Piggott was an archaeologist rather than Vedic Sanskrit scholar, he averred that the Vedic god Indra was an "apotheosis of an Aryan fighting leader" and the Vedic *dasas* were almost certainly the inhabitants of the Indus Valley cities.[377] The conclusions arrived at by both archaeologists enjoyed great popularity for a long time and they have remained present in the Czech scholarship ever since.[378] Wheeler later admitted that there apparently were more causes for the destruction and downfall of Harappa, Mohenjo-daro, and other cities, but he insisted that that the demise of Mohenjo-daro culminated in a massacre.[379] The interpretation of the Mohenjo-daro findings as a massacre was first doubted by G. Dales by proving different dating of the skeletal remains of the supposedly single battle.[380] In the following years, Wheeler's theory was archaeologically disproved since some of the skeletons bear the marks of healing wounds, the excavation lacks findings of weapons as well as skeletal remains of invaders, among others.[381]

The sum of recent research shows that the Late Harappan Period exhibits a fundamental continuity in terms of human skeletal remains, architecture, and technology. Having researched the site for a long time, Jonathan Kenoyer concluded: "One of the most important results of the current work at Harappa is that there continues to be no support for the earlier interpretations of Vedic-Aryan invasions and the destruction of Harappan settlements."[382] Many other discovered sites of the Indus Valley Civilisation have not yielded any evidence of great fights or radical

---

376 Stuart Piggott, *Prehistoric India to 1000 B.C.* (Harmondsworth: Penguin Books, 1950).

377 Piggott, *Prehistoric India to 1000 B.C.*, 260.

378 For example, see the "coup de grâce" cited at the beginning of this chapter, which the Aryans allegedly dealt the Indus Valley Civilisation. It is almost a literal rendition of Wheeler's "final blow." Wheeler, *Civilization of the Indus Valley and Beyond*, 74–83.

379 Wheeler, *Civilization of the Indus Valley and Beyond*, 53.

380 G. F. Dales, "The Mythical Masacre at Mohenjo-daro," *Expedition* 6, no. 3 (1964): 36–43.

381 See, for instance, Kenneth A. R. Kennedy, "Identification of Sacrificial and Massacre Victims in Archaeological Sites: The Skeletal Evidence," *Man and Environment* 19 (1994): 247–251; S. P. Gupta, "The Indus Saraswati Civilization. Beginnings and Developments," 196–200; B. B. Lal, "Aryan Invasion of India: Perpetuation of a Myth," in *The Indo-Aryan Controversy*, 52–53.

382 Jonathan M. Kenoyer, "Cultural Change during the Late Harappan Period at Harappa. New Insights on Vedic Aryan Issues," in *The Indo-Aryan Controversy*, 44.

changes suggestive of the massive arrival of new inhabitants in the Late Harappan Period.

Further attempts at identifying the Aryans with other archaeological sites have not produced any satisfactory results. Apart from the above mentioned hypothesis concerning Cemetery H, there appeared another theory before World War II. First P. Mitra and later R. Heine-Geldern considered some bronze tool depots dated to the period of the Indus Valley Civilisation's demise as Aryan. Heine-Geldern compared these tools with findings in Iran and Russia that he thought to be similar in shape. He developed these ideas after World War II, while B. B. Lal argued against them as early as 1951.[383]

Efforts to associate the Aryans with a specific archaeological culture or period in Southern Asia are a series of uncertain guesses. In some cases, they were phrased in a highly tentative manner and later abandoned by their authors. Some examples include the Ahar Culture in north-western Rajasthan (D. P. Agraval); the Gandhara Grave Culture (Erdosy, who distanced himself from his theory); Painted Grey Ware (B. B. Lal, who also abandoned the hypothesis); Chalcolithic sites in Rajasthan, Maharashtra, and Andhra Pradesh (H. D. Sankalia), the Ochre Coloured Pottery Culture, the Black and Red Ware culture, or the Northern Black Polished Ware. Since the 1960s, archaeologists have been criticising attempts at identifying any sites as Aryan and doubting the usefulness of the invasion and migration theories for interpreting findings in India.[384]

The Painted Grey Ware Culture is apparently the most popular candidate for being identified with the Aryans. The Czech Indologist Filipský also claimed that "the excavations of this culture suggest the presence of a new people due to a cultural inventory of an ostensibly West-Asian origin, its chronological classification and geographical distribution, although scholars oppose a definite identification of the Painted Grey Ware users with Aryan tribes . . ."[385] It will be useful to mention the reasons why scholars oppose the hypothesis since Filipský did not give any in *Dějiny Indie*. For instance, Jim Shaffer noted that the hypothesis has been refuted by Thapar's objection, although the Painted Grey Ware seemed to fit the accepted chronology. Thapar remarked that if

383 Kennedy, "Have Aryans Been Identified in the Prehistoric Skeletal Record from South Asia?," 42–43.
384 Dilip K. Chakrabarty, "The Aryan Hypothesis in Indian Archaeology," *Indian Studies: Past and Present* 9 (1968): 343–358.
385 Strnad et al., *Dějiny Indie*, 43.

the Painted Grey Ware culture was Aryan, similar earlier specimens of such ceramics would have been found further westwards from the Ganges-Yamuna Doab according to the invasion/migration theory, which has not been the case. In fact, the opposite is true, as the Painted Grey Ware style exhibits continuity with the material found in earlier local layers.[386] On what basis did Filipský give the Painted Grey Ware sites as evidence of "continuing contacts"[387] with Iran and Central Asia?

As early as the end of the 1970s, Jerome Jacobson concluded in an overview article that any associations of the surviving Vedic texts with specific archaeological findings remain unsubstantiated and controversial. "To every single connection between textual testimony and archaeological fact there is a counter-argument."[388] *Further discoveries and their recent evaluation show that archaeological findings in Pakistan and India speak against the theories of invasion or large-scale migration.* What appeared to be a gap between the demise of the Indus Valley Civilisation and the archaeological cultures of the Ganges began to be filled up with discoveries in the 1970s, when newly uncovered Late Harappan settlements were dated as late as 1000 BC.[389] As of today, archaeologists tend to speak of a gradual movement of material culture from the Indus Valley into the valley of the Ganges, and the disappearance of the advanced urban civilisation seems to have resulted from long-term geological and ecological developments (such as changes in the Indus watercourse, soil desiccation, and extensive deforestation). An important moment in the study of Indian prehistory came with the excavations conducted at Mehrgarh, Balochistan in 1974–1986 and again in 2000.[390] Long-term research at Mehrgarh and other locations supports a cultural continuity from the seventh millennium BC to the rise of the Indus Valley Civilisation and onwards.

The French and Pakistani researchers thus contributed to a gradual shift in archaeological and anthropological understanding: 1) The Indus

386 Jim Schaffer, "The Indo-Aryan Invasions: Cultural Myth and Archaeological Reality," in *The People of South Asia: The Biological Anthropology of India, Pakistan, and Nepal*, ed. John R. Lukacs (New York: Plenum Press, 1984), 84.

387 Strnad et al., *Dějiny Indie*, 43.

388 Jerome Jacobson, "Recent Developments in South Asian Prehistory and Protohistory," *Annual Review of Anthropology* 8 (1979), 490.

389 See, for instance, K. N. Dikshit, "The Late Harappan in North India," in *Frontiers of Indus Civilisation: Wheelers Volume*, ed. B. B. Lal and S. P. Gupta (New Delhi: Books on behalf of Indian Archaeological Society, 1984), 253–269.

390 Jarrige, et al., *Mehrgarh: Field Reports 1974–1985, form Neolithic Times to the Indus Civilisation* (Karachi: Dept. of Culture and Tourism, Govt. of Sindh and French Ministry of Foreign Affairs, 1995).

Valley Civilisation grew on local basis. Although there is evidence of trade with other regions as far as Mesopotamia, former ideas of a Western invasion or a strong Mesopotamian influence on the development of this advanced culture are entirely unsubstantiated. 2) The theories of invasion or huge Aryan migration is not supported by archaeological findings. During the period of the supposed invasion (1500–1000 BC), no fundamental divide in skeletal remains or material culture is in evidence. On the contrary, there is abundant proof of a long-term continuity. This is what Kennedy, Shaffer, and Lichtenstein have to say on the matter:

> What the biological data demonstrate is that no exotic races are apparent from laboratory studies of human remains excavated from any archaeological site, including those accorded Aryan status. All prehistoric human remains recovered thus far from the Indian subcontinent are phenotypically identifiable as ancient South Asians. Furthermore, their biological continuity with the living peoples of India, Pakistan, Sri Lanka, and the border regions is well established across time and space.[391]

> The modern archaeological record for Southern Asia indicates a history of significant cultural continuity; an interpretation at variance with earlier 18th through 20th century scholarly views of South Asian cultural discontinuity and South Asian cultural dependence on Western culture influences. . . . The current archaeological and paleoanthropological data simply do not support these centuries old interpretative paradigms suggesting Western intrusive cultural influence as responsible for the supposed major discontinuities in the South Asian cultural prehistoric record.[392]

The conclusion is obvious. Archaeology and physical anthropology can hardly yield any real weighty evidence concerning the homeland or the migration of the Aryans, since under the current state of research all attempts at associating the Aryans with archaeological material are based

---

391 Kennedy, "Have Aryans Been Identified in the Prehistoric Skeletal Record from South Asia?" 60.
392 Jim G. Schaffer and Diane A. Lichtenstein, "South Asian Archaeology and the Myth of Indo-Aryan Invasions," in *The Indo-Aryan Controversy*, 93. Similarly, Kenoyer spoke of strong cultural and historical continuity for which there is no need to seek analogies outside the subcontinent, see J. M. Kenoyer, "Early City States in South Asia: Comparing the Harappan Phase and the Early Historic Period," in *The Archaeology of City States: Cross Cultural Approaches*, ed. D. L. Nichols and T. H. Charlton (Washington: Smithsonian Institute, 1997), 52–70.

solely on linguistic hypotheses, while the connection of language with archaeological findings cannot be proven. Moreover, the present archaeological research disproves important elements of the invasion theory; there is no evidence of a massive and violent invasion of the Aryans. On the contrary, at the time of their supposed arrival in the Indus Valley in around 1500 BC, the findings bear out a continuity in both skeletal remains and material culture.

What arguments can be put forward then in favour of the coming of a new people and the dramatic scenario involving the subjugation or ousting of the Dravidians? Kenneth Kennedy has a point in saying that if there are no biological criteria that would characterise the Aryans, "how could one recognise an Aryan, living or dead?"[393] We do not possess such criteria today. However, European scientists were convinced for a long time that they knew the biological criteria of the Aryan race. How did they arrive at this opinion?

Physical Anthropology and the Racial Theory

A significant phase in the development of theories concerning the Aryans was a period of controversy between linguists and anthropologists in the second half of the 19th century. My overview will mainly focus on speculations about certain passages in the Vedic corpus that were for a long time considered evidence of the racial characteristics of the Aryans. It will gradually become manifest that speculations about Aryan physiology along with preceding linguistic inferences are bound up with attempts at explaining the so-called caste system of India. To this day, Czech scholarship reiterates speculations that derive from racial theories:

The Vedas condemn these impious and phallus-worshipping (as is the ambiguous term *śiśnadēva* sometimes interpreted) adversaries of the Aryans, who some authors identify with people of Dravidian or Munda origins, for their enmity, their black complexion, their snub noses, and their ungodly manners, for their failure to observe rites and sacrifices, disobedience of moral principles, and ignorance of prayers.[394]

---

393 Kennedy, "Have Aryans Been Identified in the Prehistoric Skeletal Record from South Asia?," 61.
394 Strnad et al., *Dějiny Indie*, 38.

Indological works still translate the word *varna* as colour (of skin), which was originally used as evidence that the victorious Aryans of lighter complexion assigned the lowest place in society to the subjugated dark-skinned population. The only difference from the explicit claim of older publications consists of a more careful formulation that is expressive of political correctness in post-war academia. While Lesný wrote that the translation of *varna* as colour makes it clear that the word originally differentiated two races, "the white conquerors and the dark natives,"[395] Filipský maintained that that "the use of varna for social classes could suggest that their origin derived from an ethnic division (texts contain terms that seem to express a contrast between the appearance of the Aryans and that of the Dasas)."[396]

In order to better understand the context, it must be noted that the Aryan debate took place within a wider reassessment of religion and culture in the West which saw the encounter of two theories of human progress and civilisation—that of the Enlightenment and that of Darwin. Along with linguistics and ideas concerning the characteristics of law, the earlier Enlightenment theory dominated the debate until the mid-19th century. As A. Kuper has shown, the Enlightenment conceptualisation of civilisation was accompanied by speculations about evolutionary stages from the primitive phase to the highest degree of civilisation which Europe was thought to have achieved. Montesquieu, Turgot as well as Scottish Enlightenment scholars supposed that in the primitive phase people were hunters, gradually advancing to pastoral farming, agriculture, and eventually, to trade and division of labour.[397] E Tylor's work presented a classical formulation of the theory of progress from the primitive to the civilised:

> The educated world of Europe and America practically settles a standard by simply placing its own nations at one end of the social series and savage tribes at the other, arranging the rest of mankind between these limits according as they correspond more closely to savage or to cultured life.[398]

---

395 Lesný, *Indie a Indové*, 19.
396 Strnad et al., *Dějiny Indie*, 48. The topic of racially defined Aryans and Dasas is a long-lasting staple of the Czech scholarship; it is sufficient to connect the above mentioned quotes from works of O. Pertold, I. Fišer, and J. Filipský.
397 Adam Kuper, *The Reinvention of Primitive Society* (New York: Routledge, 2005), 28–31.
398 Edward B. Tylor, *Primitive Culture* (1871), 1:26, quoted in Kuper, *The Reinvention of Primitive Society*, 37.

At that time, the older theories of progress started to be supplemented with Darwin's theory of man as a biological species. Trautmann has demonstrated how initially linguistically oriented anthropology began to tend towards the study of physiology, mainly under the influence of Darwin's theory and the increasing number of archaeological discoveries.[399]

A prominent figure at the time of the controversy between linguists and physical anthropologists in the second half of the 19th century was Friedrich Max Müller. While the well-known Orientalist never stopped emphasising the difference between language and the physiology of its speakers, he did not refuse the nascent physiological classification as such.[400] Although he protested the association of language and physiology, he searched the Vedic texts for such evidence. His findings were later used in H. H. Risley's and other physical anthropologists' theories. Thus, a racial theory of noble conquerors of ancient India came into being, conforming to the British ideas of the second half of the 19th century. The British were the most advanced nation, the best representatives of the white race. As it is well known, French and German speculations of this kind did not lag behind.[401]

What ethnological evidence did Müller find in *the Vedas*? Trautmann's and Hock's arguments remain unsurpassed in this respect: It was a composite picture of the three "noble" (*arya*) castes of the twice-born and an allusion to a hostile group, sometimes called the *dasas*. The bearers of the Vedic ritual would apparently distance themselves from various groups on the basis of ritual differences, as the term *anagnitra* (those who do not keep the fire, most probably the ritual fire) suggests. There are also mentions of "eaters of (raw) meat" and the not easily translatable appellation *rakshasa*.

F. M. Müller introduced his search for evidence of different physical features of the Aryans and the subjugated natives by noting that the Vedic texts do not contain any references to specific physical characteristics. He nevertheless proposed that there might be an allusion to the shape of the nose. Whereas Aryan gods have beautiful noses (*sushipra*), the Dasas are sometimes called *vrshashipra*, which could be rendered

399 Trautmann, *Aryans and British India*, 165–189.
400 Trautmann, *Aryans and British India*, 196.
401 See, for instance, the influential works: León Poliakov, *The Aryan Myth: A History of Racist and Nationalistic Ideas in Europe* (New York: Barnes and Noble Books, 1996); and Stefan Arvidsson, *Aryan Idols: IndoEuropean Mythology as Ideology and Science* (Chicago: University of Chicago Press, 2006).

"bull-nosed" or "goat-nosed." However, he soon found out that the word *shipra* referred to the mouth or the face and put the matter to rest. However, another Müller's interpretation of a single Vedic passage (RgV 5.29.10) enjoyed great reception.

The passage calls the enemies of the Vedic ritual *anas*, which Müller interpreted as *a-nas*, i.e. "nose-less" or "snub-nosed" in contrast to the Aryans. Somewhat earlier, H. H. Wilson noted the traditional Indian etymology which analyses the word as *an-as*, i.e. "mouthless" or "face-less," meaning "lacking (correct) speech." This is similar to the old Czech ethnonym *němci* applied to the Germanic neighbours, which means "mute," "dumb," or "those who do not speak (our tongue)." However, the nascent racial anthropology preferred Müller's interpretation. Although this was a dubious interpretation of a single passage from the large Vedic corpus, the promoter of anthropometry H. H. Riesly claimed that the Vedic Aryans referred to their enemies as nose-less. Consequently, he boosted the significance of the nasal index in the late 19th and early 20th centuries anthropology and gave rise to a frequently repeated error.[402]

Müller's "proof" was later supplemented by Macdonell and Keith who referred to two passages (RgV 1.130.8 and 6.40.1) that mention hostile beings of dark complexion (*krsna-tvac*). To this, Trautmann pointed out that the two references cannot constitute evidence of a characteristic physiology of the Dasas. Not only are there only two of them, there is more to it: The first one does not refer to a human being but to an *asura* (a creature of traditional stories) according to a traditional Indian explanation.[403] Hans H. Hock has produced a very convincing analysis of the German intellectuals Zimmer, Geldner, and others' part in interpreting the Vedic passages as evidence of differences between the natives and the Aryans in colour of skin and shape of nose.[404] A thorough reading and contextualisation of the passages on the Dasas' skin colour offers more plausible explanation than physiological. These references are linked to

---

402 Thomas R. Trautmann, "Constructing the Racial Theory of Indian Civilisation," in *The Aryan Debate*, 100–101. A proponent of anthropometrical methods and the classification of people into races based on this criterion, H. H. Risley studied the social groups of India. He was a census commissioner in India in 1901, an office that he used to pursue his anthropometrical research. See Nicholas Dirks, "Castes of Mind," 68–72; and Trautmann, *Aryans and British India*, 198–211.

403 Trautmann, "Constructing the Racial Theory of Indian Civilisation," 102.

404 Hans H. Hock, "Philology and the Historical Interpretation of the Vedic Texts," 282–290. The remaining part of the chapter provides detailed arguments concerning the Vedic passages that are frequently used to defend the Aryan migration hypothesis and the astronomical evidence.

the Vedic contrast between light and darkness, between the forces of light and darkness in this world. Hock concluded:

> The evidence of the Rig-Vedic passages just examined thus does not establish a difference in "race" or phenotype between *aryas* and *dasas/dasyus*. Whether there was such a difference or not will have to be argued out on the basis of other evidence which, of course, must likewise be subjected to close scrutiny.[405]

The European ideas concerning the invasion theory and the reconstruction of Aryans' physical appearance by the end of the 19th century were also connected with attempts to explain the emergence of the so-called caste system. The Vedic collections were considered one of the oldest documents describing the social organisation, as A. Macdonell supposed:

> We are here presented with an authentic account in broad outline of the actual social conditions of the time: *viz.* that the Aryan population, still inspired with a lively sense of opposition to the non-Aryan, consisted of a double aristocracy exercising respectively a spiritual and a temporal dominion, the third position being occupied by the Aryan freemen whose normal occupations were pastoral pursuits and agriculture. To this threefold Aryan community were added the non-Aryan plebeians and slaves; while outside these four groups were to be found the aboriginal tribes unaffected by Aryan civilization.[406]

Macdonnell considered the Aryan community representative of a simple social organisation where division of labour had just begun to emerge: "The general organization of society here presented is a primitive one, occupations being but little differentiated, and every man being for the most part able to supply his simple wants himself."[407] The tacitly accepted ideas of the Enlightenment regarding the primitive state of society were a natural starting point. Under the theory of progress from primitive to more advanced societies, the "nomadic" Aryans appeared on a higher scale of civilisation than the "native tribes" who were supposedly hunters and gatherers.

---

405 Hock, "Philology and the Historical Interpretation of the Vedic Texts," 290.
406 Arthur A. Macdonell, "The Early History of Caste," *American Historical Review* 19, no. 2 (1914): 237.
407 Macdonell, "The Early History of Caste," 240.

The birth of Indian culture was explained as a clear victory of the incoming nomads over the savage locals (hunters and gatherers). Macdonell also introduced the above mentioned "evidence" concerning the skin colour of the conquered Dasas and gave an analysis of contemporary opinions on the matter. How did those classes of ancient Indian society become castes? Macdonnell had a ready ad hoc answer: It was because of a difference of blood between the invading and the subjugated races.[408]

But efforts to keep purity of blood would have been insufficient as history abounds in examples of invaders who have merged with subdued people. Comparing the contemporary segregation of the white and black races in the US and in South Africa, Macdonnell claimed that the dividing line must have been the colour of skin. As the Aryans were divided into professional "classes," there arose a system which united the white conquerors and the subjugated "dark natives" in one society whilst preserving segregation.[409] It is truly amazing how the racial segregation in the US and in South Africa before World War I explained to Macdonell the formation of Indian society more than three thousand years ago. Yet, this explanation was widely accepted and only the horrors of the Nazi regime led the Western intellectuals to necessary self-reflection, resulting in the rejection of the concept of race in post-war science:

> Since the 1950s, physical anthropology has been abandoning the idea of race in favour of the idea of biological populations each having its own statistical range of variation of traits which overlap with the ranges of other biological populations. It is now understood that there are no discrete races clearly distinct from one another, and this explains the notorious fact that race science experts of the past could never agree on what the number of different races was.[410]

Speculations about the progress of civilisation from a primitive society to its supposed culmination, represented by the Western world,

---

408 Macdonell's claim resonates in recent Czech scholarship; for example, Hana Preinhaelterová wrote: "The first Aryans who invaded India singing *the Vedas* and crushing the non-Aryans had the exalted idea that their blood . . . must not be mixed with the blood of the natives." Hana Preinhaelterová, *Hinduista od zrození do zrození* [A Hindu from a birth to another birth] (Prague: Vyšehrad, 1997), 41. The theme of blood is specifically European debate, and many thinkers, including F. Max Müller, wrote about it before Macdonell. Lacking a proper analysis, a link was made between the recommendations of the *Dharmashastras* on marriage and the preservation of blood purity (19th century anthropology paid a great attention to the blood relationships).
409 Macdonell, "The Early History of Caste," 242–243.
410 Trautmann, *The Aryan Debate*, xxxvii.

together with the racial theories were the main shaping ideas in the creation of the AIT. These considerations formed a basis for distinguishing the Aryans from the Dasas. As has been noted, the Vedic corpus does not provide any evidence supporting racial interpretations. Unfortunately, relics of those ideas can be found in contemporary scholarship to this day.

From the "Brahminical Invasion" to the Aryans

The preceding analysis has yielded two important findings: 19th century physical anthropologists used linguistic knowledge in an arbitrary manner, indulging in racial speculations. The invasion theory was to provide an explanation for the emergence of the so-called caste system, interpretation of which has not ceased to fuel controversy among Western scholars. What part did linguistics play in these discussions, having supposedly procured proof of the invasion theory? At least, so is it claimed in many prestigious works. One example for all:

> The Aryan invasion of India is recorded in no written document and it cannot yet be traced archaeologically, but it is nevertheless firmly established as a historical fact on the basis of comparative philology. The Indo-European languages, of which Sanskrit in its Vedic form is one of the oldest members, originated in Europe, and the only possible way by which a language belonging to this family could be carried all the way to India was a migration of the people speaking it.[411]

The formation of the theory must be understood in the context of European linguistic research and speculations of the 17th and 18th centuries. As it is well known, these discussions focused on three mutually related questions: What was the primary language of humankind (the language of Paradise)?[412] How did languages come to separate from each other and spread in the world? And is it possible to find or create an ideal language?[413] Of course, these questions were based on the acceptance of

---

411 Burrow, "The Early Aryans," 21.
412 See, for instance, Maurice Olender, *The Language of Paradise: Race, Religion and Philology in the Nineteenth Century* (Cambridge and London: Harvard University Press, 1992), 15.
413 See e.g. Patrik Ouředník, *Hledání ztraceného jazyka* [Searching for the lost language] (Středokluky: Zdeněk Susa, 1997), 18–24.

Genesis as a truthful account of global history in which the European nations were usually considered the descendants of Japheth. The Catholic Church's teaching about Hebrew as the language of Paradise was called into doubt as early as the 17th century due to missionaries' reports from China that informed Europeans of the great antiquity of the local culture and language. Furthermore, scholarly efforts to enhance the importance of particular languages and countries led to the identification of the language of Paradise with Irish, Castilian, Dutch, Flemish, Swedish, Danish, and other languages.[414] A direct predecessor of the Indo-European theory is the so-called Scythian hypothesis. Johannes Goropius Becanus (1519–1572) was probably the first to suggest that Scythian was the primary language out of which other European languages had developed. A series of attempts followed to prove the relatedness of European languages and to derive them from this candidate, all of them exhibiting huge differences and no satisfactory results.[415] Some of the most prominent scholars, including Newton and Leibniz, at the turn of the 17th and 18th centuries engaged in speculations about the original language and its gradual degeneration as well as the classification of language groups.[416]

William Jones reaped the somewhat undeserved praise for being the first to determine the relatedness of Indo-European languages.[417] These are his famous words from an annual lecture for the Asiatic Society:

---

414 Ouředník, *Hledání ztraceného jazyka*, 27.
415 G. J. Metcalf, "The Indo-European Hypothesis in the Sixteenth and Seventeenth Centuries," in *Studies in the History of Linguistics: Traditions and Paradigms*, ed. D. H. Hymes (Bloomington: Indiana University Press, 1974), 234–240.
416 Tulio De Mauro and Lia Formigari, *Leibniz, Humboldt, and the Origins of Comparativism* (Amsterdam: John Benjamin Publishing Company, 1990).
417 In fact, William Jones had several predecessors who noticed the relationship between Indian and European languages. The first of those was apparently the Venetian merchant Filippo Sassetti, who wrote as early as the mid-16th century of similarities between Sanskrit and Italian words. Sassetti was also intrigued to discover the Indian claim that different pronunciations were caused by different movements and positions of the mouth and tongue. Some Jesuit missionaries acquired a substantial knowledge of Sanskrit and other Indian languages and were able to write and debate in Sanskrit and to translate from it. Some outstanding examples include Roberto Nobili and J. F. Pons. In all probability, Pons was the author of the Latin grammar of Sanskrit written c. 1733. The British Orientalist N. Halhed had noticed similarities of Sanskrit with Persian, Latin, and Greek several years before Jones. See Jean Claude Muller, "Early Stages of Language Comparison from Sassetti to Sir William Jones," *Kratylos* 31 (1986), 131; Pierre-Sylvain Filliozat, "The French Institute of Indology in Pondicherry," *Wiener Zeitschrift für die Kunde Süd- und Ostasiens* 28 (1984): 133–147; Trautmann, *Aryans and British India*, 39.

The *Sanscrit* language, whatever be its antiquity, is of a wonderful structure; more perfect than the *Greek*, more copious than the *Latin*, and more exquisitely refined than either, yet bearing to both of them a stronger affinity, both in the roots of verbs and in the forms of grammar, than could possibly have been produced by accident; so strong indeed, that no philologer could examine them all three, without believing them to have sprung from some common source, which, perhaps, no longer exists: there is a similar reason, though not quite so forcible, for supposing that both the *Gothick* and the *Celtick*, though blended with a very different idiom, had the same origin with the *Sanscrit*; and the old Persian might be added to the same family.[418]

However, when Jones had been speaking to the members of the Asiatic Society, he had only been learning Sanskrit for a few months then, besides his duties as a judge and other interests. How could he postulate the Indo-European family of languages with the beginner level of knowledge of Sanskrit? S. N. Mukherjee's observation concerning the wider context of Jones' comparative project will explain this puzzle: The British Orientalist was not interested in linguistic research as such but rather in reconstructing the earliest history of humankind. His comparison of languages was only one of four areas of comparison between the ancient cultures known to Europeans and India. The others included philosophy and religion, remains of ancient sculpture and architecture, and the surviving records of their sciences and arts.[419] By means of these comparisons, Jones aimed at discovery of the original, the oldest religion of humankind. Urs App has produced a detailed analysis of Jones' comparative project and concluded:

The entire thrust of Jones's third discourse is thus directed toward a primeval homeland of humanity, a motherland with and ur-race speaking an ur-language, confessing an ur-religion, performing ur-science, and enjoying ur-art. In view of this broad and startling argument it is hardly surprising that no one, Jones included, paid much attention to the sphere of linguistics where Jones' considerable knowledge of languages led to a more limited claim of an unknown parent language of Sanskrit, Persian, and some European idioms.[420]

---

418 Jones, *The Works of Sir William Jones*, 1:26.
419 Mukherjee, *Sir William Jones*, 98.
420 App, "William Jones's Ancient Theology," 45.

On close reading of Jones' work, one finds many more speculative identifications of Biblical and Graeco-Roman characters with Indian ones than comparative linguistics endeavours. Jones only gave a few words now and then to illustrate some similarities between the languages in question. However, *his work does not contain any systematic large-scale attempt to provide linguistic proof of the postulated relationship between languages of the Indo-European family*. It is worth noting that such a proof was only given several decades afterwards due to the inspiration from traditional Indian linguistics (*Vyakarana*). The author of the analysis, which one would have expected from Jones in the first place, was the German linguist Franz Bopp (1791–1867).[421] However, Bopp adopted the most important insights from Wilkins' English summary of Panini's Sanskrit grammar. Wilkins used traditional Indian methods of linguistic analysis, especially the analysis of words into smaller units, i.e. stems, roots, prefixes, and suffixes. Until then, European linguistics relied on the Alexandrian School's analyses, supplemented with philosophical and logical classifications of the Middle Ages and early modern times. Only Panini's insights enabled Bopp, R. Rask, and other Europeans to develop a truly systematic and comparative grammar.[422]

What does this imply for the creation of the AIT and its linguistic evidence? There are three preliminary conclusions to be made: 1) The idea of language family was part of Jones' quest for the primordial state of humankind, not only with regard to original religion but also to science and arts. 2) Similarly, speculations about the Indo-European homeland stemmed directly from centuries-long discussions which aimed at a precise description of events in the aftermath of the Flood, an effort to establish a precise geographical description of Noah's and his descendants' movements. As mentioned in the first chapter, Jones followed Newton's and Bryant's speculations in this regard. 3) Although the idea of relatedness of Indo-European languages was well-received in the European salons at the end of the 18th and the beginning of the 19th centuries, a truly linguistic proof was presented only by Franz Bopp, who had been inspired by traditional Indian linguistics. *It must be noted that Bopp's and*

---

421 Bopp's *Über das Conjugationssystem der Sanskritsprache in Vergleichung mit jenem der griechischen, lateinischen, persischen und germanischen Sprache* (1816) was a revolutionary work in the development of European linguistics.
422 Cf. Frits Staal, *Ritual and Mantras*, 34–36, and Thieme's introduction in Betty Shefts, *Grammatical Method of Panini: His Treatment of Sanskrit Present Stems* (New Haven: American Oriental Society, 1961), ix.

others' works confirmed only one component of Jones' theory: the relatedness of Indo-European languages. The other three ideas, namely the existence and character of primitive religion, Indo-European homeland, and the arrival of the ancients in India from Persia remained purely speculative. However, as the theological paradigm determined the interpretations of Indian traditions for several more decades, these unproven ideas were supported and maintained by the scientifically proven linguistic component of the theory.

Marianne Keppens had the following observations important to further analysis of the theory: 1) In the AIT, the direct predecessor of the Aryans was the tribe or tribes of the Brahmins who according to many Europeans are thought to have come to India from the north. 2) The idea of Brahminical tribes' invasion is older than the proof of the distinctiveness of Dravidian languages from Sanskrit and other mainly north-Indian languages put forward by Ellis. It was the background against which the newly found differences between Sanskrit and Dravidian speakers were explained. 3) However, rather than explaining the linguistic and ethnic differences, the idea was meant to elucidate the specific social organisation of India—the so-called caste system.[423]

The interpretation of the Brahmins' and their role in Indian society and history reappears here. Some interpretations of the Brahmins have already been noted above, including their image as power-mongering priests. One has to remember that until the mid-19th century, the Biblical model of Noah's descendants' dispersion and the gradual population of the Earth had been a debated but generally accepted paradigm of history. Due to an apparent etymological similarity in names, the Brahmins were considered the descendants of Abraham and placed within the family tree model of the dispersion of peoples across the globe. In the Biblical perspective, the Brahmins occupied a very early stage of human history in which a common religion and the first phase of diversification of one original language were supposedly involved. Besides Newton, Bryant, and Leibniz, discussions about the location of the cradle occupied intellectuals in France and elsewhere. For example, upon reading Holwell's and Dow's works, Voltaire became enthusiastic about India as the cradle of civilization, while J. S. Bailly argued against it:

---

423 Marianne Keppens, "The Aryans and the Ancient System of Caste," in *Western Foundations of the Caste System*, 221–251.

Not only must we seek around these mountains the origin of the Persians; but we must equally, though with less positive proofs, locate there the origin of the Indians and Chinese. Has not the Sanscrit language shown, Monsieur, that the Brahmans (Brames) are strangers to India? Has Mr. Gentil not told you that they had come from the north?[424]

The Biblical narrative seemed to suggest that much. At the beginning of the 17th century, Melchior Coting started off a series of speculations according to which the Brahmins were the descendants of one of the tribes of Israel.[425] For another three hundred years, Europeans thought that the Brahmins were originally a priestly family and later a tribe, in an analogy to the priestly tribe of Levi:

It was from the ranks of these three orders that the Hindu caste of Brahmins and the Hebrew tribe of Levi were formed.[426]

The idea of the Brahmins' advent to India from the outside foreshadowed the arrival of the Aryans. It only remained to notice that the bearers of the Vedic rituals referred to themselves as the "noble ones" (*arya*) and to re-describe the priestly tribe as an ethnical group.

Now to the second point raised by M. Keppens: The difference of Sanskrit from Dravidian languages only appears to be an argument in favour of the invasion theory. As late as the beginning of the 19th century, Ch. Wilkins, T. H. Colebrooke, and W. Carey endorsed Jones' claim concerning the relatedness of all Indian languages that they supposed to have stemmed from Sanskrit. Only in 1819 did F. W. Ellis produce the so-called Dravidian proof of the distinctive nature of South-Indian language Telugu, identifying a group of important verb roots that could in no way be derived from Sanskrit verb roots of the same meaning. It should be noted that Ellis used a grammar of Telugu composed by an Indian scholar Mamadi Venkayya.[427] However, a detailed elaboration of the Dravidian proof took another few decades and it became more widely

424 Bailly cited in App, "William Jones's Ancient Theology," 53.
425 Gelders and Balagangadhara, "Rethinking Orientalism," 124.
426 J. F. Hewitt, *The Ruling Races of Prehistoric Times in India, South-Western Asia and Southern Europe* (London: Archibald Constable, 1894), 1:xvii.
427 Those were actually Ellis' notes to Campbell's grammar of Telugu that was used in the schooling of junior officials of East India Company. See a reprint of a major part of Ellis' text in Trautmann, *The Aryan Debate*, 6–13.

known only after the publication of Campbell's *Comparative Grammar of the Dravidian or South-Indian Languages* (1856).[428]

Brahmins' invasion as an explanation of the origin of the caste system had already become a widespread idea by the time that the distinctive nature of the Dravidian languages began to be established. The Dravidian proof was thus hardly more than a welcome addition. Keppens mentioned several half-forgotten authors who associated the idea of invasion with the introduction of the caste system. Mark Wills was among the earliest of those. In 1810, he surmised that "the establishment of castes was not the effort of a single mind, but the result of successive expedients for retaining in subjection the conquests of the northern Hindoos."[429]

French scholars of the first decades of the 19th century also thought that the caste system had resulted from a foreign invasion. For example, in his *Monuments anciens et modernes de l'Hindoustan* (1821), Louis Langlés claimed that the ancient Hindus "had supplanted the Indigenous people of India, of which the caste of Pariahs probably offers us the sad remains."[430] Keppens also referred to works by Abel Rémusat, Eugène Burnouf, and others who shared this idea in the mid-19th century. In addition, the British historian of India, Elphinstone read some passages from *the Vedas* and the *Manava-dharamashastra* and concluded that the twice-born were a race of conquerors, although he also pointed out the lack of evidence for an Indian homeland outside the subcontinent.[431]

In the second half of the 19th century, these ideas were supplemented with the racial theories of physical anthropology, as we have seen in the preceding passage. The linguistically proven differences between Indo-European and Dravidian languages which later also included another specific group, the Munda languages, were directly linked to the physiology of their speakers. The originally theological model of the post-diluvian dispersion of nations was secularised in linguistic and

---

428 Trautmann, *The Aryan Debate*, 6–7.
429 Mark Wilks, *Historical Sketches of the South of India*, 1810, quoted in Marianne Keppens, "Indians are Aryans, so What?" Position paper, *Rethinking Religion in India I*, New Delhi, January, 2009, 5. Wilks based his idea on an interpretation of a narrative, which describes the defeat of Pariah king by a foreign ruler.
430 Louis Langlés, *Monuments Anciens et Modernes*, 1821, quoted in Keppens, "Indians are Aryans, so What?," 5.
431 Keppens, "Indians are Aryans, so What?," 6. The Belgian scholar noted that the German orientalists Rudolf Roth, Martin Haug, and Albrecht Weber were convinced that Brahmin invasion explained the emergence of the caste system.

anthropological speculations about the noble Aryan race that subjugated the uncivilised peoples of India.

The theological suppositions also preceded linguistic findings regarding the dating of the alleged Aryan invasion. Like earlier Orientalists, F. M. Müller considered the development of Indian religion in terms of a short biblical chronology. Among others, the famous Orientalist followed the work of Abbé Dubois, a Catholic missionary in India, whom he considered "a trustworthy authority . . . which will always retain its value."[432] The reliable Dubois claimed that the Indians are the descendants of Japheth and located their homeland in the vicinity of the Caucasus from where they set for India shortly after the Flood.[433]

Genealogical calculations placed the upper limit of the dates of events immediately following the Flood around 2500 BC. Müller established the lower limit supposing that the development of the Vedic corpus had been finalised by the Buddha's time, because the Pali Buddhist texts mentioned Upanishadic ideas. In Müller's time, the Buddha's lifetime was dated into the 6th century BC. As the British Orientalist supposed that the composition of each layer of the Vedic corpus lasted over the period of two hundred years, he established by reverse calculation that the *Rigveda* had been composed c. 1200 BC.[434] The Aryan invasion must have taken place in the preceding centuries, starting c. 1500 BC. Although Müller admitted towards the end of his life that *the Vedas* might be of a much earlier date,[435] his original estimation became part and parcel of the by now classical invasion theory.

In conclusion, the idea of Aryan invasion is rooted in theological discussion which presupposes the universal truth of the Biblical accounts. Regarding the image of Brahminical tribes who were supposed to have descended from one of the sons of Noah, it became a widely spread and accepted idea before the difference of Indo-European and Dravidian languages was established. Newton, Bryant, Jones, and other scholars tried

---

432 Klaus Klostermaier, "Questioning the Aryan Invasion Theory and Revising Ancient Indian History," *ISKCON Communications Journal* 6, no. 1 (1998), 2.

433 Abbé Dubois, *Hindu Manners, Customs and Ceremonies* (Oxford: Clarendon Press, 1906), quoted in Klostermaier, "Questioning the Aryan Invasion Theory and Revising Ancient Indian History," 2.

434 See e.g. Navaratna Rajaram, *The Politics of History: The Aryan Invasion Theory and the Subversion of Scholariship* (New Delhi: Voice of India, 1995), 91–96.

435 Klostermaier, "Questioning the Aryan Invasion Theory and Revising Ancient Indian History," 2.

to establish whether the Indians had descended from Japheth or Ham. The Brahmins of India were interpreted as a priestly tribe of foreign origin, in the manner of the Hebrew tribe of Levi. These considerations were to resolve the European puzzlement concerning the origin of the caste system in India. Another important component of the picture was the explanation of *the Vedas* as the world's oldest sacred scripture, proving the primordial monotheism of humankind. Religious and linguistic characteristics thus became linked, defining the Aryans in opposition to the Dravidians and the Mundas.

In the second half of the 19th century, the nascent physical anthropology contributed racial characteristics that had been derived from highly dubious readings of a few Vedic passages. Archaeology entered this discussion only after the discovery of the Indus Valley Civilisation. At this stage, the diffusionist model of the origin and spread of civilisation played a major part, founded as it was on the theological idea of *translatio studii*. Its influence is evident in the works of G. Childe, B. Hrozný, M. Wheeler, W. Burrow, and many others (civilisation came to India from the West). The discovery of an advanced urban civilisation in the Indus Valley that had flourished long before the date of the Aryan invasion, as proposed by Max Müller, did not correspond with the contemporary belief in the barbarian state of the Dravidians. As a consequence, the theory was changed to fit the findings: The barbarian Dravidians became the creators of an advanced urban civilisation, although other explanations were also possible, e. g. that of B. Hrozný.

Until the 1960s, archaeological findings had been interpreted in terms of the accepted invasion theory. However, an increasing number of findings and their assessment lead to two conclusions that do not support the invasion theory. The continuity in skeletal remains and material culture in the archaeological sites of Southern Asia is positively established, without evidence of any large invasion or migration. On the other hand, the earlier attempts at associating archaeological material with the Aryans is evaluated negatively since there are no well-founded criteria for such an identification.[436] The only scientifically established fact of the entire invasion theory is the relatedness of Indo-European languages. However, their wide geographical distribution remains an open question.

---

436 Besides the above mentioned scholars, the association of material remains with linguistic theories without written documents has been dismissed by Dilip K. Chakrabarty, "Power, Politics and Ariya Mayai or 'Aryan Illusion' in the study of Indian History," position paper at the 2nd Roundtable Session, *Rethinking Religion in India II*, New Delhi, January, 2009.

In a nutshell, the theological paradigm endowed speculations about the Aryans with the belief in a linguistic and religious unity of nations or ethnicities, which ultimately derives from the idea of a common origin of humankind based on Genesis. These principles were instrumental in the development of linguistic discussion, which was only later joined by physical anthropologists and archaeologists. Theological assumptions formed the basic structure of ideas of the theory. Linguistic, and later also archaeological discoveries have been interpreted through the prism of the presupposed invasion hypothesis for a long time.

Did Ram Mohan Roy Understand Western Religion?[437]

Ram Mohan Roy . . . the first earnest minded investigator of the science of comparative religion that the world has produced.
Monier Monier-Williams,
Religious Thought and Life in India

As the British East India Company advanced in its conquest of South Asia, many fundamental changes were installed in the life of the people of India. Their traditions became the subject of study and criticism of both East India Company officials and Protestant missionaries. In the first decades of the 19th century, Ram Mohan Roy was probably the most well-known Indian thinker who reacted to the criticism of the British colonizers. He was certainly an important personality, because he has been described as "the father of modern India" and "the founder of modern Indian philosophy."[438] Ram Mohan Roy has been praised as the reformer of Hinduism and the traditional Indian society. His work is taken as the beginning of the rise of Hinduism as a global religion; some authors talked about "the renaissance of Hinduism" which this reformer

---

437 The main part of argumentation of this chapter was originally published as my article in the Polish journal of religious studies *Nomos. Czasopismo Religioznawcze* 77 (2012): 64–86. I thank here to its Editor-in-Chief Henryk Hoffmann for his approval of the use of the original text as the basis for this chapter.

438 Hem Chandra Sarkar, *Rammohan Roy: The Father of Modern India* (Calcutta: Srimati Sakuntala Rao, 1910); Halbfass, *India and Europe*, 291; Jan Gonda, *Die Religionen Indiens* (Stuttgart: Kohlhamer, 1963), 2:302. Jan Gonda offers a very useful overview of the older literature to the topic.

should have started.[439] Ram Mohan Roy is thus depicted as the religious reformer of Hinduism.

The argumentation of previous chapters denies existence of the religion called Hinduism; how should we than understand the ideas and activities of Ram Mohan Roy? It was his dealing with the concept of Hinduism as a religion, possibly as the first of the modern Indian thinkers, that enabled him to write about "theology of Hinduism," "God," "Hindu Theism," etc. It is evident today that his concept of Hinduism was based on the ideas taken from the British colonizers. Ram Mohan Roy strived to understand and accept inspiration from the Western religions, mainly from the Unitarian teaching. However, if we want to understand precisely his thoughts, we should inquire into the central problem of any inter-cultural dialogue: *How much did this Bengali reformer really understand the Western conceptual framework of religion?*

It is a worthy question to pursue, because most researchers have presupposed so far that Roy understood the Western concept of religion without problems, and their attention was focused on the characterization of Roy's opinions. There are basically three explanations of Roy's thought and activities that I was able to identify. While speaking of his period of public involvement and growing fame (1815–1833), this influential man was basically a Unitarian Christian according to some,[440] he strived for a renewal of ancient Indian tradition in the opinion of others,[441] or he is depicted as a person taking "a difficult middle path"[442] between Western Christianity and domestic Hinduism.

Yet a close reading reveals a very confusing picture. Although different scholars are inclined to describe Ram Mohan Roy's thoughts in one of the above mentioned ways, they also tend to include other positions in their explanations. In some cases, I found vague and confusing statements. I will summarize several problems of these different explanations in the first part of this chapter. Having gone through these different interpretations, at first, I came to the conclusion that Roy basically

---

439 Flood, *An Introduction to Hinduism*, 250–251.
440 J. T. F. Jordens, "Hindu Religious and Social Reform in British India," in *A Cultural History of India*, 367; Lynn Zastoupil, "Defining Christians, Making Britons: Rammohun Roy and the Unitarians," *Victorian Studies* 44, no. 2 (2002): 215–243; but see also David Kopf, *The Brahmo Samaj and the Shaping of the Modern Indian Mind* (Princeton: Princeton University Press, 1979), 9–15.
441 Ajit Kumar Ray, *The Religious Ideas of Rammohun Roy* (New Delhi: Kanak Publications, 1976), 64.
442 Kopf, *The Brahmo Samaj and the Shaping of the Modern Indian Mind*, 314.

accepted the Western monotheistic frame, deism in the beginning and the Unitarian ideas later.[443] There was much evidence for this conclusion that I shall summarize in the second part of this chapter. This conclusion was only strengthened by my first discussions with Jakob De Roover, Polly Hazarika, and other colleagues who have dealt with Roy's ideas in their research.

Somewhat later, De Roover came with a more promising insight. His thesis clarifies the problems with explanation of Roy's position by asking: How did Ram Mohan Roy understand his Western masters, friends, and enemies speaking of religion? De Roover basically pointed out the difficulties which Ram Mohan Roy must have encountered while he tried to understand a cluster of Western concepts connected with religion. Although Ram Mohan Roy strived to enter the Western framework of understanding, as a native Brahmin he could hardly understand the alien Western concepts in their original meaning. Apparently, his studies of Islam and of the Jewish tradition did not help in this regard.

Although Ram Mohan Roy might have thought he understood the Western framework of ideas, it can be shown that the opposite is true. The individual concepts of this framework, which are connected together in a very particular way, and thus understandable to people grown in the Western view of the world, were used by Ram Mohan Roy in a meaningless or grotesque way. The goal of my analysis here is not to deride the Bengali reformer, of course. I want to show how precisely these moments of misunderstanding are important referents to a different way of thought, which caused the distortions in question. It is here that we can track the influence of the traditional Indian understanding: The distortions of the Western understanding of religion were done on the basis of Roy's deeply rooted cluster of traditional Indian ideas. More accurately, these distortions are not accidental, they are systematical results of the thinking formed by the traditional Indian structure of ideas. Would it be possible to identify these important Indian ideas in this way?[444]

---

443 Historical facts concerning Roy's association with the Unitarians were elaborated by Zastoupil, "Defining Christians, Making Britons: Rammohun Ray and the Unitarians," 215–243, and "Notorious and Convicted Mutilators: Ram Mohan Roy, Thomas Jefferson, and the Bible," *Journal of World History* 20, no. 3 (2009): 399–434.

444 Jakob De Roover presented his analysis "The Colonial Dialogue on Religion" at the conference *Rethinking Religion in India III. European Representations and Indian Responses* in Pardubice, Czech Republic, October 12, 2011. I am grateful to him both for this inspiring approach and for the valuable comments he offered on the first draft of this text. I would also like to thank Mary I. Bockover, who read the second draft with careful attention and who commented on it with enthusiasm.

If yes, these traditional structures of ideas would be so deeply rooted and so 'natural' that even such an educated thinker as Ram Mohan Roy would not be able to reflect their functioning properly. I am going to take this new thesis, the most promising from all known to me, and I will test its explanative power. First, I will look for other examples of Roy's distortions, different from those used by Jakob De Roover. Should I find them, I will strive to explain their background. Before that, it will be useful to look at several problems of the older discussions and to reconsider arguments for Roy's acceptance of the Western, dominantly Unitarian ideas about religion.

Problems in the Debate about Roy's Ideas of Religion

Although explanations of Roy's ideas by the 19th century Indologists like F. Max Müller or Monier-Williams might be an interesting task for an analysis, I am going to consider the opinions of more recent authors.[445] In a still influential compendium *A Cultural History of India*, J. T. F. Jordens ascribed much of Roy's ideas to the strong influences of European deism and ideology of the Unitarians, concluding: "In fact his very schematic religious creed has, apart from the name of Brahma, practically no specifically Hindu content."[446] But on the next page the same scholar wrote that "Ram Mohan never parted ways with Hinduism" and that "he felt reform had to be carried out from within the Hindu community."[447] If Roy's "religious creed" did not have any Hindu content, how should we understand the claim that Roy "never parted with Hinduism?" It is not clear either whether Jordens indicated a possibility of coexistence of the Western religious credo and Hinduism, or what was the exact meaning of the reform "carried out from within the Hindu community." Both claims are very problematic when we consider the traditional "Hindu" reactions to the efforts of Ram Mohan Roy: His community considered the reformer to be a man who rejected many traditional practices and accepted the Western ones. From this perspective,

---

445 It is important to note that F. M. Müller understood Roy's attempts according to his own vision for Christianizing India, which can happen by the Hindus' acceptance of the alleged monotheism of *the Vedas*. See Friedrich Max Müller, *Biographical Essays* (London: Longmans, 1884), 23 and 43.
446 Jordens, "Hindu Religious and Social Reform in British India," 367.
447 Jordens, "Hindu Religious and Social Reform in British India," 368.

such a reform consists of the acceptance of external criticism, alien to domestic traditions.

David Kopf argued that Roy "might have reacted to the West by ardently defending the defects, the abuses, the weaknesses of quotidian Hinduism. He might have taken the opposite course and subscribed totally to the Western culture, either by converting to Christianity or by adopting a secular style of life. But he chose the more difficult middle path through which he sought to wed modernization in the West with Hindu institutions and traditions."[448]

However, Kopf also recognised the importance of the Unitarian ideas for Ram Mohan Roy, be it in the faith in a rational religion, a monotheism and specific forms of worship, or in the field of social reforms. Kopf even considered seriously the possibility that Brahmo Sabha might have been the direct successor of the Unitarian Committee of Calcutta and thus "a domesticated form of the Unitarian Church."[449] In this case, it is not at all clear where in Ram Mohan Roy's thought and efforts do we find the Hindu traditions and institutions, especially when Kopf at the same time argued that the British Orientalists' scholarship had been the main source of Ram Mohan's basic arguments for his reforms of Hindu traditions.

Stephen Hay understood Roy as a modernizer who attempted to renovate both Christianity and Hinduism with the guidance of reason. Hay emphasized the role of reason in Roy's efforts to increase "the enlightenment and well-being of the members of his society;" this Indian reformer did not formulate his interpretations "on a predilection for either Western or indigenous traditions."[450] It looks as if the rationality is a culture-transcending platform; a non-partisan position, which would enable the reformer to reconsider both domestic and Western traditions. Yet the closer reading of his works reveals how much he was indebted to the Western cultural understanding of rationality, taken from his encounters especially with Baptists and Unitarians. We were following some of these debates about the "proper" rationality, allegedly being present only in the Western culture, in the chapter on historical debates of Indian past.

---

448 Kopf, *The Brahmo Samaj and the Shaping of the Modern Indian Mind*, 314.
449 Kopf, *The Brahmo Samaj and the Shaping of the Modern Indian Mind*, 3–15, but see also 48.
450 Stephen N. Hay, "Western and Indigenous Elements in Modern Indian Thought: The Case of Rammohun Roy," in *Changing Japanese Attitudes Toward Modernization*, ed. Marius B. Jansen (Princeton: Princeton University Press, 1972), 324–327.

Ajit Kumar Ray offered a puzzling interpretation: Although Ram Mohan Roy "welcomed new ideas," he did not accomplish "a synthesis of ideas old and new, but a reappraisal of India's ancient faith."[451] This is confusing: What was the source of Roy's alleged "reappraisal" if not those new, that is Western, ideas? Did Roy appreciate and welcome new ideas, but refused to build on them?

Bruce C. Robertson elaborated on a comparison of Roy's Bengali and English works and he concluded that Roy was an *Advaita Vedanta* thinker, who was later misunderstood by his own followers and by the Western scholars alike.[452] However, this scholar himself pointed to important conclusions where Roy completely departed from the traditional positions of Shankara, his main authority. It is, for example, the opinion about a qualification necessary to obtain the knowledge of the highest (*brahma*). Whilst for Shankara, the life of wandering ascetic (*sannyasin*) was the necessary condition, Ram Mohan Roy claimed that a family life is qualifying a person in the same, or even better, way.

Another difference lies in the opinion about the way how to achieve the highest knowledge. To put it briefly, for Shankara it was the result of human striving, whereas Ram Mohan Roy considered the highest knowledge a gift awarded by Atman.[453] It is important to note in this connection that Shankara was the main authority for Roy and apparently, he did not consider, nor did he know other, mainly Vaishnava, schools of Vedanta. There is also evidence that Roy based his monotheistic interpretation of *Vedanta Sutras* on the works of H. T. Colebrooke, one of the first British Orientalists.[454] Moreover, the reactions from the traditional scholars of Vedanta to Roy's efforts were rejecting. They considered his interpretations unacceptable modernization, motivated by greed and desire for success. All these facts contradict the conviction that Roy's thinking continued the line of the traditional Vedanta.

Wilhelm Halbfass propagated the concept of different horizons of languages and thought, inspired by ideas of H. G. Gadamer.[455] The most important questions of Halbfass in this connection are the ways in which Indians and Europeans could understand each other, and also,

451 Ray, *The Religious Ideas of Rammohun Roy*, 64.
452 Bruce Carlisle Robertson, *Raja Ram Mohan Ray. The Father of Modern India* (New Delhi: Oxford University Press, 2001), 176–177.
453 Robertson, *Raja Ram Mohan Ray*, 78, 135, 145, 147.
454 David Kopf, *British Orientalism and the Bengal Renaissance. The Dynamics of Indian Modernization 1773–1835* (Calcutta: K. L. Mukhopadhyay, 1969), 198.
455 Halbfass used the concept of horizon from the philosophy of Hans Georg Gadamer.

how did they treated the otherness of the other. In Roy's case, Halbfass stressed that "historical surveys and psychological and biographical analyses of 'influences' . . . alone do not suffice for the understanding of the central hermeneutical question."[456] He also considered any reduction to Western models to be "simplifications as inappropriate as the neo-Hindu mythicizing is unacceptable."[457] I can agree with him so far. But when Halbfass said that it is important to understand Roy's use of alien concepts as the means of self-understanding and self-presentation, problems arise. If Ram Mohan Roy should have used the Western ideas as the framework of self-understanding,[458] how would it have been possible for him to do that? Given the historical situation, that is the meeting of two very different cultures with very different conceptual frameworks, it should be, first of all, analysed whether their members understood each other at all. Only then can we consider the possibility of using an alien framework for understanding anything. From the part of the book concerning Roy, it is quite clear that Halbfass implicitly presupposed that the Bengali reformer understood Western ideas without problems. This will turn out to be a false presupposition, as we will see in the third part of this chapter.[459]

Halbfass, Killingley, and then Zastoupil have all basically claimed that Roy was able to move between different languages and cultural horizons, namely Hindu, Muslim, and Christian horizons. According to this explanation, Roy could "speak from within" these respective traditions in order to respond to the audience of a particular cultural horizon he entered.[460] His knowledge of several languages should have enabled him to do so. Having followed this interpretation, Zastoupil suggested

---

456 Halbfass, *India and Europe*, 200.
457 Halbfass, *India and Europe*, 200–201.
458 Halbfass, *India and Europe*, 215.
459 I found other problematic statements of Halbfass. For example, he basically accepted the Western notion about the degenerated state of Hindu religion and society, promoted by both Protestant Missionaries and Orientalists in the times of Ram Mohan Roy (see Halbfass, *India and Europe*, 214, part 20). This is hardly acceptable as a scholarly thesis. The early rule of the East India Company in Bengal would explain much about the dark picture of Northen India in Roy's time; the consequences of great famine of 1767–69 were horrific and long-lasting. See Ramesh Chandra Majumdar, *British Paramountcy and Indian Renaissance* (Bombay: Bharatiya Vidya Bhavan, 1970), 412–417; and Kopf, *British Orientalism and the Bengal Renaissance*, 13–16 for overview and direction to other sources on these events.
460 Halbfass, *India and Europe*, 207–208; Dermot H. Killingley, *Ram Mohan Ray in Hindu and Christian Traditions: The Teape Lectures 1990* (New Castle upon Tyne: Grevatt and Grevatt, 1993), 33–38, 44–45, 58–59, 160; Zastoupil, "Defining Christians, Making Britons: Rammohun Ray and the Unitarians," 222.

the possibility of multiple religious affiliations for Roy.[461] Following the discussions with S. N. Balagangadhara and Jakob De Roover, however, I have to repeat this objection: *How did Roy understand the clusters of the Western ideas which constitute the background of the respective languages and their cultural horizons?* Before anybody can enter a foreign cultural horizon and speak from within it, he must properly understand the basic structures, or the clusters of ideas that are connected in a certain way. This structure of connections gives specific meaning to a culture's particular ideas. For this task, linguistic competence in several languages is not enough, as Balagangadhara convincingly argued. If somebody from a very different culture encountered the Christian ideas of the West expressed by words like 'God,' 'religion,' 'worship,' etc., how could he make sense of them?

> The issue is not so much about the meaning of specific words. In the absence of a background set of beliefs, is it possible to pick out what they are referring to, something, which is constituted as a "totality" due to the interrelationship between these concepts?[462]

The answer is obviously "no." Without an understanding of the specific cluster of ideas in its specific structure in a given culture, it is not possible to understand the meaning of individual concepts in the respective language use of this culture. We are concerned here, of course, with abstract thinking, not with words referring to objects of common daily experience. This insight forms a solid base for questioning Roy's understanding of the Western religion. Having followed it, De Roover came recently with this promising approach:

> Ram Mohan Ray indeed appears to have collaborated with the Europeans in characterizing the Hindu traditions as a religion with its own set of doctrines about the divine and its own practice of worship. . . . Ray adopts certain sets of ideas from the British and appears to use the relevant terms in much the same way. But this goes only so far. . . . Always, there comes a point where he begins to draw on other ideas to make sense of these and to give shape to his use of English words. Consequently . . . we keep bumping into instances where he suddenly uses a term completely differ-

461 Zastoupil, "Defining Christians, Making Britons: Rammohun Ray and the Unitarians," 222.
462 Balagangadhara, *"The Heathen in His Blindnes..."*, 229.

ently than expected or writes sentences that do not make sense against the background of the commonplace ideas he appears to have adopted.[463]

De Roover pointed to the examples of Roy's strange understanding of "idolatry," to his use of the opposites "false and true" in connection with doctrines, and to his ideas about worship. De Roover showed how these examples illustrate the fact that when Europeans and Indians met at the time of Roy, they in many ways did not understand the basics of the other's culture. While Europeans made sense of their experiences with Indian people by understanding indigenous traditions within a Christian religious framework, the people of India tried to understand their experience with Europeans on the base of an Indian framework. Thus when a member of one culture spoke about the ideas of a person from the other culture, he inevitably distorted them. Both partners did not understand the whole structure that gave position and particular meaning to the individual ideas of the other. Somebody might take this view as a resignation on the possibility of understanding between members of different cultures. But this insight is rather a promising starting point for research.

Let us suppose that these distortions are not just individual, or arbitrary; rather, that they are systematic at certain level. If we can trace such distortions in the description of "the other" and then show what it tells us about the important ideas in the structure of understanding of the describer, we will be able to study and understand the ideas of the describer. In our case, Ram Mohan Roy's attempts to use the Western concepts would show us some important ideas of the traditional Indian framework of thought.

Firstly, I will take De Roover's example of idolatry and test how much it really proves his thesis. Secondly, if this direction of research shows promise, I should be able to find some more examples of Roy's distortions of the important ideas from the Western framework of ideas concerning religion. If I will find such examples, I shall try to suggest what Roy's distortions reveal to us about the traditional Indian cluster of ideas. Yet, before going for this aim, let me first summarise what Ram Mohan Roy seemingly accepted from the Christian ideas about religion and religious practices. It will be useful for the later tests of De Roover's claims.

---

463 Jakob De Roover, "The Colonial Dialogue on Religion," a position paper in the first Roundtable Session, *Rethinking Religion in India III. European Representations and Indian Responses*, Pardubice, Czech Republic, October 12, 2011.

Western Monotheistic Framework Accepted . . .

Several important arguments can be presented in order to show that Roy accepted the Christian Unitarian framework in his fight with "idolatry," his attempt to reconstruct the "pure monotheism" of *the Vedas* and Vedanta, his appreciation for Christ, and his defence of the Unitarian position in theological debates with Baptist missionaries. We shall also note his activities that led to the establishment of the Unitarian committee and the Unitarian Press in Calcutta, and finally his engagement with the Unitarians during his last two years on the British Isles.

The acceptance of the concept of idolatry as the source of immorality is a good point to start with. Europeans found people in India practicing many different rituals that very often involved a statue or an image of a god (*deva*), or goddess (*devi*); for example, offering food to these statues and images (*bhoga-arati*), ritual bathing of a statue (*abhisheka*), singing and dancing in front of it, etc.

These practices were domestic traditions for Roy, a descendant of a Brahminical family. Later, he stopped doing *puja, abhisheka* and other practices, allegedly under the influence of his studies of Islam. And later, having followed criticism of the Protestant Missionaries and the British Orientalists alike, Roy found the Brahmins of India guilty of the misguidance of masses to idolatry:

> I have had ample opportunity of observing the superstitious puerilities into which they have been thrown by their self-interested guides, who, in defiance of the law as well as of common sense, have succeeded but too well in conducting them to the temple of Idolatry; and while they hid from their view the true substance of morality, have infused into their simple hearts a weak attachment for its mere shadow.[464]

According to the Bengali reformer, the so-called idolatry was "fatal" and "inducing the violation of every humane and social feeling' of otherwise mild and patient Indians.[465] "Hindoo idolatry," said Roy, "more than any other pagan worship, destroys the texture of society"[466] and "prescribes

---

464 Ram Mohan Roy, "Translation of the Ishopanishad," in *The English Works of Raja Rammohun Roy,* ed. Jogendra Chunder Ghose (Calcutta: Srikanta Roy, 1906), 1:101–102. From this footnote on, all the titles of texts that will be mentioned without an author will be Roy's.
465 Roy, "Translation of the Ishopanishad," 103.
466 "Abridgment of the Vedant," in *The English Works of Raja Rammohun Roy,* 1:6.

crimes of the most heinous nature, which even the most savage nations would blush to commit."[467] "Idolatry" was to be blamed for everything bad happening in the Bengali society.

> Idolatry, as now practiced by our countrymen, and which the learned Brahmun so zealously supports as conductive to morality, is not only rejected by the Shastras universally, but must also be looked upon with great horror by common sense, as leading directly to immorality and destructive of social comforts.[468]

Roy's acceptance of the Western monotheistic stance seems to be obvious: The worship of images is the source of immorality, a criminal act even, because it is a worship of false gods. In order to justify his programme of rejection of "idolatry," Roy argued that this worship was not what *the Vedas* and Vedanta had originally taught. He also disapproved of the traditional notion that scriptures, especially *the Puranas, Tantras*, and *Agamas*, mandate the worship of God in material form; according to him, these are only the objects of imagination and these scriptures declare them as such.[469] The Bengali reformer claimed that the unlimited, transcendental Lord cannot be perceived by senses, nor even limited by some image.[470] In this way, we arrived at Roy's monotheistic concept of the Deity.

The Bengali reformer declared his belief in the "one true and eternal God,"[471] "a wise and uncreated Being, the supporter and Ruler of the boundless universe."[472] This is a clear monotheistic credo, especially when he contrasted it with the "idolatry" and belief in the "innumerable gods and goddesses" of his countrymen.[473] His descriptions of the "one true God" as the designer of the universe, of the human body, and of nature as one whose majesty can be seen through the works of nature are the same as Western Christian ideas.[474] Ram Mohan Roy interpreted

467 "Translation of the Kuth-opunishud," in *The English Works of Raja Rammohun Roy*, 1:62.
468 "Second Defence of the Hindoo Theism," in *The English Works of Raja Rammohun* Roy, 1:158.
469 Robertson, *Raja Ram Mohan Ray*, 100–101.
470 Compare translation of the original text Vedantagraha by Bruce Robertson (ibid.) with the translation and explanation of the same Roy's text by Dermot H. Killingley, *The Only True God. Works on Religion by Rammohun Roy. Selected and Translated from Bengali and Sanskrit, with an Introduction and Notes* (Newcastle upon Tyne: Grevatt and Grevatt, 1982), 10–11.
471 "Translation of an Abridgment of the Vedant," in *The English Works of Raja Rammohun Ray*, 1:3.
472 "Translation of an Abridgment of the Vedant," 5.
473 "Translation of an Abridgment of the Vedant."
474 Compare with "Translation of the Moonduk Upanishad," in *The English Works of Raja Rammohun Roy*, 1:28.

the teachings of Vedanta in this way: *brahma* of *the Upanishads* is actually the true invisible God worshipped in different religious traditions of the world. In order to support his position, Roy stated that *the Vedas* "are of unquestionable authority amongst all Hindoos"[475] and thus he followed the British Orientalists' ideas about central scriptures of ancient India. In his search for the original and pure monotheism of *the Vedas*, Roy followed the Orientalists' interpretations. These were William Jones, Henry T. Colebrooke, and others who put Indian texts within biblical chronology, stating that the original and pure monotheism of *the Vedas* had been corrupted into polytheism.[476] In order to support his position, he also pointed to a worship of other communities—the "non-idolatrous" worship of God by Muslims, Protestants, and Sikhs. On the other hand, if there was a community that he criticised most often, it was the Vaishnava community and its practices. Ram Mohan Roy chose the worship of Krishna as an example of immoral idolatry:

> I begin with Krishna as the most adored of the incarnations. . . . His worship is made to consist in the institution of his image or picture, accompanied by one or more females, and in the contemplation of his history and behaviour, such as his perpetration of murder upon a female of the name of Putana; his compelling of a great number of married and unmarried women to stand before him denuded; his debauching them and several others, to the mortal affliction of their husbands and relations; his annoying them, by violating the laws of cleanliness and other facts of the same nature. The grossness of his worship does not find a limit here.[477]

In this criticism, we can hear the words of the Baptist missionaries of Shrirampur. In the same manner as these missionaries, Roy showed either disregard or ignorance of the Vaishnavite understanding of the above mentioned stories about Krishna. Puranic story about Putana stressed the fact that she wanted to kill Krishna, when he was a toddler. She smeared her breasts with poison, befriended Krishna's mother Yashoda and offered her breast to feed small Krishna. Yet he was not affected by her poison and sucked the life from her. Such a story is hardly "a perpetration of murder"; would we feel morally offended by hearing

475 "Translation of the Cena Upanishad," in *The English Works of Raja Rammohun Roay*, 1:47.
476 Kopf, *British Orientalism and the Bengal Renaissance*, 35–41.
477 "A Defence of Hindoo Theism," in *The English Works of Raja Rammohun Roy*, 1:140.

such a story, we could judge the Greek stories about Heracles' or Perseus' "murders" as well.

The moral judgement of the songs and stories about love between Krishna and *gopis* is another categorical mistake. The criticism of missionaries is based on the assumption that Christ, as an incarnation of the all-perfect God, is also a model for moral behaviour of people. Therefore, it made sense to ask what kind of example do the allegedly divine incarnations of the Hindu gods give. The theological idea was ground for comparisons of Krishna with Christ, which became an important topic in the 19th century.[478] Obviously, stories about Krishna cannot be judged well in such a comparison. However, when Vaishnavas enjoy listening to the stories, they certainly do not take them as activities to be imitated in their daily lives. We cannot elaborate here on the teaching of different tastes (*rasa* in Sanskrit), the emotional and aesthetic experiences of the listeners that will explain much about the role of stories describing Krishna-lila.[479] What is important for our discussion is that it again seems as if Roy accepted the British criticism of such stories. Protestant missionaries such as William Carey and William Ward compared Christian morality with the example set by Krishna. The idolatry concerning this "false god" of the Hindus seemed to celebrate all activities that were seen as evil and disgusting by these missionaries.[480] Ram Mohan Roy often had discussions with these missionaries in Shrirampur and his opinions in this regard were clearly influenced by them.

Roy accepted the Western explanation of the allegedly original monotheism of *the Vedas*. All *devas* (gods) have supposedly risen from the one Supreme Being. He also accepted the Western idea of personification of natural forces, which were turned into gods by the Ancient people.

---

478 See, for example, John P. Jones, *India's Problem: Krishna or Christ* (New York: Flemming H. Revell, 1903).

479 It would be better, perhaps, to read a song in the original Sanskrit, accompanied by a good translation and comments, to get a sense of emotional experience built by songs about Krishna, than to start with theoretical elaborations of the same. One such good work is Barbara Stoler Miller, *The Gitagovinda of Jayadeva: Love Song of the Dark Lord* (Delhi: Motilal Banarsidass, 1984). For an interesting study into literary and aesthetic ideas of the Indian traditions, see Róbert Gáfrik, *Od významu k emóciám: Úvaha o prínose sanskritskej literárnej teórie do diskurzu západnej literárnej vedy* [From meaning to emotions: An essay about the contribution of the Sanskrit literary theory for the discourse of the western studies of Literature] (Trnava: Trnavská univerzita, 2012).

480 See for example George Smith, *The Life of William Carey. Shoe Maker and Missionary* (London: J. M. Dent, not dated), 52–53, and William Ward, *A View of the History, Literature, and Religion of the Hindoos* (London: Baptist Missionary Society, 1817), 1:xlvi–xlix.

Compare the ideas of Ram Mohan Roy with H. T. Colebrooke's opinion on the "real doctrine of the Indian scriptures."[481] In his fight for the distinction between the one true God and the false gods, Roy also participated in the linguistic discussions about the correct translation of the term *God* to Sanskrit. He opposed William Hodge Mill's proposal based on the linguistic similarity of *deva* to Greek *theos* or Latin *deus*: "In my humble opinion the introduction of the word *deva* to signify *God* . . . would require a change in the vernacular language of this country which would unintentionally tend to confirm irrevocably polytheism among the Hindoos."[482]

Roy's acceptance of Western ideas did not stop here, as the famous controversy around his book *The Precepts of Jesus, the Guide to Peace and Happiness* reveals. The Bengali reformer tried to extract moral teaching of Jesus from the historical and the dogmatic context of the Gospels. No wonder that several Christian missionaries reacted to this attempt with outrage, notably Joshua Marshman of the Baptist mission in Shrirampur. The public debate in newspapers raised considerable interest also in Britain and in the United States, because Roy defended his understanding of the "unity of God" against the Trinitarian teaching of many churches. It is understandable that this attempt was highly appreciated especially by the Unitarians, whose efforts to purify Christianity by its return to the allegedly pure original form Roy supported greatly. In this spirit he wrote to Thomas Rees, praying for success of the new reformation:

> I have no language to express the happiness I derive from the idea that so many friends of truth, both in England and America, are engaged in attempting to free the originally pure, simple, and practical religion of Christ from the heathenish doctrines and absurd notions gradually introduced under the Roman power; and I sincerely pray that the success of those gentlemen may be as great as (if not greater than) that of LUTHER and others, to whom the religious world is indebted for laying the first stone of religious reformation, and having recommended the system of distinguishing divine authority from human creeds, and the practice of benevolence from ridiculous outward observances.[483]

---

481 "The Second Defense of the Hindoo Theism," in *The English Works of Raja Rammohun Roy*, 1:156; Colebrooke, *Miscellaneous Essays*, 1:110–111.

482 See a long quote from a letter written by Roy which was not published in the edition of Collet: R. F. Young, *Resistant Hinduism: Sanskrit Sources on anti-Christian Apologetics in Early Nineteenth Century India* (Vienna: Gerold, 1981), 42.

483 From a Letter to Thomas Rees, in *The English Works of Raja Rammohun Roy*, 2:349.

Some scholars stressed only the fact that he criticised concepts of Christ's divinity, atonement, and the doctrine of the Trinity in a printed exchange with Joshua Marshman from the Baptist mission in Shrirampur. Because of that it seemed to some scholars that Roy's position was not Christian. However, is not the discussion about the nature of Christ a discussion *within the framework of Christian theology*? Has this issue not been one of the main themes of Christian theology from its beginning, and also the cause of the schismatic battles? Roy defended the idea of "unity of God" against Trinitarian teaching which is clearly the Unitarian position in this Christian debate. Roy attacked some Christian dogmas, true, but at the same time he believed that Jesus was the first born creature, superior even to the angels in heaven, who "like Adam lived with God before his coming into this world" and who alone "deserves a special honour."[484]

Let us also notice Roy's great esteem for Christian ethical teaching. His intention of publishing *The Precepts of Jesus*, the starting point of the above mentioned controversy, can be described by a quote from Roy's letter to John Digby: "The consequence of my long and uninterrupted researches into religious truth has been that I have found the doctrine of Christ more conductive to moral principles and better adapted for the use of rational beings than any others which have come to my knowledge."[485] In the introduction to his *Precepts of Jesus*, Roy considered the moral law to be the essential characteristic of Christianity in which the moral code of behaviour between human beings is revealed in a way superior to other religions: "The latter (i.e. morality, M. F.), albeit partially taught in every system of religion with which I am acquainted, is principally spread by Christianity."[486]

Lynn Zastoupil pointed to the way Roy used Unitarian arguments in the controversy around *The Precepts of Jesus* as textual criticism involving comparison with Greek and Hebrew originals and rational scepticism. London Unitarians understood Roy's controversy with Baptists as identical with their own.[487] Robertson characterised the whole controversy as "a public confrontation between deism and Evangelical Protestantism" and he noted that at the same time, a parallel confrontation between

---

484 See M. M. Thomas, *The Acknowledged Christ of the Indian Renaissance* (London: SCM Press, 1969), 19, 25.

485 Roy's letter quoted in Thomas, *The Acknowledged Christ of the Indian Renaissance*, 8–9.

486 *The Precepts of Jesus: The Guide to Peace and Happiness*, London: Unitarian Society, 1823), xxv.

487 Zastoupil, "Defining Christians, Making Britons: Rammohun Ray and the Unitarians," 228–234.

Calvinists and Unitarians was taking place in New England.[488] There are other Roy's activities that are noteworthy for our debate. Roy was not only the companion of the Unitarians in theological debates and an admirer of the Christian ethical teaching, he actually convinced originally Baptist missionary William Adam about the truth of Unitarianism, and together with Dwarkanath Tagore established the Calcutta Unitarian Committee in 1823. Starting a Unitarian Press, setting up a library, worship services with W. Adam as a minister, and plans to build a chapel followed. It is still unclear whether Ram Mohan Roy wanted to establish Brahmo Sabha (1829) as an Indian form of the Unitarian Church or not.[489] Roy had long years of correspondence with the leading British and American Unitarians, such as Thomas Rees, W. E. Channing, and Joseph Tuckerman. One of the reasons for his visit to the British Isles was a long time prepared meeting of Unitarians of three continents.

It is also noteworthy that Roy was most probably ready to swear in public that he is a good Christian. Lynn Zastoupil argued rather convincingly for this claim when he put the question of Roy's Unitarian/Christian identity in the context of political ambitions of the British Unitarians. Bentham or Bowring put forward Roy as a candidate for Parliament elections in 1831; this was a part of crucial attempts of the Unitarians to enforce fundamental changes in the British law, especially laws concerning the emancipation of the Jews and greater separation of the Anglican Church from the state. When Roy agreed to this proposition, he most probably knew that in the case of his victory, he would have to take the oath containing the words "upon the true faith of a Christian." Thus it seems that Roy contemplated the possibility of publicly swearing to being a true Christian.[490]

All these ideas from Roy's works and the facts about his life seem to make for a strong argument that this Bengali reformer basically accepted the Western, especially the Unitarian framework of understanding as his own. It is certainly reasonable to conclude that Roy embraced

---

488 "The *cause celebre* in New England was the election of Henry Ware Sr, a Unitarian, to the Hollis Professorship of Divinity at Harvard Divinity School. . . . The similarity between these two confrontations made Ram Mohan Roy a companion in struggle, a welcome ally of the American Unitarians, as Ralph Waldo Emerson himself understood." Robertson, *Raja Ram Mohan Ray*, 55–56.

489 Compare Kopf, *The Brahmo Samaj and the Shaping of the Modern Indian Mind*, 4, 15, with Zastoupil, "Defining Christians, Making Britons: Rammohun Ray and the Unitarians," 234.

490 Zastoupil, "Defining Christians, Making Britons: Rammohun Ray and the Unitarians," 236–237.

Christian Unitarian ideas and practices and strived to apply them in his life and society. But this finding is not sufficient for answering the more important question: *Did he really understand the meaning of Western ideas in their specific structure?* Did he understand the concept of religion, God, idolatry, and other fundamental ideas of Christianity as perceived by Europeans? Although many authors portrayed Roy as a genius who studied and understood several religions very well, we should be careful to accept this view just because many had said so.

... but not Understood: "Good Idolatry" and "Evil in the Name of God"

For the following debate, let us keep in mind that Roy specifically mentioned his efforts to change the ritual practices of Indian people as the main reason for his translations of important traditional texts. He accepted the conviction of the British Orientalists about the legitimacy of practices coming from the old scriptures. When Ram Mohan Roy pondered over the origin of many practices of his times, he was guided by the Western argument which cast doubt on many rituals in India, because the "ancient scriptures" did not mention them.

> My constant reflections on the inconvenient, or rather injurious rites introduced by the peculiar practice of Hindoo idolatry, which, more than any other pagan worship, destroys the textures of society, together with compassion for my countrymen, have compelled me to use every possible effort to awaken them from their dream of error: and by making them acquainted with their Scriptures, enable them to contemplate with true devotion the unity and omnipresence of Nature's God.[491]

The Vedanta Sutras and *Upanishads* known to Roy did not mention different kinds of *puja*, or large festivals of his times. On the other hand, *the Puranas, Agamas,* and *Tantras* contained descriptions of these practices in large detail. Because Roy did not want to reject the authority of the latter texts, he faced at least two problems. How to explain the degeneration of the alleged monotheism of *the Vedas*? How to keep the authority of these different texts if some of them are describing at length the practices he

---

[491] "Translation of an Abridgement of the Vedant," in *The English Works of Raja Rammohun Roy*, 1:5.

rejected? The first question was answered for him by the British Orientalists. In the first chapter we could see how the first Orientalist developed ideas about the originally pure monotheism of India. The different gods of the country were originally only personifications of various attributes of the God and of his amazing creations, such as the heavenly bodies. This personification was supposedly only an allegorical expression of the one True God's might and glory. However, people were said to have gradually forgotten the original meaning of the personification and began to regard these gods as real, giving rise to polytheism. This popular idea of the 18th century was projected on Indian traditions by J. Z. Holwell and H. T. Colebrooke.[492] Ram Mohan Roy took these ideas over from the British Orientalists:

> In the most ancient times the inhabitants of this part of the globe (at least the more intelligent class) were not unacquainted with metaphysical subjects; that allegorical language, or description, was frequently employed, to represent the attributes of the Creator, which were sometimes designated as independent existences; and that, however suitable this method might be to the refined understandings of men learning, it had the most mischievous effect when literature and philosophy decayed, producing all those absurdities and idolatrous notions.[493]

We have been following Roy's argumentation which, so far, looks as if it was solely confined to the Christian framework of thought. It looks as if the Bengali reformer accepted the monotheistic idea and because of that, he fiercely fought the Indian idolatry. And yet, as Dermot Killingley noted, this Bengali reformer surprisingly did not refuse *puja* and other ritual practices labelled as "idolatry" altogether.[494] But the importance of this fact was elaborated only by De Roover: Under the word "idolatry," Roy understood something different than Europeans. He considered "idolatrous" practices as acceptable for those who are not able to adore

---

492 This allegorical explanation was applied to the traditions of India by J. Z. Holwell, whose works were very influential at the time of the first British Orientalists, as we saw in the first chapter. T. H. Colebrooke accepted the same explanation as Holwell and Roy took it from Colebrooke later. Compare Holwell, *A Review of the Original Principles, Religions and Moral, of the Ancient Bramins*, especially 110–112, and Colebrooke, *Miscellaneus Essays I*, 110–111, with the following quote.

493 "Translation of the Cena Upanishad," in *The English Works of Raja Rammohun Roy*, 1:49.

494 Dermot Killingley already noted that it had been often wrongly stated that Roy condemned idolatry entirely. Killingley, *The Only True God*, 4, 22.

the invisible Supreme Being. "To him, idol worship is not false, because it is the worship of false gods who deceive their followers and lead them to eternal damnation. It is false only in the sense that it is not acceptable for those competent of worshiping the invisible Supreme Being."[495]

As Jakob De Roover proposed, a close reading of Roy's work reveals surprising distortions of Western ideas. First, I will sum up Roy's dealing with idolatry following De Roover's analysis and then I will examine three other instances of distortions I found. The first is Roy's consent to do "evil in the name of God" for those who do not wish to find about the true God. The second is his extraction of moral teachings of Jesus out of the dogmatic and historical contexts of the New Testament and, the third, Roy's comparison of different levels of worshippers in Christian and Hindu traditions. We will see how the Bengali reformer did not understand the basic framework of the Western ideas about religion, albeit he studied and discussed these ideas for many years.

> I cannot admit that the worship of these attributes under various representations, by means of consecrated objects, has been prescribed by the Veda to the HUMAN RACE; as this kind of worship of consecrated objects is enjoined by the Sastra to those only who are incapable of raising their minds to the notion of an invisible Supreme Being.[496]

On the one hand, it seems that the Western universalism is expressed here, because Roy was assuming *the Vedas* are prescribing something to the whole humankind. On the other hand, he accepted that the worship of the "consecrated objects" is helpful for some kind of people (which goes against the clear-cut division between true and false religion in the Western understanding). Roy continued the idea with his loose translation of the traditional texts, which should have supported his explanation:

> The vulgar look for their God in water; men of more extended knowledge in celestial bodies; the ignorant in wood, bricks, and stones; but learned men in the Universal Soul. Thus corresponding to the nature of different power or qualities, numerous figures have been invented for the benefit of those who are not possessed of sufficient understanding.[497]

---

495 De Roover, "The Colonial Dialogue on Religion."
496 "A Defence of Hindoo Theism," in *The English Works of Raja Rammohun Roy*, 1:96.
497 "A Defence of Hindoo Theism," in *The English Works of Raja Rammohun Roy*, 1:96.

Roy considered the worship of the "Supreme Being" the universal message of *the Vedas*. His description of this special being echoes the Western ideas about its transcendental nature, its creation of the world, etc. It seems that Roy accepted the Christian concept of the true religion, which considers other religions to be polytheistic (paganism). However, how should one reconcile this stance with his approval of the worship of images, which should help people with "limited understanding" and which is better than if these people remained in the "rough condition" without any religious principles?[498] Roy's answer is surprising: The people who are not qualified can gradually purify their minds throughout the worship of images! He basically said that "idolatry" is good for those who have "limited understanding," because these practices would gradually bring them to wish to know God:

> If people who do not yet wish to know God worship these representations instead of God, their minds will become purified and they can then wish to know God; once they know God, however, they have no need to worship representations.[499]

Not only can "idolatrous" practices purify the mind of the less qualified; "by fixing their attention on those invented figures, they may be able to restrain themselves from vicious temptations."[500] This is a truly amazing statement when you compare it with his claims that seemed to accept the Western notion of idolatry as the source of immorality and decay. In the structure of ideas where the concept of idolatry makes sense, it is simply not possible to say that it is the source of immoral behaviour for some and yet the way for purification and moral improvement for others. Christian theological framework does not allow this; either you worship the true God or false gods who are deified heroes at best and the Devil in his seducing activities at worst. The implications within this framework are also either-or: either the true worship resulting in mercy and salvation or the false worship leading to confusion and damnation. Apparently, Roy was not able to grasp this structure of meaning. In order to see the difference more clearly, imagine the following situation: One of the Roy's Unitarian friends in England talks to some villagers in Scotland. When the highly educated Unitarian finds out that the

---

498 "Translation of the Cena Upanishad," in *The English Works of Raja Rammohun Roy*, 1:49.
499 "Reply to a Gosvamin," in Killingley, *The Only True God*, 43.
500 "Translation of the Ishopanishad," in *The English Works of Raja Rammohun Ray*, 1:88.

concept of invisible God and the subtle worshipping of this being is difficult to grasp for these people, he recommends them to keep some of the surviving pagan rituals. He also suggests to carve new idols for sacrifices and ritual dances around them, because in this way, the villagers would purify their minds for later contemplation of the only true God. This would be a ridiculous suggestion even for the liberal Unitarians. As Thomas Rees wrote in the introduction to Roy's book *The Precepts of Jesus*, it is sufficient to look at his strong condemnation of idolatry in India and elsewhere.[501]

I have found other startling examples of Roy's distortion of the Western ideas. The first is his interpretation of "evil" activities that seemed to be sanctioned by the Shastras. Roy's criticism of traditional stories, songs, and dramas connected with Krishna has already been mentioned. It is especially the erotic part of Krishna-lila that horrified many Britons and subsequently Roy as well. I have mentioned that the traditional Vaishnava understanding of erotic Bhakti does not imply that the Vaishnavas should imitate erotic pastimes of their beloved Krishna. About the stories concerning Krishna's dealing with women of Vraja that are sung in *Bhagavata Purana*, Roy said: "For someone who instead of believing in the supreme God longs for women and pleasure, instructions have been provided for worship based on the delights of sex."[502] Similar explanations were given about instructions concerning the ritual use of alcohol, killing goats or other animals, and "doing evil" in different *Tantras* and other texts. Roy concluded:

All these instructions belong to the lower knowledge. But the intention behind them is that all those who are not interested in the true nature of God and who have a natural liking for unclean food, alcohol, erotic talk, violence, and so on, instead of indulging in these abominations as unbelievers, should practice them in the name of God, on the strength of texts quoted above; since if unbelief became widespread, it would be a great disaster for the world.[503]

In short, Roy was advocating in the religious language of the Western framework of ideas that if you are not qualified to worship the one true

501 Thomas Rees was the Secretary of the Unitarian society in Britain. See his introduction in *The Precepts of Jesus*, v–xi.
502 "Preface to the Mandukya Upanisad," in Killingley, *The Only True God*, 27.
503 "Preface to the Mandukya Upanisad," in Killingley, *The Only True God*, 27.

God, you should worship at least the idols. If you have the inclination to immoral, or even criminal acts, you should sin in the name of God! Imagine again the Unitarian friend of the Bengali reformer, who explains to the villagers that it is better to do "evil" activities "in the name of God" than just act badly without belief. In Christianity, including the broad understanding of the Unitarians, you are either doing evil, disobeying God's commandments, and thus in the state of disgrace, or you strive to live in accordance with the Ten Commandments and other morals, and then you are blessed. But how can one do "evil" things "in the name of God?"

The discussed quote proves to be a distortion of the Western understanding of "belief" in connection with the either good or bad actions. From the Christian point of view, a very strange connection has been made. Belief seems to be equal to following the particular injunctions of the Shastras, whatever they are, whereas the opposite of belief means that people do "evil" just because they can. And this should be a greater disaster for the world than immoralities done on the basis of scriptural injunctions! I am not going to delve into the cause of these confusing statements yet. At this moment, I just want to illustrate how Roy's thought missed the Western point and distorted the basic ideas of its framework, where a distinction between good and evil activities makes sense from the doctrinal point of view.[504]

Another example of distortions of the originally clear structure of ideas is Roy's approach to Christological debates. I already mentioned his theological battles with Baptist missionaries of Shrirampur. It is in this case, one might say, that Roy understood the Western framework of ideas very well. He was in agreement with the Unitarian doctrine of Jesus Christ being a human being, not God, and he gave many arguments from the Bible, in the fashion of the most educated Western theologians. Yet again, it is questionable whether Roy understood the foundations of Christological debates and its crucial role in the Western religious thinking well. Let us begin with his lament:

---

504 Objection can be raised on the grounds of the fact that it is Killingley's translation from Roy's original Bengali which I am using for this example of distortion. But Killingley himself strived to translate the texts to English in the very same manner as Roy did. The British scholar explained his efforts to follow Roy's use of words and phrases in a great detail. Following this, I can assume that it is very similar or even the same as if Roy himself had translated the text, as he did with several other works.

I regret only that the followers of Jesus, in general, should have paid much greater attention to inquires after his nature than to the observance of his commandments, when we are well aware that no human acquirements can ever discover the nature even of the most common and visible things, and moreover, that such inquiries are not enjoined by the divine revelation.[505]

Let us consider his claim carefully. *Although Roy participated in the debates about the nature of Christ, at the same time he did not think it was possible to come to any conclusion in this matter.* Moreover, this questioning is "not enjoined by the divine revelation." The last statement was probably in accordance with the arguments of the Unitarians. But even though Roy may have accepted certain ideas from the Christological debate, I still consider his statement to be a good example of distortion. Consider a simple fact: While the nature of Christ had been one of the core issues in the Christian theological debates for centuries, it was both unimportant and insolvable problem for Roy. Here is the difference between his understanding and the ideas of the Unitarians. The conclusion that Jesus was a human being was a solution of the Christological disputes for the Unitarians, the solution arrived at by means of reasoning and critical examination of the New Testament. It was important for them to prove that Jesus was a human being. However, precisely these Christian doctrinal debates were the problem which prevented Roy for a long time to understand "the core" of Christianity, that is the moral teaching of Christ, according to the Bengali reformer's own words. Roy specifically claimed that the metaphysical speculations and historical events could be doubted by different critics, but the moral teaching of Christ could be not.[506]

It is well-known that the debate about the nature of Jesus has been one of the main conflicts in the Christian thought, present from the very beginnings of Christianity. The Unitarian stance was one of the positions in the debate, one possible answer to the important question of Western religious thought. Yet Roy did not consider the debate important. Although his approach to religious matters was often described as rational, in reality, he considered human reason a limited and problematic tool, and not only "while searching for the theological truth."[507] The theme of

---

505 Roy's letter in *The English Works of Raja Rammohun Ray*, 1:346.
506 *The Precepts of Jesus*, xxv–xxviii.
507 See, for example, the introduction to "Translation of the Cena Upanishad," in *The English Works of Raja Rammohun Roy*, 1:50.

the Christological debates and the position of Unitarians in them needs much more elaboration than the focus of this chapter allows.[508] The same is true for the difference between the position of the Unitarians' and Roy's understanding. But one thing is clear: Even though Roy was often credited with his rational approach to these debates in the same way that the Unitarians were, he actually denied that any "human acquirements" could solve the issue.[509]

What was the purpose of his involvement in this discussion, then? He said it clearly: Instead of such a hopeless engagement, people should follow the practical teachings of Christ. The practical recommendations and examples that Jesus gave to the Apostles and to people in general were to Roy the core of Christianity. This was actually the point of controversy created by his book *The Precepts of Jesus, the Guide to Peace and Happiness*. Roy envisioned the book to be a compendium of moral teachings of Jesus that would convince his countrymen about the great value of Christianity. He thought that separating its moral precepts from other issues in the New Testament "will be more likely to produce the desirable effect of improving the hearts and minds of men of different persuasions and different degrees of understanding."[510] However, it is precisely this extracting of practical morality from historical and dogmatic contexts of the New Testament that brought about the heated reactions from Baptist missionaries. Roy was called "injurer of the cause of truth" and "a heathen." Roy's reaction to Joshua Marshman's criticism clearly shows that the Bengali reformer did not understand the framework of Christian ideas.

Baptist missionaries were particularly critical of Roy's presumption that it is possible to separate moral teachings from the dogmas;

---

508 The Christological dilemma is discussed by Balagangadhara, *"The Heathen in His Blindness..."*, 180–185. The critical examinations of the New Testament by the Unitarians were following the disputes in early Christianity. The true nature of Jesus was, as it is well known, one of the central issues in the theological battles between the raising orthodoxy and "heretics" like the Ebionites or Marcion. A concise introduction into the diversity of early Christian opinions concerning the issue offers Bart D. Ehrman, *Lost Christianities: The Battles for Scripture and the Faith We Never Knew* (Oxford: Oxford University Press, 2003). For the internal understanding of the Unitarians, see Earl M. Wilbur, *A History of Unitarianism: Socianism and Its Antecedents* (Cambridge: Harvard University Press, 1945). It is also necessary to contrast Roy's rejection of the possibility to inquire into the nature of "even most common and visible" things with the Western ideas about the "book of Nature." According to the latter, an inquisitive mind can read the laws and will of God in the creation. This idea was very popular especially because of the works of Isaac Newton and it was embraced by the Unitarians.

509 Roy repeated that reason alone is incompetent to solve important problems of "searching for the theological truth," see for example Introduction to the "Translation of the Cena Upanishad," in *The English Works of Raja Rammohun Roy*, 1:50.

510 *The Precepts of Jesus*, xxvii.

they considered this presumption as "radically false." Roy defended his approach by stressing that he understood morals as the fulfilling of "various duties to God, to oneself, and to society."[511] And thus, based on the authority of Jesus, moral precepts must suffice for securing the peace and happiness of mankind, said Roy. How exactly he understood the authority of Jesus is not clear at all. Nevertheless, these moral teachings include "all the revealed law and the whole system of religion adopted by the prophets, re-established and fulfilled by Jesus himself."[512] The controversy reveals several distortions of the Western ideas: Jesus was a great teacher according to Roy, empowered by God perhaps, but no more than that; historical narratives and dogmas concerning the life of Christ were not an important part of the tradition, and as such could be discarded. To him what really mattered was the moral teaching of Jesus, or better to say, practical directions for human conduct. As we shall soon see, the practical principles of human conduct were what Roy understood by the words "religious principles."

Finally, there is Roy's comparison of three levels of worship between Christians and Hindus that proves to be a distortion of Western ideas. The Bengali reformer argued that particular kinds of worship in the Christian and Hindu traditions are on their respective levels the same. According to him, the best worship is that which is performed "in one's thoughts," along with service to others. Such worship believers perform in "God that is in every sense one."[513] On the second and third levels, we find evidently those "less qualified" that I discussed earlier in connection with the theme of idolatry. On those two levels find themselves believers in the Holy Trinity, who can be compared with believers in Rama and other *avatars* of Vishnu. What made the distinction between the last two levels of either Christian or Hindu worshippers for Roy is very interesting. It was the simple fact whether they create "various external images" of Jesus and Rama or not.

At first glance, it is not clear to what extent Ram Mohan dealt with doctrines in this model of three levels of worshippers. He did mention the unity of one God in contrast with the number of divine personalities. But ultimately, these doctrines were not important at all for him; the distinction was made on the grounds of what particular practices looked like—whether they imagine the worshipped deities in mind only

---

511 *The Precepts of Jesus*, 106–107.
512 *The Precepts of Jesus*, 109.
513 "Humble suggestions," in *The English Works of Raja Rammohun Ray*, 1:300.

or in the world perceptible by senses as well. How are we otherwise going to make sense of Roy's conclusive words that "the religious principles of the two last mentioned sects of foreigners are one and the same with those of the two similar sects among Hindoos, although clothed in different garb?"[514]

Roy was obviously missing the particular kind of connection between doctrine and worship in Christianity. True worship can be based only on belief in one true God. All other gods are simply false gods and to worship them means to perform "idolatry." There is no doubt about this theological conclusion. There were attempts made to include the Indian traditions into the large plan of salvation, especially through the interpretation of *praeparatio evangelica*. However, within the Christian framework of understanding the matter, it cannot be stated that worship of a picture of Jesus and worship of a picture of Rama are *exactly* one and the very same kind of worship.[515] If all the above mentioned distortions are summarized, it is therefore doubtful that Roy really did understand the Western belief in one God and in Christ as the "Son of God." However, one thing is becoming clear: "Religious principles" meant to him mainly the specific ways in which people performed their worship, irrespective of their particular beliefs.

The Traditional Indian Framework of Roy's Thoughts

We have discussed several examples of Roy's distortions of fundamental Western concepts such as "idolatry," "worship," "evil," and "religious principles." It is also doubtful whether Roy understood the Western cluster of ideas about the "one true God" and Jesus Christ. This can be a task for a future analysis. Let us now consider the second part of the examined theses, considering what do the examples of Roy's distortions of understanding Western ideas tell us about the traditional Indian thought. Let us suppose that the distortions of this Western cluster of ideas were made on the grounds of another, traditional Indian frame of understanding. This framework had its own specific structure of ideas bound together in a cluster that was intelligible for members of Indian culture. Following

---

514 "Humble suggestions," in *The English Works of Raja Rammohun Ray*, 1:301.
515 I am very well aware of the Protestant criticism of Catholic use of paintings and statues in churches. But if you consider the debates carefully, their focus suports the argument about Roy's incomprehension of the meaning of idolatry in Western religious thought.

Roy's distortions, we can propose some of the characteristics of his native Indian structure of ideas.

Let me first summarise what we have learnt about Roy's understanding of worship from his distortions of Western ideas. There is worship with the use of material images, or forms, and worship without them. Albeit necessary for some people, the first kind of practice is not the best thing to do, but much better than to "let them remain idle."[516] There are different levels of worship accordingly, and also the goals attained by the means of practice at the respective levels are different, as the Bengali reformer clearly stated:

> Passages recommending the worship by means of form and passages dissuading from such worship should be separately applied to those who entertain different sentiments.[517]

According to the Bengali reformer, different ways of worship lead to different outcomes:

> After death, this class of devotees enjoys eternal beauty in the highest heaven. . . . . While those worshipping by means of form, as the Vedanta affirms, enjoy only temporary bliss.[518]

Thus, when Ram Mohan Roy spoke about "idolatry," he actually meant particular ritual practices that are appropriate for some people. It is clear from his descriptions that it was *puja*, *abhisheka*, and other rituals in the same form as we know them even today. What should the best worship, or the highest level of it, look like? He described it as "adoration of the Supreme Being in one's thoughts,"[519] meaning a variety of practices from "meditation on the soul being of divine origin"[520] to recitation of the *Gayatri mantra* or *Pranava* (Om).[521]

---

516 "Abridgement of the Vedant," in *The English Works of Raja Rammohun Ray*, 1:17.

517 "Translation of the Sunskrit Tract on the Different Modes of Worship," in *The English Works of Raja Rammohun Roy*, 1:295–296.

518 "Translation of the Sunskrit Tract on the Different Modes of Worship," in *The English Works of Raja Rammohun Roy*, 1:294.

519 "Second Defence of the Monotheistical System of the Veds," in *The English Works of Raja Rammohun Roy*, 1:154.

520 "Translation of the Sunskrit Tract on the Different Modes of Worhsip," in *The English Works of Raja Rammohun Roy*, 1:294.

521 "Prescript for Offering Supreme Worship by Means of the Gayutree," in *The English Works of Raja Rammohun Roy,* 1:113–122; see also Robertson, *Raja Ram Mohan Ray*, 132.

From all this we can make a preliminary conclusion that Roy was above all concerned with ritual and meditative practices suitable for different kinds of people. Inevitably, we are coming to the issue of the relationship between practices and doctrines, or beliefs. Although it looks at the first sight that the three kinds of worshippers are discerned by their various doctrines, the closer analysis of the characterizations of these kinds of worship reveal a different picture: *Ram Mohan Roy discerned the different kinds of worshippers according to different practices.* The crucial point was whether they used any image for their rituals and meditative practices or not. The same criterion was used by Roy to compare different Indian traditions and Christian practices, without giving much importance to their particular beliefs.

We should connect this insight with the fact that the traditional Indian thought enabled Roy to separate the principles of moral conduct form the Christian doctrines. Beliefs (doctrinal content) are a subject of the critical analysis and therefore, they can be changed or rejected, whereas the principles of human behaviour are a really important part of any religion, according to him. These principals of conduct were the basic criterion for a "searching person" to discern between different religions, whereas doctrinal controversies were not important:

> To those who are not biased by prejudice . . . a simple enumeration and statement of the respective tenets of different sects may be a sufficient guide to direct their inquires in ascertaining which of them is the most consistent with the sacred traditions, and most acceptable to common sense. For these reasons I decline entering into any discussion on those points (i.e. doctrinal controversies, M. F.), and confine my attention at present to the task of laying before my fellow-creatures the words of Christ (i.e. moral principles, M. F.).[522]

Let us summarize our findings so far: The traditional Indian framework of thought enabled Roy to separate the principles of human conduct from the doctrinal context and to compare Christian and Hindu worship on the basis of external observances or non-observances of certain activities without really considering the difference in doctrines. We can derive from this finding that *Roy's traditional Indian thinking either did not*

---

[522] *The Precepts of Jesus*, xxvii. Roy's use of words "tenets" and "words of Christ" may seem confusing in this quotation, but from the context it is clear that by both expressions he meant moral principles or a code of behaviour.

connect doctrines to practices or it did, but in a way very different to the Western Christian framework of thought. How would it be otherwise possible to freely change or even discard doctrines without any impact on practices and morality? How can any "earnest-minded investigator of the science of comparative religion" just compare practices of different religious groups without considering the differences between their doctrines? How can you consider principles of moral conduct to be the essence of Christianity and resign to the very possibility to find out who Jesus was?

I find the best available explanation in the work of S. N. Balangangadhara. This scholar explained the crucial difference in the connection of beliefs and practices between Western Christianity and the Indian traditions. While in the Western framework of thought worship is understood as an expression of belief, Indian culture did not develop this connection. In order to explain this and other questions of modern research, Balangangadhara developed a thesis of the specific configuration of knowledge characterising the Indian culture. According to this thesis, each culture develops several different ways of dealing with humans and the world, that is, of "going about the world." These ways are a theoretical knowledge, a performative knowledge, or songs, poetry, and other forms of arts. In each culture all these ways of going about the world are present, but in a different constellation. Usually one particular way is dominant and the others are subordinated to it. Imagine a culture where performative knowledge subordinates other kinds of knowledge, including doctrines as a kind of theoretical knowledge. The Indian culture can be characterised as such a configuration of learning where practices themselves dominate as the way to access knowledge, to get to know the world, and to learn more about it. And consequently, Indian thought has the following particular characteristics:

> Performative knowledge must subordinate other kinds of knowledge. That is to say that the subject of considerations must be the actions of treating the world and the people in it; the purpose of thinking is to improve these actions; but because these activities are the dominant ones in this configuration, thinking about these actions does not provide the foundation of treating the world, on the contrary, it serves as its critic.[523]

---

523 Balangangadhara, *"The Heathen in His Blindness..."*, 412. It is necessary to read the whole part of Balangangadhara's book to understand the argumentation properly; because of the focus of this chapter I am taking just one part of his arguments.

Roy's distortions of Western framework of thoughts, caused by his traditional Indian thinking can be explained in this way. As we have seen, the main focus of his contemplations and writing was indeed on practices, because he was concerned with the following questions: Which ritual and meditative practices are the best for this or that kind of people; what goals can be achieved by different kinds of "worship"; what kind of behaviour can his fellow countrymen learn from the moral teachings of Christ; what kind of "evil" and "good" activities are described in the Shastras, and to what purpose they should serve. As Roy explicitly stated many times, his aim was to improve the actions taken by his fellow countrymen, a fact that was undoubted by his contemporaries. Obviously, his thought functioned as a critic of practices as such. The only departure from Indian tradition was Roy's effort to provide for a doctrine as the foundation for going about the world in order to support his preference of certain "modes of worship." His new interpretation of Vedanta would have been this "basic doctrine" as it clearly followed the British cluster of ideas. It is no wonder that the traditional Vedanta scholars of his time rejected it.

To conclude: It is reasonable to see Roy's ideas and work as an honest effort to embrace the Christian Unitarian framework of ideas and practices by which he hoped to improve the life of people in India. In this Unitarian manner, he reinterpreted Vedanta and tried to reform his contemporaries. Hence Roy's support in the banning of *sati* by the decree of the East India Company, his support for the introduction of the British model of education in Bengal, his engagement in the debates about the property law, enthusiastic writing for the newspapers, etc. However, although the Bengali reformer strived to understand the Western conceptual framework of religion, his distortions of fundamental Western ideas such as "worship," "idolatry," and "evil" prove that he could not understand them.

The analysis of these distortions is a promising way to understand the traditional Indian framework of thought. Roy's distortions indicate the fundamentally different Indian understanding of the activities that Westerners explained as "worship," "idolatry," "prayer," etc. They also indicate a different relationship between practices and doctrines, or beliefs, in Roy's culture.

I have briefly shown that it actually supports Balagangadhara's theses about cultures as configurations of learning. Indian culture can be understood as a configuration of learning where the performative knowledge as such dominates other kinds of knowledge. As a consequence,

Ram Mohan Roy was concerned with thinking about practices of his contemporary Bengali society. This is why he could disconnect doctrines from practices in a way unacceptable within the Western framework of religion. This is the reason why he did not understand the concepts of "worship," "idolatry," and others. And why his effort to provide a reinterpretation of Vedanta as the foundation for the best practices was almost unanimously rejected by his Indian contemporaries but celebrated in the West. Analysis of more examples of Roy's distortions of the Western ideas about religion with special attention to the relationship between doctrines and practices in his writings is therefore a promising direction to achieve a better understanding of the traditional Indian thought.

Conclusions

If all (or even most) individual descriptions of some non-Western culture
exhibit a common structure or a shared pattern, then this structure
or pattern allows us to formulate questions for research that reveal
the nature of the Western culture.
S. N. Balagangadhara

We began with the question: What role did the European religious
thought play in the explanation of Indian culture? Another question
followed: How does the religious conceptualisation of a remote culture
enable us to understand its differences? *At this stage of research, I can only*
confirm the conclusions of Balagangadhara's analyses: European explanation
of "the other" creates, in fact, only a picture of "just another," a shadow of the
Europeans' understanding of themselves and the world. The conceptualisation
of Indian traditions as a religion is one of the most significant processes that
have led to this intercultural misunderstanding. This explanation of Indian
traditions was shaped within the structures of originally Christian theological framework, which is hardly explicit and not easily recognizable
in the humanities and social sciences today. Despite the secularization
of European thought, the structures of theological ideas laid the basis
for our research questions and also told us where and how to look for
answers to these questions.

The themes discussed in the individual chapters brought particular problems of the originally theological foundations of our theorizing Indian culture to light. First, I was testing the validity of Balagangadhara's observations regarding the problems of explaining the Indian

traditions as Hinduism and Buddhism in the Czech Indological scholar-ship. I found out that the Czech Indologists shared the same fundamental structure of religious interpretations with the first British Orientalists, although especially the last generation of the Czech scholars did not know their works much.[524] The same structure of ideas and the concomitant problems are clearly pointing towards the roots of Western Indology, which needs to be analysed from the following perspective: *William Jones and other founders of modern Oriental Studies adopted the theological questions of their predecessors.* In this way, they continued the explanation of Indian traditions as religious and many other Western scholars elaborated this basic line of explanation. In addition, I argued that Western historiography is also anchored in the structures of the theological paradigm much more than it might appear at first sight. In this sense, the history of India is a European construct that does not enable us to understand the traditional Indian approach to their past.

I discussed how the formation of the Aryan Invasion Theory was fundamentally shaped by theological assumptions and questions. The constructionist argument regarding the dialogue between the British colonisers and the native scholars was considered in the case of Ram Mohan Roy. I argued that the Bengali scholar's understanding of Western thinking cannot be taken for granted as it has been done so far. Despite his sincere efforts, he failed to understand the fundamental concepts of European theological thought. However, the specific nature of his misunderstanding is the starting point of an analysis that offers insights into traditional Indian thought. Before suggesting several implications of these debates for further research, let me summarize the most important findings of each chapter.

1) *For more than eighty years, the Czech school of Indology has been basically repeating the same explanation of Indian traditions because it has failed to reflect upon the influence of the Christian theological thought properly.* The religion of India is defined by the doctrine of the law of Karman, rebirth, and the search for liberation from the cycle of lives. Czech Indologists considered the Vedic corpus and especially the *Upanishads* to be the basic

---

524 However, the earlier links between Czech Indologists' and British Orientalists' ideas can be easily documented. For example, V. Lesný and his pupil D. Zbavitel referred to earlier works by F. M. Müller, A. B. Keith, V. A Smith, and other scholars. Czech school did understandably derive even more from the German scholarship of H. von Glasenapp, M. Winternitz, and other German Indologists. I did not follow the influence of the French and other Western nations' Orientalism on the Czech Orientalists' work, which remains as one of the possible directions for a future research.

sacred scriptures of India. They also included the *Manava-dharmashastra* and other texts of similar nature among the sacred scriptures of the subcontinent. The Brahmins are said to be Hindu priests who have been jealously guarding their spiritual monopoly and their supreme position at the top of the social hierarchy for over three thousand years. Buddhists and other ascetic traditions, which allegedly started as a protest against the Brahminical orthodoxy, were gradually absorbed into the Brahminical system and thus effectively marginalised. Hinduism is to be understood as a socio-religious system. Although Buddhism successfully resists attempts at defining it, Czech Indologists spoke of it as a religion, mentioning the well-known paradox of a "religion without God."

These explanations have been criticised here and evidence has been provided for the fact that the "Hindus" of India lack conditions for establishing and maintaining such an orthodoxy. Many "Hindus" do not believe in the law of Karman and do not strive to be liberated from the cycle of lives. Remarkably, as early as the 18th century, there is evidence that a great number of Brahmins did not know *the Vedas* nor *the Upanishads*. However, the discussion yielded an important insight into Indian traditions. Horace H. Wilson and others noted that the usage of Sanskrit or other texts emphasised correct recitation and singing; however, there was little or no interest in their meaning for the dominant use in ritual. This evidence should lead us to reconsidering the relation between practices and their explanations, which is apparently different from the Christian basis of practice in orthodoxy.

Other argument concerns the misunderstanding of the role of Brahmins. Many Brahmins do not make their living as "priests." It is also not true that they exercise a monopoly on rituals, meditative practices, or other "spiritual" matters. There is neither a representative pan-Indian Brahmin organisation nor a central authority even for all the Brahminical *jatis*. Such circumstances make it hard to imagine what constitutes the supposed defining doctrinal and societal elements of Hinduism. According to the testimony of the *Pali Canon*, the Buddhist tradition engaged in the pan-Indian discussions about the ideal of a true Brahmin, which certainly does not support the idea of a Buddhist "revolt" against the priestly class. There is also another evidence that the Buddha did not fight against the social organisation that the Europeans call the caste system. He acquired a great number of ascetic followers who lived outside of society. However, the Buddha's "lay" disciples remained within the so-called caste system, living in accordance with contemporary traditions.

I found the Czech Indologists' argumentation vague and inconsistent oftentimes, such as Dušan Zbavitel's attempt at explaining the role of Brahmins or Miltner's ideas about the nature of Buddhism. Zbavitel contradicted himself, for example, by first describing the great power of the Brahmins as the basic feature of Hinduism and then admitting that the Brahmins only have a consulting role in the decision-making processes of the village *panchayats*. Vladimír Miltner offered three different explanations in succession as to what Buddhism should be: a peculiar religion, a religion that "cannot be simply defined as religion," and finally, a profoundly humanist philosophy. Such and other problems of the Czech discussions on Indian traditions do not differ fundamentally from those of many other Western explanations. Interestingly, Czech scholarship after the World War II maintained the same structures of thinking about Indian traditions across the whole range of opinions. This basic structure of the explanation of Indian traditions is the same in the works of positivist Orientalists, Marxists, and Christian theologians. None of them has questioned the understanding of Indian traditions as religious, although they differ in their treatment of specific topics.[525]

My analysis of the Czech Indological production confirms Balagangadhara's hypothesis that the explanation of Indian traditions as religion has resulted from shared, albeit not properly reflected structures of the theological ideas among various European nations. If the Czech descriptions are practically identical to the British ones and share the same kind of problems, Said's focus on the relationship between colonial power and Oriental Studies becomes secondary here. On the other hand, his hint about the continuity of theological thought from the earlier representations of the "Orient" to the works of the first British Orientalists and further is of fundamental importance.

2) It was necessary to look deeper into the past in order to explain the origins of the problems with concepts of Hinduism and Buddhism. Therefore, the first chapter also described an important formative stage

---

525 It is true that some Czech scholars considered this or that school of Indian thought to be materialistic, hence, outside of the scope of religious thought. Thus, for example, Egon Bondy explained the Budhha's original teaching as a kind of materialistic dialectics. However, these debates did not change the basic religious explanation of the Indian traditions which has been discussed in this book. In fact, even though some schools of the traditional Indian thought might have been considered materialistic, they generally were absorbed into major religious mainstream of Hinduism, Buddhism, or other "religions" of India in the Czech understanding. This was allegedly also the case with the original Buddha's teaching in the perspective of Egon Bondy (Zbyněk Fišer).

in the development of the religious interpretation of Indian traditions. It had to do with the emergence of British Oriental Studies in India since around 1760 to 1880. Although the first British Orientalists are often praised as the founders of an objective discipline, they actually asked theologically formed questions and the aims of their research were also primarily theological. Their conceptualization of Indian traditions betrays a biblical structure: Since the moment of creation, God endowed every human being with a rudimentary relationship towards Himself. After the Flood, Noah's descendants dispersed all over the world. India is said to have been settled by a nation or tribe of Brahmins, a priestly group similar to the descendants of Levi among the Jews. The testimony of their ancient religion had been enshrined in *the Vedas*. Holwell's, Dow's, Jones', and Colebrooke's main aim was to identify a precise doctrinal content in the supposedly sacred texts of the Indians. They searched them for proofs of their own religious belief, i.e. traces of "primitive monotheism."

Within the theological paradigm, *the Vedas* and *the Upanishads* appeared to be among the oldest surviving evidence regarding the state of religion in the aftermath of the Flood. In the European eyes, they thus acquired the status of the most important sacred texts of Indian religion. The central question of the research remained—until the times of Horace H. Wilson, M. Monier-Williams and F. M. Müller—whether *the Vedas* represented the primordial monotheism or its degeneration into idolatry. However, all the British Orientalists of the period in question thought that contemporary Indian traditions represent the latter. Although they admired some ideas and characters of India, those would only belong to the ancient times. The pattern of decline and split of the originally one true religion which supposedly started with *the Vedas* became the basis for characterising the historical stages of Indian "religions": Vedism, Brahmanism, and Hinduism. I showed how was this scheme created especially in the works of H. H. Wilson and M. Monier-Williams. It is noteworthy that this explanation of religious history of India is the dominant description until today, although different challenges has been raised against it.

However, how was it possible to explain the degeneration of the originally pure monotheism? Holwell's answer was an invented story about Brahmin priests who replaced the original scripture with their forgery. He painted a vivid picture of power-mongering priests controlling the poor believers. The 'Brahmin forgery' remained an important topic for Jones' successors Thomas Maurice, Horace H. Wilson, and other

Europeans. The power-hungry priestly class became an ever repeated explanation of the emergence of the caste system and its functioning in India until today. However, the British Orientalists did not invent this interpretation; they continued a centuries old representation of the Brahmins as priests in European literature.

The ideas of the primordial monotheism of the Indians were not created by the British Orientalists either. There were medieval speculations about how many members of the Holy Trinity the Brahmins knew, whether they knew God the Father, the Ten Commandments, and so on. If William Jones found that the Upanishadic teaching confirmed his belief in one God the Creator, the Jesuit Roberto Nobili saw the true God in the Upanishadic concept of *brahma* more than one hundred and fifty years before Jones. Catholics and Protestants alike projected their beliefs based on the book of Genesis into Indian texts. The Deist tendencies of the Enlightenment scholars did not change much in this respect. When the British Orientalists embarked on their studies in the last third of the 18th century, the image of Indian religion had got its basic structure already. Jones' research aimed at discovering the primordial religion as well as the primordial arts, sciences, and language of humankind after the Flood, as was presupposed in the Biblical exegesis of history. *Said was therefore correct in suspecting that the first generations of British Orientalists did not create any fundamental change in this explanation. The theological structure of the explanation of Indian traditions remained intact in modern Oriental Studies.* In the works of Friedrich Max Müller, Monier Monier-Williams, and others, it also became part of the nascent religious studies and other humanities.

3) The basic structure of ideas in European historiography adopted all the important ideas that stemmed from the theological paradigm: the framework of the global chronicle along with the single linear chronology which expresses the progress of human history towards a desired goal. A basic act of historiography is to date events and place them on the temporal axis. Belief in the specific character of each particular period remains, based as it was, on the ideas of divine pedagogy and the exegetical principle of accommodation. The ideas of *translatio imperii* and *translatio studii* keeps reappearing in various interpretations of history to this date, e.g. in the diffusionist model of the spread of civilisation. A specific legacy of ancient apologetics is the strongly historical nature of doctrines, bound up with the figure of Jesus. The European narrative derives its truth value from the events having really occurred, whereas this does not have to be a criterion at all in the Indian narrative as we

have seen in the discussion about the truthfulness of *Ramayana* stories. The works of William Jones, James Mill, Georg Friedrich Hegel, and others contain also a problematic idea of the contrast between freedom and "oriental despotism." The alleged freedom and reasonable form of government in the Western countries was pitched against the idea of theocratic or aristocratic rule over masses of misguided people. In this view, the degenerated Hindu religion is a tool for enslaving people.

The controversy over the ancient Indians' historical consciousness or lack thereof is misguiding. Instead of piling evidence which should support one of the stances in this debate, we should step back and ask how and why historiography developed in the West. European historiography is constrained by the structures of Christian theological paradigm so much that it can hardly capture the traditional Indian treatment of memories of the past. The polarity between true history and myth has constrained the understanding of human past since the emergence of the Christian historical thinking and this framework does not allow us to even consider a possibility of an entirely different approach to the past. *European historiography dismisses any different understanding of the past as sheer myth that may at best contain a historical core.* The Indians had, and some communities still have, a very different way of dealing with the past, as the anthropological research of rural areas testify. Our universalising history represents a specifically European way of rewriting a very different understanding of the past by warping it to fit structures of ideas that are alien to Indian traditions. In this sense, the history of India is indeed a European legacy to modern India. In order to understand the Indian treatment of the past better, a different type of research is needed. This research will analyse the role of stories seriously and it will not relegate them to a sphere of myths, legends, or fantasies.

4) What is the result of the discussion about the Aryan Invasion Theory? From its whole structure, only one single well established claim remained: The relatedness of the Indo-European languages has been convincingly established, independent of any other than linguistic analysis. In the terms of the history of science, it is an interesting fact that the fundamental insights which made the scientific comparison of the Indo-European languages possible came from the traditional Indian grammatical thought. Although the other parts of its explanation, i.e. the reconstruction of a proto-Indo-European language and the localisation of this hypothetical language speakers' homeland are ultimately based on the Biblical tree model of the spread of peoples after the Flood, there is currently no better theory. Moreover, the model remains

as the foundation upon which both AIT advocates and proponents of the autochthonous origin of the Aryans build their arguments. Both theories contain the problematic conjunction of religion and language as the main characteristics of human groups.

The development of the AIT is a good example of the problems that modern philosophy of science has pointed out: A) a strong exemplum—the discovery of the Indo-European family of languages and later that of the different Dravidian language group were interpreted in the light of the presupposed idea of a priestly tribes' invasion of India; B) all subsequent findings were interpreted in the same vein while a quantitatively small number of facts was employed to prove the theory, including the dubious translations of some Vedic passages or the problematic interpretation of archaeological discoveries, for example, the Cemetery H at Harappa. Significantly, the discovery of the advanced Indus Valley Civilisation could not falsify the theory. For example, immediately after the publication of some of the first findings, G. V. Childe produced three different interpretations in order to integrate the new facts into the current theory. Some time later, Bedřich Hrozný inserted a Dravidian invasion between the assumed two Indo-European invasions so that he would not have to abandon the widespread contemporary belief about the primitive state of the Dravidians. This belief was rooted in the diffusionist idea of the originally only source of advanced civilisation in the West.

5) My discussion of Ram Mohan Roy's ideas about religion is an attempt to find a better way of understanding Indian traditions. Is it at all possible to transcend the limitations created by the European self-understanding of the culture that was consequently projected on the Indian "other?" This new way consists of testing the hypothesis that the encounters between Europeans and Indians result in a mutual distortion of the other's thought structures. It is not a matter of arbitrary wilfulness, but an encounter of two very different traditions of thought. If we wish to study Indian traditions, we shall focus on the way Indians have distorted European concepts by exhibiting a fundamental lack of understanding of the connections between them. These concepts are bound together in a very specific way, which creates a larger structure of ideas within which each concept acquires a specific meaning. It can be shown that Ram Mohan's distortions of these concepts are systematic, based on the traditional Indian structures of thought. In this way, the patterns of Indian thinking can be detected and analysed. Rather than an obstacle to understanding, such analyses of the distorted ideas will open a way towards a fruitful intercultural dialogue.

Although there are several reasons to say that Roy adopted the Unitarian worldview, a closer examination of his texts has revealed a fundamental lack of understanding of the Western religious concepts. On the one hand, the Bengali reformer vehemently protested against the negative impact of "idolatry" on Hindus. On the other hand, he thought that the "worship" of images or statues was beneficial to "less qualified" people. It is clear that Roy did not understand the structure of European Christian thought that endowed the term "idolatry" with its meaning. He opined that "evil" deed was better carried out in the name of God than in other ways, because people at a certain level of development needed such practices. Accordingly, he divided "worshippers" into two categories: those who do not make any representations of the deity (not even in their mind) and those who do. These are two levels of the path of those who seek knowledge of the *brahma*. Furthermore, he divided the people who need some representations for worship into two subsequent grades: the higher grade represents those who worship images only in their mind and the lower grade consists of those who make material representations.

This typology enabled him to compare Christian and Indian worshippers without attributing any significance to the doctrines that those "worshippers" profess. He separated Jesus' ethical teachings from the question of who Jesus was and he evidently did not grasp the significance of the Christological controversies in the West. His debate with the Baptists appears to merely defend the Unitarian position in Christological issues, but after closer analysis, I have argued that Ram Mohan Roy actually considered this question unimportant and hardly solvable. In his view, the essence of Christianity was Jesus' ethical teachings. These distortions reveal deeply rooted Indian thinking which does not ground practices in a belief system as we are used to doing in Europe. *Therefore, research of distortions of thought structures that occur in the dialogue on both sides is paradoxically a step forward towards a better intercultural understanding.*

From all these particular points, several interesting observations can be made and their consequences considered. Firstly, we have seen how within the Orientalist paradigm, certain questions were asked and others not. And even more importantly, questions about the very questions pursued by the researchers were seldom raised. Concerning the first point, there is a close link between the framework of reference, sources used, and the questions asked. When the Western scholars ponder about the original belief system of *the Vedas*, about Brahminical monopoly in religious matters, or about Upanishadic Atman being akin to the Christian debates of human soul, they adopt the whole framework of Christian ideas which are needed in order to have any meaningful debate of these matters. All these questions presuppose the validity of Christian assumptions about many issues involved. Consider the finding of the first chapter as an example. Unless the assumptions are recognized, it is puzzling why (not only the Czech) Orientalists' descriptions of the doctrinal core of Indian traditions keep the basic inconsistency over many decades: On the one hand, Hinduism should have the most liberal doctrinal system imaginable, because the Hindus are not obliged to believe literally anything. Even agnosticism, Marxism, or atheism are suggested as acceptable beliefs for the Hindus. On the other hand, the trio Atman, law of Karman, and reincarnation keep the central role in the Western explanations. They truly became the core beliefs of Hinduism. Why should have such inconsistency remained in the dominant explanation for centuries by now?

The typical answer aimed at the elusive nature of the alleged Hindu doctrines; and sometimes this served also as an illustration of the amazing ability of the "cunning Brahminhood" to incorporate every and any belief into their "monstrous" system. However, if we consider the question itself, a different explanation of problems at hand emerges. These are Westerners who need to know a doctrinal core of other peoples' religion in order to understand them. These are Christians who have been assuming for centuries that there is basically one Paganism all around the globe, with basically one Pantheon of gods and godesses, which must have the same kind of impact on thinking of its adherents. In other words, there must be a search for the one true God in each and every human soul, expressed also in the form of Paganism. Whether the Western findings in India were explained by degeneration, evolutionary models of religion, or by other means, they presupposed the truth of many such ideas. With all these interconnected assumptions, it is a must to try and find out about the doctrines of other people in order to understand them. It is hard to imagine the possibility of a very different cultural world, where doctrines are playing a different role than in the West or where they are absent in the sense we talk of doctrines in Europe. And much harder to make any serious research into. Therefore, the Orientalist paradigm needs to keep the description of the core beliefs of Hinduism (or other "Indian religions"), however problematic and inconsistent it is. It does not matter, if respective scholars reject the strong criticism of earlier Christian missionaries and call for more sensitive approach to "Hindu beliefs and practices." The basic framework of ideas remains.

It is also possible to draw some preliminary conclusions regarding the relationship of theory and observation in the Orientalist paradigm. The theoretical assumptions of the originally theological ideas shaped what could be observed in a fundamental way. Roberto Nobili found the biblical God in the *Upanishads* as did the first British Orientalists one hundred and fifty years later. In less clear form, many scholars until today speculate about the transcendence of *brahma*. Linguistic competence was by no means a decisive or particularly determining factor in the lack of reflection about the basic assumptions of such a theorizing. Holwell and Dow had no knowledge of Sanskrit. Jones was well-versed in the language, but he became familiar with the *Upanishads* and studied them for a long time via a Persian translation. Judging by Wilson's translation of the *Vishnu Purana* and other texts, Horace H. Wilson apparently knew Sanskrit better than Jones. Despite these differences, all of them looked at the Indian traditions in the light of Christian narrative about the one true God and his peculiar way of communication with different people. In the same way, they perceived the supposed degeneration of the "primordial monotheism" which was thought to have been caused by the Brahmins' textual forgeries. These ideas are not just a collection of random concepts, rather the opposite; they form specific structures of ideas which are meaningful only in such connections and hardly in others. These structures created a deep layer, or foundation, of many scholarly debates which ensued over the last two centuries. We can visualize some later developments as the next layers of ideas, much closer to the surface of the totality of our current debates. Take the theory of degeneration, or the evolution of religion in India as an example. It rests on the set of earlier assumptions about the search of people for the biblical God, but it also became an "of course" grounds for many other discussions.

About non-questioning the questions which are guiding the research into traditions of India: Problems with the concepts of Christian theological framework were hinted, here and there, but these hints were usually not developed into a systematic critique of the whole background of Christian ideas behind the understanding of Indian traditions. Why is that? Is it because the sense of cumulative progress in the studies of India, by which I mean understandable appreciation of the enormous amount of the historical, ethnological, and other facts about the "Oriental other," is blinding many scholars towards the problems in the fundaments of the dominant explanations? Is it also because the postmodern thought has shaken the earlier confidence in building a large theory, which brought about a wide-spread resignation on any larger theorizing? Many other disturbing questions emerge with the insights we have gained so far. On the one hand, we should strive for better analysis of the secularization of the European thought, because it evidently did not free itself from the grip of Christian theological assumptions. On the other hand, let us reconsider the theoretical thought which grounds other concepts in the description of different cultures. We often used them in a good faith that these concepts are "general," "neutral," or even "scientific" tools for analysing the other. Law as a provision and execution of justice is one such concept; the link between worship of god(s) and morality another. How did the colonized people and their daughters and sons of the decolonized world understand such concepts? How have they been applying them in the organization and rule of their contemporary societies? Our answers to these questions will be crucial for both Europe and India in the changing world of the 21st century.

Bibliography

Almond, Philip C. *The British Discovery of Buddhism*. Cambridge: Cambridge University Press, 1988.

App, Urs. *The Birth of Orientalism*. Philadelphia: University of Pennsylvania Press, 2010.

App, Urs. *William Jones's Ancient Theology*. Sino-Platonic Papers 191. Philadelphia: University of Pennsylvania Press.

Appleby, Joyce, Lynn Hunt, and Margaret Jacob. *Telling the Truth about History*. New York: W. W. Norton, 1994.

Arvidsson, Stefan. *Aryan Idols: Indo-European Mythology as Ideology and Science*. Chicago: University of Chicago Press, 2006.

Balagangadhara, S. N. *"The Heathen in His Blindness . . ." Asia, the West and the Dynamic of Religion*. Leiden: Brill, 1994.

Balagangadhara, S. N. *"The Heathen in His Blindness . . ." Asia, the West and the Dynamic of Religion*. 2nd ed. New Delhi: Manohar, 2005.

Balagangadhara, S. N. *Reconceptualizing India Studies*. New Delhi: Oxford University Press, 2012.

Balagangadhara, S. N. "Translation, Interpretation and Culture." Unpublished article (2012).

Balagangadhara, S. N. "What Do Indians Need: A History or the Past," http://xyz4000 .wordpress.com/2012/02/16/what-do-indians-need-a-history-or-the-past-s-n -balagangadhara.

Basham, Arthur L., ed. *A Cultural History of India*. 10th ed. New Delhi: Oxford University Press, 1996.

Bhaktivedanta Swami Prabhupada, A. C. *Srimad Bhagavatam. Third Canto, Part One*. 2nd ed. Los Angeles: Bhaktivedanta Book Trust, 1993.

Bhaktivedanta Swami Prabhupada, A. C. *Srimad Bhagavatam. Seventh Canto*. 2nd ed. Los Angeles: Bhaktivedanta Book Trust, 1993.

Bharati, Agehananda. *Hindu Views and Ways and the Hindu-Muslim Interface*. New Delhi: Munshiram Manoharlal, 1981.

Blaut, James M. *The Colonizer's Model of the World. Geographical Diffusionism and Eurocentric History*. New York: Guilford Press, 1993.

Bondy, Egon. *Indická filosofie* [Indian philosophy]. Prague: Vokno, 1991.

Boublík, Vladimír. *Teologie mimokřesťanských náboženství* [Theology of the non-Christian religions]. Prague: Karmelitánské nakladatelství, 2000.

Bowler, Peter J. *The Invention of Progress: The Victorians and the Past.* London: B. Blackwell, 1989.

Brooks, Douglas R. "The Thousand-Headed Person: The Mystery of Hinduism and the Study of Religion in the AAR." *Journal of the American Academy of Religion* 62, no. 4 (1994): 1111–1126.

Burrow, T. "The Early Aryans." In *A Cultural History of India,* edited by A. L. Basham, 20–29. Oxford: Clarendon Press, 1996.

Butterfield, Herbert. *Man on His Past: The Study of the History of Historical Scholarship.* Cambridge: Cambridge University Press, 1955.

Chakrabarty, Dilip K. "The Aryan Hypothesis in Indian Archaeology." *Indian Studies: Past and Present* 9 (1968): 343–358.

Chakrabarty, Dilip K. "Power, Politics and Ariya Mayai or 'Aryan Illusion' in the study of Indian History." Position paper at the 2nd Roundtable session *Rethinking Religion in India II.* New Delhi, January 2009.

Chesnut, Glenn F. *The First Christian Histories: Eusebius, Socrates, Sozomen, Theodret and Evagrius.* 2nd ed. Macon, GA: Mercer University Press, 1986.

Childe, Gordon V. *The Aryans: A Study of Indo-European Origins.* London: Kegan Paul, Trench, Trubner, 1926.

Childe, Gordon V. *New Light on the Most Ancient East.* New York: D. Appleton-Century Company, 1934.

Cohn, Bernard. "The Pasts of an Indian Village." In *Time: Histories and Ethnologies,* edited by Diane Owen Hughes and Thomas R. Trautmann: 21–30. 4th ed. Ann Arbor: University of Michigan Press, 1998.

Colebrooke, Henry T. "On Ancient Monuments, Containing Sanscrit Inscriptions." *Asiatic Researches* 9 (1807): 398–444.

Colebrooke, Henry T. "On the Philosophy of the Hindus. Prat I." *Transactions of the Royal Asiatic Society of Great Britain and Ireland* 1 (1824): 19–43.

Colebrooke, Henry T. *Miscellaneous Essays.* Vol. 1. London: W. H. Allen, 1837.

Collet, Sophia Dobson. *The Life and Letters of Raja Rammohun Roy.* 3rd ed. Calcutta: Sadharan Brahmo Samaj, 1962.

Dales, G. F. "The Mythical Massacre at Mohenjo-Daro." *Expedition* 6, no. 3 (1964): 36–43.

Deák, Dušan. *Indický svätci medzi minulosťou a prítomnosťou. Hľadanie hinduistov a muslimov v Južnej Ázii* [Indian sages between the past and present: On seeking for Hindus and Muslims in South Asia]. Trnava: Univerzita Sv. Cyrila a Metoda, 2010.

Deliyannis, Deborah M. *Historiography in the Middle Ages.* Leiden: Brill, 2003.

De Mauro, Tulio, and Lia Formigari. *Leibniz, Humboldt, and the Origins of Comparativism.* Amsterdam: John Benjamin, 1990.

De Roover, Jakob. "The Colonial Dialogue on Religion." 1st Roundtable session *Rethinking Religion in India III.* Pardubice (October 2011).

De Roover, Jakob. "Incurably Religious? *Consensus Gentium* and the Cultural Universality of Religion." *Numen* 61, no. 1 (2014): 5–32.

Dhammapadam: Cesta k pravdě [Dhammapadam: A way to the truth, translated by Karel Werner]. Prague: Odeon, 1992.

Dikshit, K. N. "The Late Harappan in North India." In *Frontiers of Indus Civilisation: Wheelers Volume,* edited by B. B. Lal and S. P. Gupta, 253–269. New Delhi: Books and Books on behalf of Indian Archaeological Society, 1984.

Dirks, Nicholas B. "Castes of Mind." *Representations. Special Issue: Imperial Fantasies and Postcolonial Histories* 37 (1992): 56–78.

Dobiáš, Josef. *Dějepisectví starověké* [The historiography of the ancients]. Prague: Historický klub, 1948.

Dow, Alexander. *A History of Hindoostan, translated from the Persian: To which Are Prefixed Two Dissertations, the First Concerning the Hindoos, and the Second on the Origin and Nature of Despotism.* New ed. London: J. Walker, 1812 (1st ed. 1772).

Eaton, Richard. *The Rise of Islam and the Bengal Frontier, 1204–1760.* Berkeley: University of California Press, 1993.

Edwardes, Michael. *British India 1772–1947: A Survey of the Nature and Effects of Alien Rule.* London: Sidgwick & Jackson, 1967.

Ehrman, Bart D. *Lost Christianities. The Battles for Scripture and the Faith We Never Knew.* Oxford: Oxford University Press, 2003.

Eidlitz, Walther. *Krsna Caitanya. Sein Leben und Seine Lehre.* Stockholm: Almqvist & Wiksell, 1968.

Fajkus, Břetislav. *Současná filosofie a metodologie vědy* [Contemporary philosophy and methodology of science]. Prague: Filosofia, 1997.

Fajkus, Břetislav, *Filosofie a metodologie vědy. Vývoj, současnost a perspektivy* [The philosophy and methodology of science: Developments, current situation and the perspectives]. Prague: Academia, 2005.

Fárek, Martin. "Did Ram Mohan Ray Understand Western Religion?" *Nomos* 77 (2012): 64–86.

Fárek, Martin. *Haré Kršna v západním světě: Setkání dvou myšlenkových tradic* [Hare Krishna in the western world: meetings of two traditions of thought]. Pardubice: Univerzita Pardubice, 2004.

Fárek, Martin. "Hinduismus: reálné náboženství, nebo konstrukt koloniální vědy?" [Hinduism: A real religion or a construct of the colonial science?] *Religio* 14, no. 2 (2006): 227–242.

Fárek, Martin. "Were Shramana and Bhakti Movements against the Caste System?" In *Western Foundations of the Caste System*, edited by Martin Fárek, Dunkin Jalki, Sufiya Pathan and Prakash Shah, 127–172. Cham: Palgrave Macmillan, 2017.

Feuerstein, Georg, Subhash Kak, and David Frawley. *In Search of the Cradle of Civilization.* New Delhi: Motilal Banarsidass, 1999.

Filipský, Jan et al. *Dějiny Bangladéše, Bhútánu, Malediv, Nepálu, Pákistánu a Šrí Lanky* [History of Bangladesh, Bhutan, Maledives, Pakistan and Sri Lanka]. Prague: Nakladatelství Lidové noviny, 2003.

Filliozat, Pierre-Sylvain. "The French Institute of Indology in Pondicherry." *Wiener Zeitschrift für die Kunde Süd- und Ostasiens* 28 (1984): 133–147.

Fišer, Ivo, and Kamil Zvelebil. *Země posvátných řek* [The country of sacred rivers]. Prague: Mladá fronta, 1959.

Fišer, Zbyněk. *Buddha.* Prague: Orbis, 1968.

Flood, Gavin. *An Introduction to Hinduism.* New Delhi: Cambridge University Press, 1998.

Frykenberg, Robert E. "The Emergence of Modern Hinduism as a Concept and as an Institution: A Reappraisal with Special Reference to South India." In *Hinduism Reconsidered*, edited by Günther-Dietz Sontheimer and Herman Kulke, 29–49. New Delhi: Manohar, 1989.

Fulbrook, Mary. *Historical Theory.* 2nd ed. London: Routledge, 2008.

Fuller, C. J. *The Camphor Flame: Popular Hinduism and Society in India.* 2nd ed. Princeton: Princeton University Press, 2004.

Funkenstein, Amos. *Theology and the Scientific Imagination from the Middle Ages to the Seventeenth Century.* Princeton: Princeton University Press, 1986.

Gáfrik, Róbert. *Od významu k emóciám: Úvaha o prínose sanskritskej literárnej teórie do diskurzu západnej literárnej vedy* [From Meaning to Emotions: An essay about the contribution

of the Sanskrit literary theory for the discourse of the western studies of literature].
Trnava: Trnavská univerzita, 2012.

Gáfrik, Róbert. "Representations of India in Slovak Travel Writing during the Communist Regime (1948–1989)." In *Postcolonial Europe? Essays on Post-Communist Literatures and Cultures*, edited by Dobrota Pucherová and Róbert Gáfrik, 283–298. Leiden: Brill Rodopi, 2015.

Gelders, Raf. "Ascetics and Crafty Priests." Unpublished Ph.D. dissertation. Ghent University, 2010.

Gelders, Raf. "Genealogy of Colonial Discourse: Hindu Traditions and the Limits of European Representations." *Comparative Studies in Society and History* 51, no. 3 (2009): 563–589.

Gelders, Raf, and S. N. Balagangadhara. "Rethinking Orientalism: Colonialism and the Study of Indian Traditions." *History of Religions* 51, no. 2 (2011): 101–128.

Ghose, Jogendra Chunder. *The English Works of Raja Rammohun Roy*. Vol. 1. Calcutta: Srikanta Roy, 1906.

Ghose, Jogendra Chunder. *The English Works of Raja Rammohun Roy*. Vol. 2. Calcutta: Srikanta Roy, 1901.

Ghosh, Ranjan. "India, *Itihasa*, and Inter-historiographical Discourse." *History and Theory* 46 (2004): 210–217.

Godfrey-Smith, Peter. *Theory and Reality: An Introduction to the Philosophy of Science*. Chicago: University of Chicago Press, 2003.

Gonda, Jan. *Die Religionen Indiens: Der jüngere Hinduismus*. Vol. 2. Stuttgart: W. Kohlhammer, 1963.

Grant, Charles. *Observations on the State of Society among the Asiatic Subjects of Great Britain, articularly with Respect to Morals; and on the Means of Improving It*, 1796.

Grierson, G. A. "The Monotheistic Religion of Ancient India and Its Descendant: The Modern Doctrine of Faith." 3rd International Congress of History of Religion. Oxford (1908).

Gupta, S. P. "The Indus-Sarasvati Civilisation. Beginnings and Developments." In *The Aryan Debate*, edited by Thomas R. Trautmann. New Delhi: Oxford University Press, 2007.

Haberman, David. "Divine Betrayal: Krishna-Gopal of Braj in the Eyes of Outsiders." *Journal of Vaisnava Studies* 3, no. 1 (1994): 83–111.

Halbfass, Wilhelm. *India and Europe. An Essay in Understanding*. Albany: SUNY Press, 1988.

Hall, Fitzedward. *Works of the Late Horace Hayman Wilson*. Vols. 1, 2, 6. London: Trübner, 1864.

Hart, George L. *A Rapid Sanskrit Method*. 3rd ed. New Delhi: Motilal Banarsidass, 1989.

Hastings, James. *Encyclopaedia of Religion and Ethics*. 13 vols. Edinburgh: T. and T. Clark, 1908–1926.

Hay, Stephen N. "Western and Indigenous Elements in Modern Indian Thought: The Case of Rammohun Roy." In *Changing Japanese Attitudes Toward Modernization*, edited by Marius B. Jansen, 311–328. Princeton: Princeton University Press, 1972.

Heesterman, J. C. "Brahmin, Ritual and Renouncer." *Wiener Zeitschrift für die Kunde Süd- und Ostasiens* 8 (1964): 1–31.

Heesterman, J. C. "Vratya and Sacrifice." *Indo-Iranian Journal* 6 (1962): 1–37.

Hegel, Georg Wilhelm Friedrich. *Lectures on the History of Philosophy*. Vol. 1. London: Kegan Paul, Trench, Trubner, 1892.

Heller, Jan, and Milan Mrázek. *Nástin religionistiky: Uvedení do vědy o náboženství* [A sketch of religious studies: An introduction into the science of religion]. 2nd ed. Prague: Kalich, 2004.

Hewitt, J. F. *The Ruling Races of Prehistoric Times in India, South-Western Asia and Southern Europe*. Vol 1. London: Archibald Constable, 1894.

Hock, Hans Henrich. "Philology and the Historical Interpretations of the Vedic Texts." In *The Indo-Aryan Controversy*, edited by Edwin Bryant and Laurie L. Patton, 282–308. London: Routledge, 2005.

Hodgen, Margaret. *Early Anthropology in the Sixteenth and Seventeenth Centuries*. Philadelphia: University of Pennsylvania Press, 1964.

Hodgen, Margaret T. "Sebastian Muenster (1489–1552): A Sixteenth Century Ethnographer." *Osiris* 11 (1954): 504–529.

Holba, Jiří. "Buddhova nauka o ne-Já (*an-átman*)" [Buddha's teaching about non-self]. In *Pojetí duše v náboženských tradicích světa* [Concept of soul in the religious traditions of the world], edited by Radek Chlup, 295–329. Prague: DharmaGaia, 2007.

Holwell, John Zephaniah. *A Review of the Original Principles, Religious and Moral, of the Ancient Bramins: Comprehending an Account of the Mythology, Cosmogony, Fasts and Festivals, of the Gentoos, Followers of the Shastah. With a Dissertation on the Metempsychosis, Commonly, though Erroneously, Called the Pythagorean Doctrine*. London: Vernor, 1779.

Hooykaas, Christiaan. *Balinese Bauddha Brahmans*. Amsterdam: North Holland, 1973.

Hrozný, Bedřich. *Nejstarší dějiny přední Asie, Indie a Kréty* [Ancient history of Western Asia, India and Crete]. 4th extended ed. Prague: Melantrich, 1945.

Hyam, Ronald. *Britain's Imperial Century 1815–1914: A Study of Empire and Expansion*. London: B. T. Batsford, 1976.

The Imperial Gazetteer of India. The Indian Empire. Vol. 2, *Historical*. 2nd ed. Oxford: Clarendon Press, 1909.

Inden, Ronald. *Imagining India*. Oxford: Blackwell, 1990.

Irschick, Eugene. *Dialogue and History: Constructing South Asia 1795–1895*. Berkeley: University of California Press, 1994.

Jacobson, Jerome. "Recent Developments in South Asian Prehistory and Protohistory." *Annual Review of Anthropology* 8 (1979): 490.

Jarrige, C. et al. *Mehrgarh: Field Reports 1974–1985, from Neolithic Times to the Indus Civilisation*. Karachi: Department of Culture and Tourism, Government of Sindh, and French Ministry of Foreign Affairs, 1995.

Jones, Anna Maria. *The Works of Sir William Jones in Six Volumes*. Vols. 1, 6. London: G. G. and J. Robinson, 1799.

Jones, John. *India's Problem: Krishna or Christ*. New York: Flemming H. Revell, 1903.

Jones, William. *Institutes of the Hindu Law; Or, the Ordinances of Menu, according to the Gloss of Culluca: Comprising the Indian System of Duties, Religious and Civil*. 3rd ed. London: W. H. Allen, 1869.

Jordens, J. T. F. "Hindu Religious and Social Reform in British India." In *A Cultural History of India*, edited by A. L. Basham, 365–382. 10th ed. New Delhi: Oxford University Press, 1996.

Karfíková, Lenka. "Křesťanské pojetí božství" [Christian concept of god]. In *Bůh a bohové: Pojetí božství v náboženských tradicích světa* [God and gods: The concept of a deity in the religious traditions of the world], edited by Radek Chlup, 59–81. Prague: DharmaGaia, 2004.

Keay, John. *India Discovered. The Recovery of a Lost Civilisation*. 3rd ed. London: HarperCollins, 2001.

Keith, A. B. *A History of Sanskrit Literature*. London: Oxford University Press, 1920.

Kennedy, Kenneth A. R. "Identification of Sacrificial and Massacre Victims in Archaeological Sites: The Skeletal Evidence." *Man and Environment* 19 (1994): 247–251.

Kennedy, Kenneth A. R. "Have Aryans been identified in the Prehistoric Skeletal Record from South Asia?" In *The Indo-Aryans of Ancient South Asia. Language, Material Culture and Ethnicity*, edited by George Erdosy, 32–66. New Delhi: Munshiram Manoharlal, 1997.

Kenoyer, Jonathan M. "Cultural Change During the Late Harappan Period at Harappa. New Insights on Vedic Aryan Issues." In *The Indo-Aryan Controversy. Evidence and Inference in Indian History*, edited by Edwin F. Bryant and Laurie L. Patton, 21–49. London: Routledge, 2005.

Kenoyer, Jonathan M. "Early City-States in South Asia: Comparing the Harappan Phase and the Early Historic Period." In *The Archaeology of City States: Cross Cultural Approaches*, edited by D. L. Nichols and T. H. Charlton, 52–70. Washington: Smithsonian Institute, 1997.

Keppens, Marianne. "Indians are Aryans, so What?" Position paper at Rethinking Religion in India I. New Delhi, January 2009.

Keppens, Marianne. "The Aryans and the Ancient System of Caste." In *Western Foundations of the Caste System*, edited by Martin Fárek et al., 221–251. London: Palgrave Macmillan, 2017.

Killingley, Dermot Hastings. *The Only True God: Works on Religion by Rammohun Roy*. Selected and Translated from Bengali and Sanskrit, with an Introduction and Notes. Newcastle upon Tyne: Grevatt and Grevatt, 1982.

Killingley, Dermot Hastings. *Rammohun Roy in Hindu and Christian Tradition: The Teape Lectures 1990*. Newcastle upon Tyne: Grevatt and Grevatt, 1993.

King, Richard. "Colonialism, Hinduism and the Discourse of Religion." Position paper in the Roundtable sessions, *Rethinking Religion in India I*, New Delhi, January 2008.

King, Richard. "Orientalism and the Modern Myth of 'Hinduism'." *Numen* 46, no. 2 (1999): 146–185.

King, Richard. *Orientalism and Religion. Post-Colonial Theory, India and "the Mystic East"*. London: Routledge, 1999.

Klostermaier, Klaus. "Questioning the Aryan Invasion Theory and Revising Ancient Indian History." *ISKCON Communication Journal* 6, no. 1 (1998): 1–7.

Knotková-Čapková, Blanka. *Základy asijských náboženství: Judaismus, islám, hinduismus, džinismus, buddhismus, sikhismus, pársismus* [The basics of Asian religions: Judaism, Islam, Hinduism, Jainism, Buddhism, Sikhism, Parsism]. Vol. 1. Prague: Karolinum, 2005.

Kopf, David. *The Brahmo Samaj and the Shaping of the Modern Indian Mind*. Princeton: Princeton University Press, 1979.

Kopf, David. *British Orientalism and the Bengal Renaissance: The Dynamics of Indian Modernization 1773–1835*. Calcutta: K. L. Mukhopadhyay, 1969.

Kopf, David. "Hermeneutics Versus History." *Journal of Asian Studies* 39, no. 3 (1980): 495–506.

Kopf, David. "The Wonder That Was Orientalism: In Defense of H. H. Wilson's Defence of Hinduism." In *Bengal Vaisnavism, Orientalism, Society, and the Arts*, edited by Joseph T. O'Connell, 75–90. Ann Arbor: Michigan State University, 1985.

Král, Oldřich. *Čínská filosofie: Pohled z dějin* [Chinese philosophy: A view from the history]. Lásenice: Maxima, 2005.

Krása, Miroslav, Dagmar Marková, and Dušan Zbavitel. *Indie a Indové. Od dávnověku k dnešku* [India and the Indians: From the ancient times till today]. Prague: Vyšehrad, 1997.

Kubalík, Josef. *Dějiny náboženství* [A history of religions]. 2nd ed. Prague: Česká katolická charita, 1988.

Kuhn, Thomas Samuel. *The Structure of Scientific Revolutions*. Chicago: Chicago University Press, 1970.

Kuper, Adam. *The Reinvention of Primitive Society. Transformation of a Myth.* 2nd ed. New York: Routledge, 2005.

Kutnar, František, and Jaroslav Marek. *Přehledné dějiny českého a slovenského dějepisectví: Od počátků národní kultury až do sklonku třicátých let 20. století* [Synoptical history of the Czech and Slovak historiography]. Prague: Nakladatelství Lidové noviny, 1997.

Küng, Hans, and Heinrich von Stietencron. *Křesťanství a hinduismus* [Christianity and hinduism]. Prague: Vyšehrad, 1997.

Lach, Donald F. *Asia in the Making of Europe.* Vol 1. Chicago: Chicago University Press, 1965.

Lakatos, Imre. "Falsification and the Methodology of Scientific Research Programmes." In *Criticism and the Growth of Knowledge,* edited by Imre Lakatos and Alan Musgrave, 91–196. Cambridge: Cambridge University Press, 1970.

Lal, B. B. "Aryan Invasion of India: Perpetuation of a Myth." In *The Indo-Aryan Controversy,* edited by Edwin Bryant and Laurie Patton, 50–74. New York: Routledge, 2005.

Latief, Hilman. "Comparative Religion in Medieval Muslim Literature." *American Journal of Islamic Social Sciences* 4, no. 23 (2006) 28–62.

Laudan, Larry. *Science and Relativism: Some Key Controversies in the Philosophy of Science.* Chicago: Chicago University Press, 1990.

Le Goff, Jacques. *History and Memory.* New York: Columbia University Press, 1992.

Le Goff, Jacques. *Medieval Civilization 400–1500.* Oxford: Blackwell, 1992.

Léon-Dufour, Xavier et al. *The Dictionary of Biblical Theology.* 2nd ed. London: Word Among Us Press, 1995.

Lesný, Vincenc. *Buddhismus.* Prague: Jaroslav Samec, 1948.

Lesný, Vincenc. *Duch Indie* [Spirit of India]. Prague: Státní nakladatelství, 1927.

Lesný, Vincenc. *Indie a Indové: Pouť staletími* [India and Indians: A journey through centuries]. Prague: Orientální ústav, 1931.

Lincoln, Bruce. "Isaac Newton and Oriental Jones on Myth, Ancient History, and the Relative Prestige of Peoples." *History of Religions* 42, no. 1 (2002): 1–18.

Llewellyn, J. E. *Defining Hinduism: A Reader.* London: Routledge, 2005.

Macdonell, Arthur A. "The Early History of Caste." *American Historical Review* 19, no. 2 (1914): 230–244.

Macnicol, Nicol. *Indian Theism from the Vedic to the Muhammadan Period.* London: Humphrey Milford / Oxford University Press, 1915.

Mahāparinibbānasutta. Velká rozprava o Buddhově úplné nibbáně [Mahaparinibbana-sutta, translated by Miroslav Rozehnal]. Prague: DharmaGaia, 1995.

Majumdar, Ramesh Chandra. *British Paramountcy and Indian Renaissance.* Mumbai: Bharatiya Vidya Bhavan, 1970.

Malek, Abdel Anwar: "Orientalism in Crisis." *Diogenes* 44 (1963): 103–140.

Mánavadharmašástra aneb Manuovo poučení o dharmě [Manava-dharmashastra, or, the Manu's Treatise on Dharma, translated by Dušan Zbavitel]. Prague: ExOriente, 2009.

Mani, Lata, and Ruth Frankenberg. "The Challenge of Orientalism." *Economy and Society* 14, no. 2 (1985): 174–192.

Marek, Jaroslav. *O historismu a dějepisectví* [About historicism and historical science]. Prague: Academia, 1992.

Marriott, McKim. "Constructing Indian Ethnosociology." *Contributions to Indian Sociology* 23, no. 1 (1989): 1–39.

Marshall, P. J. *The British Discovery of Hinduism in the Eighteenth Century.* Cambridge: Cambridge University Press, 1970.

Masuzawa, Tomoko. *The Invention of World Religions: Or, How European Universalism Was Preserved in the Language of Pluralism.* Chicago: University of Chicago Press, 2005.

Mathur, Saloni. "History and Anthropology in South Asia: Rethinking the Archive." *Annual Review of Anthropology* 29 (2000): 89–106.

Metcalf, G. J. "The Indo-European Hypothesis in the Sixteenth and Seventeenth Centuries." In *Studies in the History of Linguistics. Traditions and Paradigms*, edited by Dell H. Hymes, 233–257. Bloomington: Indiana University Press, 1974.

The Middle Length Discourses of the Buddha. A New Translation of the Majjhima Nikaya. Boston: Wisdom Publications, 1995.

Mill, James. *History of British India, with Notes and Continuation by Horace Hayman Wilson.* Vol. 2. 4th ed. London: James Madden, 1840.

Miller, Barbara Stoler. *The Gitagovinda of Jayadeva: Love Song of the Dark Lord.* Delhi: Motilal Banarsidass, 1984.

Miltner, Vladimír. *Indie má jméno Bhárat, aneb úvod do historie bytí a vědomí indické společnosti* [India's name is Bharat, or, An introduction into the history, being and consciousness of Indian society]. Prague: Panorama, 1978.

Miltner, Vladimír. *Vznik a vývoj Buddhismu* [The origin and development of Buddhism]. Prague: Vyšehrad, 2001.

Momigliano, Arnoldo. "Pagan and Christian Historiography in the Fourth Century A.D." In *The Conflict Between Paganism and Christianity in the Fourth Century*, edited by Arnoldo Momigliano, 79–99. Oxford: Clarendon Press, 1963.

Monier-Williams, Monier. *Religious Thought and Life in India. Vedism, Brahmanism, and Hinduism.* Vol. 1. London: John Murray, 1883.

Moyn, Samuel. "Amos Funkenstein on the Theological Origins of Historicism." *Journal of the History of Ideas* 64, no. 2 (2003): 639–657.

Mukherjee, S. N. *Sir William Jones: A Study in the Eighteenth-Century British Attitudes to India.* Cambridge: Cambridge University Press, 1968.

Müller, Friedrich Max. *Biographical Essays.* London: Longmans, Green, 1884.

Müller, Friedrich Max. *Chips from a German Workshop: Essays on the Science of Religion.* Vol. 1. London: Longman and Green, 1868.

Müller, Friedrich Max. *A History of Ancient Sanskrit Literature so far as It Illustrates the Primitive Religion of the Brahmans.* London: Williams and Norgate, 1859.

Müller, Georgina. *The Life and Letters of Right Honorable Friedrich Max Müller.* Vol. 1. London: Longmans, Green, 1902.

Muller, Jean Claude: "Early Stages of Language Comparison from Sassetti to Sir William Jones." *Kratylos* 31 (1986): 1–31.

Nandy, Ashis. *The Intimate Enemy. Loss and Recovery of Self Under Colonialism.* New Delhi: Oxford University Press, 1983.

Nehru, Jawaharlal. *The Discovery of India.* Delhi: Oxford University Press, 1994.

Novick, Peter. *That Noble Dream, The "Objectivity Question" and the American Historical Profession.* Cambridge: Cambridge University Press, 1988.

O'Brien, Patrick. "Historiographical Traditions and Modern Imperatives for the Restoration of Global History." *Journal of Global History* 1, no. 1 (2006): 3–39.

Oddie, Geoffrey A. "Colonialism and Religion in India." Position paper at the Roundtable Session, *Rethinking Religion in India I* (January 2008).

Olender, Maurice. *The Language of Paradise: Race, Religion and Philology in the Nineteenth Century.* Cambridge, MA: Harvard University Press, 1992.

Ondračka, Lubomír. "Védské představy o posmrtném životě" [Vedic ideas about life after death]. In *Pojetí duše v náboženských tradicích světa* [The concept of soul in the religious traditions of the world], edited by Radek Chlup, 223–266. Prague: DharmaGaia, 2007.

Orosius. *Seven Books of History Against the Pagans.* Translated with an Introduction and Notes by A. T. Fear. Liverpool: Liverpool University Press, 2010.

Ouředník, Patrik. *Hledání ztraceného jazyka* [Searching for the lost language]. Středokluky: Zdeněk Susa, 1997.

Padigar, Shrinivas V. *Vishnu Cult in Karnataka.* Mysore: Directorate of Archaeology and Museums, 1996.

Pečírka, Jan. *Dějiny pravěku a starověku* [Prehistory and ancient times]. Vol. 2. 3rd ed. Prague: SPN, 1989.

Pennington, Brian. *Was Hinduism Invented? Britons, Indians, and the Colonial Construction of Religion.* Oxford: Oxford University Press, 2005.

Pertold, Otakar. *Perla Indického oceánu. Vzpomínky ze dvou cest na Ceylon (1910 a 1922)* [Pearl of the Indian Ocean. Memories from two journeys to Ceylon in 1910 and 1922]. Prague: J. Otto, 1926.

Pertold, Otakar. *Ze zapomenutých koutů Indie* [From the forgotten corners of India]. Prague: Aventinum, 1927.

Piatigorski, A. "Some Phenomenological Observations on the Study of Indian Religion." In *Indian Religion*, edited by R. Burghart and A. Cantlie, 208–258. London: Curson Press, 1985.

Piggott, Stuart. *Prehistoric India to 1000 B.C.* Harmondsworth: Penguin Books, 1950.

Poliakov, Léon. *The Aryan Myth: A History of Racist and Nationalistic Ideas in Europe.* 2nd ed. New York: Barnes & Noble, 1996.

Popper, Karl. *The Poverty of Historicism.* 4th English ed. London: Routledge, 2002.

Pořízka, Vincenc. *Opera Minora: Studies in the Bhagavadgita and New Indo-Aryan Languages.* Prague: Oriental Institute, Academy of Sciences of the Czech Republic, 2000.

Preinhaelterová, Hana. *Hinduista od zrození do zrození* [A Hindu from a birth to another birth]. Prague: Vyšehrad, 1997.

"Proč je kráva pro hinduisty posvátná?" [Why is the cow holy for the Hindus?] *Mladá fronta dnes,* September 6 (2012): 12 A.

Rajaram, Navaratna. *The Politics of History: The Aryan Invasion Theory and the Subversion of Scholarship.* New Delhi: Voice of India, 1995.

Ray, Ajit Kumar. *The Religious Ideas of Rammohun Roy.* New Delhi: Kanak, 1976.

Renfrew, Collin. *Archaeology and Language: The Puzzle of Indo-European Origins.* 2nd ed. Cambridge: Cambridge University Press, 1988.

Renfrew, Collin "Archaeology and Language." In *The Aryan Debate*, edited by Thomas R. Trautmann, 205–229. New Delhi: Oxford University Press, 2005.

Robertson, Bruce Carlisle. *Raja Ram Mohan Ray. The Father of Modern India.* 2nd Indian ed. New Delhi: Oxford University Press, 2001.

Roy, Rammohun. *The Precepts of Jesus the Guide to Peace and Happiness, Extracted from the Books of the New Testament Ascribed to the Four Evangelists. To Which Are Added the First and Second Appeal to the Christian Public in Reply to the Observations of Dr. Marshman, of Shrirampur.* London: Unitarian Society, 1823.

Said, Edward W. *Culture and Imperialism.* 2nd ed. New York: Vintage Books, 1994.

Said, Edward W. *Orientalism. Western Conceptions of the Orient.* 2nd ed. New York: Vintage Books, 1979.

Said, Edward W. *Orientalism. Western Conceptions of the Orient.* 25th anniversary edition. New York: Vintage Books, 2003.

Sarkar, Hem Chandra. *Rammohan Roy. The Father of Modern India.* Calcutta: Srimati Sakuntala Rao, 1910.

Sarvabhavana Dasa. *Sri Siksastaka: Eight Beautiful Instructions by Sri Caitanya Mahaprabhu.* Andheri: Harmonist Publications, 1991.

Schopenhauer, Arthur. *Essays of Arthur Schopenhauer.* New York: A. L. Burt, 1893.

Shaffer, Jim G., and Diane A. Lichtenstein. "South Asian Archaeology and the Myth of Indo-Aryan Invasions." In *The Indo-Aryan Controversy. Evidence and Inference in Indian History*, edited by Edwin F. Bryant and Laurie L. Patton, 75–104. London: Routledge, 2005.

Shaffer, Jim. "The Indo-Aryan Invasions: Cultural Myth and Archaeological Reality." In *The People of South Asia: The Biological Anthropology of India, Pakistan, and Nepal*, edited by John R. Lukacs, 77–88. New York: Plenum Press, 1984.

Shefts, Betty. *Grammatical Method of Panini: His Treatment of Sanskrit Present Stems*. New Haven: American Oriental Society, 1961.

Silk, Jonathan A. *Riven by Lust: Incest and Schizm in Indian Buddhist Legend and Historiography*. Honolulu: University of Hawaii Press, 2009.

Skřivánek, Jaroslav. *Za krásami Indie* [For the beauties of India]. 2nd ed. Prague: Albatros, 1988.

Skřivánek, Milan. *K osvícenskému pojetí a výuce dějepisu ve světle rukopisů piaristické koleje v Litomyšli* [To the Enlightenment concept and teaching of history in the manuscripts from the Piarist college in Litomysl]. Pardubice: Univerzita Pardubice, 2008.

Smith, George. *The Life of William Carey: Shoe Maker and Missionary*. London: J. M. Dent, not dated.

Smith, Vincent. *The Early History of India. From 600 B.C. to the Muhammadan Conquest, including the Invasion of Alexander the Great*. 3rd ed. London: Oxford University Press, 1914.

Somadeva. *Oceán příběhů. Kathásaritságaram* [Somadeva's Ocean of Stories, translated by Dušan Zbavitel]. Vol. 1. Prague: Odeon, 1981.

Sontheimer, Günther-Dietz, and Hermann Kulke. *Hinduism Reconsidered*. 2nd Indian ed. New Delhi: Manohar, 2001.

Staal, Frits. "The Meaninglessness of Ritual." *Numen* 26 (1979): 2–22.

Staal, Frits, C. V. Somayajipad, and M. Itti Ravi Nambudiri. *AGNI. The Vedic Ritual of Fire Altar*. 2 vols. Berkeley: Asian Humanities Press, 1983.

Staal, Frits: *Ritual and Mantras: Rules without Meaning*. Delhi: Motilal Banarsidass, 1996.

Staal, Frits. "There Is No Religion There." In *The Craft of Religious Studies*, edited by Jon R. Stone, 52–75. London: MacMillan Press, 1998.

Stewart, Charles. *The History of Bengal*. London: Black, Parry, 1813.

Stietencron, Heinrich von. "Hinduism: On the Proper Use of a Deceptive Term." In *Hinduism Reconsidered*, edited by Günther-Dietz Sontheimer and Hermann Kulke, 32–53. New Delhi:

Strnad, Jaroslav et al. *Dějiny Indie* [History of India]. Prague: Nakladelství Lidové noviny, 2003.

Sugirtharajah, Sharada. *Imagining Hinduism: A Postcolonial Perspective*. London: Routledge, 2003.

Sweetman, Will. "The Prehistory of Orientalism: Colonialism and the Textual Basis for Bartholomaus Ziegenbalg's Account of Hinduism." *New Zeland Journal of Asian Studies* 6, no. 2 (2004): 12–38.

Thapar, B. K. "The Aryans: A Reappraisal of the Problem." In *India's Contributions to World Thought and Culture*, edited by L. Chandra et al., 147–164. Madras: Vivekananda Rock Memorial Committee, 1970.

Thapar, Romila. "Syndicated Hinduism." In *Hinduism Reconsidered*, edited by Günther-Dietz Sontheimer and Hermann Kulke, 54–81. 4th ed. New Delhi: Manohar, 1997.

Thomas, M. M. *The Acknowledged Christ of the Indian Renaissance*. London: SCM Press, 1969.

Topolski, Jerzy. "Pojem úpadku v dějinách a hospodářských dějinách" [The concept of decline in history and economical history]. In *Kritéria a ukazatele nerovnoměrného vývoje v evropských dějinách* [The criteria and signifiers of the uneven development in the European history], edited by Luďa Klusáková. 63–77. Prague: FF UK, 1997.

Trautmann, Thomas R. *Aryans and British India*. Berkeley: University of California Press, 1997.

Trautmann, Thomas R. *The Aryan Debate*. New Delhi: Oxford University Press, 2005.

Trautmann, Thomas R. "Constructing the Racial Theory of Indian Civilisation." In *The Aryan Debate*, edited by Thomas R. Trautmann, 84–105. New Delhi: Oxford University Press, 2005.

The Travels of Sir John Mandevilla. The Version of the Cotton Manuscript in Modern Spelling. London: Macmillan, 1915.

Treasury of Truth: Illustrated Dhammapada. Translated by Weragoda Sarada Maha Thero. Taipei: Buddha Educational Foundation, 1993.

Urwick, W. *India 100 Years Ago. The Beauty of Old India Illustrated.* 2nd ed. London: Bracken Books, 1985 (reprint of the 1st edition by Religious Tract Society, 1885).

Valtrová, Jana. *Středověká setkání s jinými: Modloslužebníci, židé, saracéni a heretici v misionářských zprávách o Asii* [The medieval encounters with the others]. Prague: Argo, 2011.

Vavroušková, Stanislava. "Tradice a moderní společnost: Hinduismus" [Tradition and modern society: Hinduism]. In *Náboženství v asijských společnostech: Tradice a současnost* [Religion in Asian societies: Tradition and present times], edited by Dagmar Marková. Prague: AV ČR, 1996.

Védské hymny [Vedic hymns, translated by O. Friš, with an article by P. Vavroušek]. 3rd extended ed. Prague: DharmaGaia, 2000.

Voltaire. *The Philosophy of History, or a Philosophical and Historical Dissertation.* London: Thomas North, 1829.

Ward, William. *A View of the History, Literature, and Religion of the Hindoos.* Vol. 1. London: Baptist Missionary Society, 1817.

Werner, Karel. *Náboženství jižní a východní Asie* [Religions of south and east Asia]. Brno: Masarykova Univerzita, 1995.

Wezler, Albrecht. "Towards a Reconstruction of Indian Cultural History: Observations and Reflections on 18th and 19th Century Indology." *Studien zur Indologie und Iranistik* 18 (1993): 305–329.

Wheeler, Mortimer. *Civilization of the Indus Valley and Beyond.* London: Thames and Hudson, 1966.

Wheeler, Mortimer. "Harappa 1946: The Defences and Cemetery R37." *Ancient India* 3 (1947): 58–130.

Wilbur, Earl M. *A History of Unitarianism: Socianism and Its Antecedents.* Cambridge, MA: Harvard University Press, 1945.

Witzel, Michael. "On Indian Historical Writing. The Role of Vamsavalis." *Journal of the Japanese Association for South Asian Studies* 2 (1990): 1–57.

Young, Richard Fox. *Resistant Hinduism. Sanskrit Sources on Anti-Christian Apologetics in Early Nineteenth-Century India.* Vienna: Gerold (De Nobili Research Library), 1981.

Zalta, Edward N. et al. *Stanford Encyclopedia of Philosophy*, http://plato.stanford.edu.

Zastoupil, Lynn. "Defining Christians, Making Britons: Rammohun Roy and the Unitarians." *Victorian Studies* 44, no. 2 (2002): 215–243.

Zastoupil, Lynn. "Notorious and Convicted Mutilitators: Rammohun Roy, Thomas Jefferson, and the Bible." *Journal of World History* 20, no. 3 (2009): 399–434.

Zbavitel, Dušan. *Bengali Literature. A History of Indian Literature Series*. Vol. 9. Wiesbaden: Otto Harrassowitz, 1976.

Zbavitel, Dušan. *Bengálská literatura. Od tantrických písní k Rabíndranáthu Thákurovi* [Bengali literature: From the tantric songs to Rabindranath Tagore]. Prague: ExOriente, 2008.

Zbavitel, Dušan et al. *Bohové s lotosovýma očima. Hinduistické mýty v indické kultuře tří tisíciletí* [The gods with lotus eyes: Myths of the Hindus in Indian culture of three millenia]. Prague: Vyšehrad, 1986.

Zbavitel, Dušan et al. *Bozi, bráhmani, lidé. Čtyři tisíciletí hinduismu* [Gods, brahmins, people: Four millenia of Hinduism]. Prague: Nakladatelství ČSAV, 1964.

Zbavitel, Dušan. *Starověká Indie* [Ancient India]. Prague: Panorama, 1985.

Zbavitel, Dušan, and Jaroslav Vacek. *Průvodce dějinami staroindické literatury* [The guide through history of the old Indian literature]. Třebíč: Arca JiMfa, 1996.

Zempliner, Arthur. *Čínská filosofie v novověké evropské filosofii* [Chinese philosophy in the modern European philosophy]. Prague: Academia, 1966.

Zvelebil, Kamil. "Decipherments of the Indus Script." In *The Aryan Debate*, edited by Thomas R. Trautmann, 254–273. New Delhi: Oxford University Press, 2005.

Index

Flavius, Josephus 112
Fleet, John Faithfull 143–144, 147
Fontenelle, Bernard le Bovier de 39
Foucault, Michel 19, 22
Friš, Oldřich 81,
Fulbrook, Mary 124,-125
Funkenstein, Amos 110–111, 113, 116–117, 119–120, 140, 148–149

G
Gadamer, Hans-Georg 188
Gayatri (*gāyatrī*) 96, 209
Gampert, Vilém 44
Gelders, Raf 30–31, 57, 104–105, 178
Geldner, Karl Friedrich 170
Gellner, Ernest André 22
Gelzer, Heinrich 112
Gibbon, Edward 34
Grant, Charles 40, 136
Grierson, George Abraham 103
Guha, Ranajit 22

H
Halbfass, Wilhelm 28, 188–189
Halhed, Nathaniel Brassey 136, 174
Hall, Fitzedward 57–58
Hastings, James 103
Hastings, Warren 23
Haug, Martin 179
Hay, Stephen Northrup 187
Hazarika, Polly 185
Heesterman, Johannes Cornelius 63, 70–71
Hegel, Georg Wilhelm Friedrich 17, 24, 123–124, 133–135, 137, 220
Heine-Geldern, Robert von 164
Heracles 195
Herder, Johann Gottfried 137
Hindoo Association 55
hipkapi 40
Hock, Hans Henrich 157–158, 169–171
Hodgen, Margaret 86–89, 104
Holwell, John Zephaniah 28, 83, 90–93, 103, 105–108, 129, 177, 200, 218, 224
Holy Trinity 81, 86, 104, 106, 197, 207, 219
Homer 25, 35, 86
Hrozný, Bedřich 161–162, 181, 221
Hugo of the St. Victor 104, 117
Hume, David 39
Hunter, William H. 132

I
Inden, Ronald 11, 22, 24, 138,
Indra 98, 163
Irschick, Eugene 23
Isaac 94, 149
Ishopanishad (*Īśopaniṣad*) 96, 192, 202
Isidor of Sevilla 86, 112
Isis 36
Iunilius Africanus 149

J
Jacobson, Jerome 165
Jain, Jainism 12, 25, 40, 48, 53, 68–69, 76, 99, 133, 146
Japheth 174, 180–181
Jatakas (*jātaka*) 63
jati (*jāti*) 22, 62, 152, 216
Jerome, St. 112
Jesus Christ 35, 85, 111, 115, 149–151, 196–197, 201, 203–208, 211, 219, 222
Joachim of Fiore 116
John, Prester 86, 128
Jones, William 12, 28, 39, 43–44, 83–84, 90–97, 107–108, 129–132, 135, 143, 149–150, 174–178, 180, 194, 215, 218–220, 224
Jordens, J. T. F. 186
Juno 36
Jupiter 36, 95

K
Kalhana 143
Karman (*karma*) 45, 53–56, 60, 62, 65–67, 70, 74–75, 215–216, 223
Keith, Arthur Berriedale 144, 170, 215
Kennedy, Kenneth 157, 160, 163–167
Kenoyer, Jonathan Mark 163, 166
Keppens, Marianne 154, 177–179
Killingley, Dermot Hastings 189, 193, 200, 204
King, Richard 22, 29
Kongudesa Rajakkal (*Koṇguḍēsarājākkaḷ*) 147
Kopf, David 22–23, 26–27, 44, 187–189, 198
Krása, Miroslav 12, 50
Krishna/Krsna 13, 101, 130, 194–195, 203
krsna tvac (*kṛṣṇa tvac*) 170
Kshatriyas (*kṣatriya*) 60, 73
Kuhn, Thomas Samuel 13–14